ENGLISH POETRY
OF THE FIRST WORLD WAR

ENGLISH POETRY
OF THE
FIRST WORLD WAR

A STUDY IN THE EVOLUTION
OF LYRIC
AND NARRATIVE FORM

BY JOHN H. JOHNSTON

PRINCETON, NEW JERSEY
PRINCETON UNIVERSITY PRESS
1964

Publication of this book has been aided
by the Ford Foundation program to support
publication, through university presses,
of works in the humanities and social sciences.

Chapter VIII is an expanded version of an article
that appeared in *The Review of Politics*,
Vol. 24, pp. 62-87.

Printed in the United States of America by
Princeton University Press,
Princeton, New Jersey

TO MY MOTHER AND FATHER
AND MY WIFE AGNES

CONTENTS

INTRODUCTION

THE PRESENT STUDY is concerned with the work of ten British soldier-poets of World War I, four of whom—Rupert Brooke, Siegfried Sassoon, Wilfred Owen, and Isaac Rosenberg—are known well enough to merit inclusion in most anthologies of modern verse. The others, for various reasons connected with the quality or quantity of their work or its date of publication, are perhaps not so well known: Julian Grenfell, Robert Nichols, Charles Sorley, Edmund Blunden, Herbert Read, and David Jones. (Blunden and Read, of course, have reputations in criticism and poetry that are independent of their war verse.) This selection is intended to represent the poets of acknowledged superiority and established reputation as well as poets of lesser reputation whose achievement seems to require a new or revised appraisal. A few other figures, such as W. N. Hodgson, Leslie Coulson, Robert Graves, and Arthur Graeme West, are treated when their verse provides convenient illustrations of certain changes in attitude or developments in technique. The work of our ten poets, therefore, represents the best or the most characteristic poetry of the war—the poetry that is most likely to be granted, according to its varying quality some place in literature.

These poets form a natural group by virtue of the fact that they were the first to deal with the kind of war peculiar to modern civilization; they were the first to attempt some assessment of the physical and spiritual effects of that kind of war. Their verse, consequently, has both a historical and a critical interest. The historical aspects of World War I poetry—that is, the general relationships between the conditions of twentieth-century warfare and the type of poetry those conditions inspired —are by now fairly obvious. No special effort, however, has yet been made to examine the literary and critical implications of that poetry: the relationships between tradition and innovation, between theory and practice, between attitude and technique, between form and materials. Since the war was such a significant factor in the remarkable literary transitions that characterize the period between 1910 and 1930, a study of the literary aspects of World War I poetry could conceivably enlarge our understanding of an important phase of those transitions—a phase that was the most dramatic symbol of the stress exerted upon the arts by the forces of modern civilization.

Almost all of the critical and scholarly writing on the subject has been devoted to brief surveys or confined to individual studies of three or four of the best-known poets. These treatments, though illuminating in some respects, fail to provide a satisfactory literary context in which the achievements of individual poets are interpreted as parts or stages of the evolutionary process leading from the sonnets of Rupert Brooke to the postwar poetry of Herbert Read and David Jones. In the light of the values it seeks to establish, the present study will attempt to unite an analysis of individual poets with a broad interpretation of their entire development as a group.

The standards invoked are those of epic and heroic literature—the traditional literature of war. Perhaps a convincing case cannot be made for viewing war literature as a genre, but Blunden's "Third Ypres" is more closely related to *The Battle of Maldon* than, say, to Masefield's verse narratives or to Eliot's *The Waste Land*. Part of Chapter I, accordingly, is devoted to a contrast between the spirit of the epic poem and the dominant moods and themes of World War I verse. The following chapters seek to demonstrate that most of the war poets, through their almost exclusive reliance on the contemporary lyric response and on the attitudes and techniques inherent in that response, were seriously hampered in their efforts to depict or evaluate their experiences. The epic poem was equal to every aspect of primitive conflict; the modern war lyric, however, was probably the medium least capable of dealing with the vastly multiplied moral and physical confusions of technological warfare. As World War I progressed, the poets themselves seemed to sense a discrepancy between the multifarious nature of their material and the limited potentialities of the lyric form; through various means most of them sought a more comprehensive, more objective mode for the communication of their experiences —a mode that could encompass, like the epic narrative, the universal as well as the particular significance of war.

Thus the reference to epic standards is not entirely arbitrary or unjust, since it is suggested both by the particular character of the limitations visible in the war lyric and by the efforts of the poets to escape some of those limitations. Such a reference is also suggested by the fact that World War I poetry must be judged in relation to standards other than sincerity and fidelity to fact; these standards, if sought in the rapidly shifting values of early twentieth-century poetry, are almost impossible to isolate and apply. Certainly much modern war verse suffers when it is examined in the light of values apparently so remote from it; conversely, other productions take on much fuller significance as they are seen to approximate the qualities inherent in the traditional literature of war. Although a study of this type usually results in revaluations, revaluation of the group or of individuals is not its major purpose. That purpose, strictly defined, is twofold: to examine the characteristic attitudes and techniques of World War I poetry, and to test the values embodied in those attitudes and techniques by reference to the large artistic possibilities inherent in the subject and in the poetic form traditionally devoted to the subject. Beyond the formal conclusions that apply to the poetry of the war, there are a number of wider implications that bear on modern poetry as a whole.

The treatment of individual writers proceeds chronologically, with the Somme battles of 1916 marking the division between the earlier and the later poets. Because of the relatively small quantity of their work, Brooke, Grenfell, Nichols, and Sorley are examined in a single chapter. The verse of the later poets —Sassoon, Blunden, Owen, and Rosenberg—was inspired, for the most part, after the Somme battles and bears a character quite different from that of the earlier poetry. Read and Jones are considered last because, properly speaking, they belong to the postwar years. A brief biographical sketch has been included in each case because reference to a poet's background and prewar poetic practice would have been somewhat awkward without it. In some instances the friendships that existed between certain authors seemed to warrant a review of their most important contacts.

This study was made possible in part by a grant (1956-1957) from The Southern Fellowships Fund, and by a Senate Summer Research Grant (1962) awarded by West Virginia University. Funds to cover permissions fees were generously provided by the Claude Worthington Benedum Foundation and the West Virginia University Foundation, Inc. Acknowledgment is made to the West Virginia University *Philological Papers*, where a greater portion of the essay on Charles Sorley first appeared, and to *The Review of Politics*, which published an abbreviated version of the chapter on David Jones. For assistance in proofreading and related matters, as well as for his steady friendship and moral support, the author owes a great debt to Professor John Hagan of Wellesley College. The author also wishes to express his special indebtedness to Professor Paul L. Wiley of the University of Wisconsin, whose advice in the matter of selection and organization has been invaluable and whose critical suggestions have helped to sharpen the treatment of individual poets; and to Professor Frank O'Malley of the University of Notre Dame, whose admiration for David Jones (communicated, in 1946, to a soldier fresh from the wars) provided the essential stimulus for the work. Finally, to the embattled young poets who in the midst of physical and spiritual extremity sang "tales of great war and strong hearts wrung," the author must humbly address a plea for tolerance: criticism was ever a peacetime art.

J. H. J.

ACKNOWLEDGMENTS

*For permission to quote copyright passages grateful
acknowledgment is made to the following:*

Edmund Blunden, Esq., for selections from POEMS, 1914-30
and for a passage from UNDERTONES OF WAR (Oxford University Press.)

Sidgwick and Jackson, Ltd., McClelland and Stewart, Ltd., and
Dodd, Mead and Co., for selections from THE COLLECTED
POEMS OF RUPERT BROOKE. Copyright, 1915, by Dodd, Mead
and Co. Copyright, 1943, by Sir Edward Marsh.

Faber and Faber, Ltd., and Harcourt, Brace and World, Inc.,
for lines from T. S. Eliot's THE WASTE LAND, from COLLECTED
POEMS, 1909-1935.

International Authors, N.V., for "A Dead Boche," from Robert
Graves's FAIRIES AND FUSILIERS (William Heinemann, Ltd.)

Lady Salmond (wife of Sir John Salmond) for lines from Julian
Grenfell's "Into Battle."

The Trustees of the Hardy Estate, The Macmillan Company
(New York), The Macmillan Company of Canada, Ltd.,
and Macmillan and Company, Ltd. (London), for lines
from "Men Who March Away," from THE COLLECTED
POEMS OF THOMAS HARDY.

John Murray, Ltd., for portions of "Before Action," from William Noel Hodgson's VERSE AND PROSE IN PEACE AND WAR.

The Society of Authors (literary representative of the Estate of
the late A. E. Housman); Jonathan Cape, Ltd., publishers
of A. E. Housman's COLLECTED POEMS; and Holt, Rinehart
and Winston, Inc., for a selection from "A Shropshire Lad"
(Authorized Edition), from COMPLETE POEMS by A. E.
Housman. Copyright © 1959 by Holt, Rinehart and Winston, Inc.

Faber and Faber, Ltd., and Chilmark Press for passages from
David Jones's IN PARENTHESIS.

ACKNOWLEDGMENTS

Jonathan Cape, Ltd., for passages from John Middleton Murry's THE EVOLUTION OF AN INTELLECTUAL.

Milton Waldman, Esq., Robert Nichols' literary executor, for selections from Robert Nichols' ARDOURS AND ENDURANCES (Chatto and Windus, Ltd.)

Harold Owen, Esq., Chatto and Windus, Ltd., and New Directions for selections from THE POEMS OF WILFRED OWEN, edited by Edmund Blunden.

Oxford University Press for a passage from Thomas Parry's A HISTORY OF WELSH LITERATURE, trans. H. Idris Bell.

Faber and Faber, Ltd., and Harold Ober Associates, Inc., for selections from Sir Herbert Read's THE INNOCENT EYE. Copyright © 1947 by Sir Herbert Read.

Faber and Faber, Ltd., and New Directions for selections from Sir Herbert Read's COLLECTED POEMS.

Chatto and Windus, Ltd., for verse and prose selections from THE COMPLETE WORKS OF ISAAC ROSENBERG, edited by Gordon Bottomley and Denys Harding. Schocken Books, Inc., for verse selections from THE COLLECTED POEMS OF ISAAC ROSENBERG, edited by Gordon Bottomley and Denys Harding. Copyright 1949 by Schocken Books, Inc.

Siegfried Sassoon, Esq., for selections from COLLECTED POEMS and SIEGFRIED'S JOURNEY (Faber and Faber, Ltd., and Viking Press), and a passage from MEMOIRS OF AN INFANTRY OFFICER (Faber and Faber, Ltd., and Doubleday, Doran and Co.)

Cambridge University Press for selections from Charles Sorley's MARLBOROUGH AND OTHER POEMS and THE LETTERS OF CHARLES SORLEY.

ENGLISH POETRY
OF THE FIRST WORLD WAR

What are the great sceptred dooms
To us, caught
In the wild wave?
We break ourselves on them,
My brother, our hearts and years.

CHAPTER I · FOREGROUND AND BACKGROUND

It is one of the ironies of English literary history that the years immediately preceding the first great modern war—the war that brought to trial the fundamental premises of Western civilization—coincided with what C. Day Lewis calls "a period of very low vitality" for poetry. There were no Edwardian or Georgian figures to match the stature of Tennyson or Browning; the main tendencies of the age were visible not in the genius of one or two master spokesmen but in the talents of a host of minor poets: "a sadly pedestrian rabble," according to Day Lewis, who "flocked along the roads their fathers had built, pointing out to each other the beauty spots and ostentatiously drinking small-beer in a desperate effort to prove their virility." This description is witty rather than just or even accurate; for among the forty-odd poets who could be loosely classified as Georgians, we find a number of individualized talents and a generally high degree of craftsmanship. However, the majority—those who would more easily qualify as "typical" Georgians—clearly embody the less attractive characteristics indicated by Day Lewis: timidity, conservatism, self-consciousness, and lack of originality and genuine imaginative power.

These poets were not alone in their deepened regard for the sanctities of tradition. The Boer War and the death of Queen Victoria in 1901 seemed to have an isolating and constricting effect on the national outlook; an era was over, it was felt, and time graciously paused while the future made ready to declare itself. The Georgian orientation toward the past was symptomatic of a general nostalgia; the gifted young men of the period all seemed intent on savoring the present as a golden, euphoric culmination of the Victorian past. Yet at the same time they apparently felt that something irretrievable was

3

passing out of English life, that a vague menace lurked on the horizon of their "sunlit, tolerant, daylight world." Rupert Brooke—the most gifted of the Georgians—summarizes this feeling in the often-quoted conclusion of "The Old Vicarage, Grantchester":

> Say, is there Beauty yet to find?
> And Certainty? and Quiet kind?
> Deep meadows yet, for to forget
> The lies, and truths, and pain? . . . oh! yet
> Stands the Church clock at ten to three?
> And is there honey still for tea?

"The Old Vicarage" appeared, appropriately enough, in the first volume of *Georgian Poetry* (1912), the periodical anthology of contemporary verse edited by Edward (later Sir Edward) Marsh. In his introductory remarks Marsh proclaimed the collection as evidence of a twentieth-century renaissance: "This volume is issued in the belief that English poetry is now once again putting on a new strength and beauty. . . . We are at the beginning of another 'Georgian period' which may take rank in due time with the several great poetic ages of the past." It is difficult to reconcile Marsh's optimism with the kind of poetry the Georgians actually produced. Since the accent was on "Beauty," "Certainty," and "Quiet kind," the tendency was "to forget/ The lies, and truths, and pain." Although the first volume of *Georgian Poetry* contained two brief realistic selections from the work of W. W. Gibson and W. H. Davies, there could be no doubt that the "new" poetry took its main inspiration from traditional pastoral themes and materials. The *Georgian Poetry* series (there were five volumes in all) represented not a renaissance but what David Daiches has aptly called a "retrenchment." Reacting to the disintegration of nineteenth-century values and conventions, the Georgian poets, according to Daiches, "adopted an eclectic traditionalism, limited, refined, carefully hedged round, and within these confines sang softly but confidently."

But if they achieved "a certain tremulous stability" in their meditative response to "the slow-beating rustic heart of England," this stability was attained by a sacrifice which is in the long run always fatal to poetry: the loss of contact with contemporary reality. One would hardly be aware, in reading the first *Georgian Poetry* volume, of the exploratory energies that were at work in Western civilization—energies manifest in the achievements of Marconi, the Wrights, the Curies, Freud, and Einstein. Nor would one be aware of England's alarming constitutional difficulties, nor of the accelerating arms race, nor of the ugly diplomatic crises that were leading the nations of Europe to the most destructive war in history. All these, together with the essential trivia of everyday existence, constituted "the lies, and truths, and pain" of life in the twentieth century; but the Georgians, neither willing nor able to confront the external reality, developed a protective subjectivity and envisioned their art as a timeless refuge wherein the church clock might always stand "at ten to three." Although Tennyson had also written of the land in which "it seemed always afternoon," he had at least warned his contemporaries of the dangers of social isolation and had praised the imperatives of toil and action. Time is part of the essence of poetry: not only the inner time of verbal rhythms but also that outer time which embodies the varied rhythms of contemporary life. Of course the individual poet is not always obliged to find his themes in the market place or the forum, but any body of poetry that deliberately ignores the pulse of contemporary society is reduced, in the end, to a tacit disavowal of its creative function, since it exists on constantly diminishing intellectual and imaginative resources.

When one considers the wide range of social, moral, and psychological problems explored by Shaw, Wells, Galsworthy, James, and Conrad, the isolation of the Georgian sensibility becomes even more obvious. The novel, of course, had a background of vigorous contact with the moral and social realities of the nineteenth century; and the drama had begun to renew its powers as a medium of satire and social criticism. The Georgian lyric, on the other hand, had been conditioned to accept only those themes and materials which could be handled in the traditional fashion. If the "retrenchment" promised security in a world threatened by continued change in nearly every area of human life, it also seriously limited the possibilities of any fresh and significant poetic response as far as the lyric was concerned.

As the characteristic medium of the romantic movement, the lyric expressed not only the poet's emotional reaction to a particular reality but also a unified imaginative vision of that reality. Much romantic theory was given to a definition of the relationship between man and the external world, between the poet and the object of his imaginative vision. According to Wordsworth, the poet "considers man and nature as essentially adapted to each other, and the mind of man as naturally the mirror of the fairest and most interesting properties of nature." The romantic vision was profound enough to transform not only man's view of nature but his view of society as well: "The Poet binds together by passion and knowledge the vast empire of human society, as it is spread over the whole earth, and over all time." This conception of the poet's powers also includes his ability to accommodate any radical change in the circumstances of life: "If the labours of Men of science should ever create any material revolution, direct or indirect, in our condition, and in the impressions which we habitually receive, the Poet will sleep then no more than at present; he will be ready to follow the steps of the Man of science, not only in those general indirect effects, but he will be at his side, carrying sensation into the midst of the objects of the science itself.

. . . If the time should ever come when what is now called science, thus familiarized to men, shall be ready to put on, as it were, a form of flesh and blood, the Poet will lend his divine spirit to aid the transfiguration, and will welcome the Being thus produced as a dear and genuine inmate of the household of man."

The range and variety of the relationships here envisioned would seem to challenge the power of the most comprehensive literary forms: the drama, the long narrative poem, or the novel. However, it is the lyric—or, in longer poems, the lyric response —which communicates the romantic poet's consciousness of the external world and the values he intuitively discerns in it. Since it grows out of the seldom more than momentary contact of the poet's sensibility with a single aspect of reality, the lyric is not a comprehensive form; it is the vision behind the lyric and not the lyric itself that is comprehensive. Thus the productions of the great English lyric poets involve a range of conceptions which lie beyond the scope or function of the particular response. The lyric statement, though devoted to the details of an emotional or sensuous experience, implies an imaginative totality, a world outlook, a philosophy of existence. Out of this fact grew Wordsworth's supreme confidence in the ability of poetry to humanize whatever scientific transformations it might choose to depict.

In the course of the nineteenth century, however, the romantic vision began to deteriorate. Man and nature no longer seemed "essentially adapted to each other"; political, religious, and economic strife divided the "vast empire of human society"; and science was producing a "material revolution" that would test the assimilative powers of poetry to a degree Wordsworth had not foreseen. As these developments broadened and accelerated, the lyric surrendered its comprehensive vision to the novel and became, in the hands of the Victorian poets, a medium for the expression of personal attitudes—doubt, disil-

7

lusionment, pessimism, nostalgia—that reflected a disintegration of romantic values. The romantic sensibility still prevailed, but it was a sensibility concerned largely with externals; romantic techniques were refined and perfected, but they lacked the vitality of authentic inspiration. Toward the end of the century, the lyric, instead of embodying any meaningful relationship between the poet and his environment, became a means of dramatizing and confirming his isolation from it.

Thus the characteristic qualities of Georgian poetry—its blandness, its decorum, its homogeneity, its simplicity of attitude, its preoccupation with rural themes (rather than with "nature" as the romantics understood the term)—all reflect the decline of a once powerful imaginative vision. The Georgians expressed themselves chiefly through what Daiches calls the "static lyric": a kind of poem in which there is no movement of ideas and no enlargement of emotions; the total meaning is registered in terms of the limited attitude with which the writer regards a limited "poetic" situation. In other words, lyric poetry had become a mere exercise of sensibility related neither to the modern reality nor to any intellectual or imaginative vision capable of assimilating it. J. M. Synge, in condemning the specialized "poetic material" that had become the stock-in-trade of the post-Victorian sensibility, remarked in 1908 that "it may almost be said that before verse can be human again it must learn to be brutal." Certain members of the Georgian fellowship—W. W. Gibson, W. H. Davies, and John Masefield—tried to revitalize their poetry by developing narrative verse forms and dealing with materials from everyday life in the contemporary idiom. Although these men did not possess the highly individualized poetic vision of Hardy or Yeats, they followed the example of the novel and drama in attempting to establish some kind of contact, however crude, between poetry and "the lies, and truths, and pain." The fact that their work is regarded today as a minor phenomenon is something of an index to the character of Georgian poetry as a whole. If poetry had to learn to be brutal before it could again be human, the lesson was supplied by circumstances that were to destroy not only the Georgian "retrenchment" but also the whole range of traditional literary attitudes and values upon which the contemporary lyric response was based.

According to the well-known judgment of Dryden, the heroic poem is "undoubtedly the greatest work which the soul of man is capable to perform." Although we no longer subscribe to rigid literary hierarchies, we still admire—perhaps the more profoundly because we find them so difficult to attain—the classic qualities of epic narrative, whether Greek or Germanic in origin: comprehensiveness, objectivity, and a sense of proportion and restraint, together with a positive, assertive attitude with respect to the values upon which motivation and action are based. In reading the poetry of World War I we are inevitably impressed by the absence of these qualities. We see a body of verse limited to a rather narrow range of personal experience, subjective and impressionistic in mode, marked by emotional excess, and motivated by disillusionment, anger, or pity. A tenuous but generic relationship exists among all types of literature devoted to the subject of war, and some of the deficiencies of modern war poetry may be assigned both to the lapse of the epic tradition and to the conditions of modern warfare which made that tradition seem impracticable and irrelevant. Other deficiencies may be traced to the immediate lyric tradition as practiced by the Georgians, for most of the young war poets shared the Georgian outlook and modeled their early verse upon established Georgian techniques. The evolution of World War I poetry is characterized by a spontaneous effort on the part of these young men to improvise some means of contact with a particularly ugly and violent revelation of the contemporary reality, and by a corresponding intensifica-

9

tion of the lyric response. Later in the war, as the result of a deepening sense of tragic involvement, most of the soldier-poets began to understand the inadequacies of mere emotional or realistic intensification; they sought, or thought of seeking, a larger and more comprehensive mode for the interpretation of wartime experience. They tried the lyric sequence; they tried the verse narrative; and they tried to enlarge and unify the vision behind the lyric by means of the theme of pity. Significantly, the purpose of these varied experiments was realized, long after the war, in a remarkable narrative poem of heroic temper and scope—proving that the epic spirit was not defunct, and that a critical invocation of epic standards with regard to World War I poetry is not altogether beside the point.

The rapid transition from the "deep meadows" of Georgian peace and security to the shocking conditions of trench warfare in France was accompanied by a powerfully negative psychological reaction. If the epic glorified primitive combat as a heroic occupation and a test of individual worth, the main tendency of contemporary war poetry has been to de-glorify modern warfare, to strip it of its falsely romantic and adventurous aspects, to emphasize its futility, and to portray it as shameful and degrading. The poets of World War I made it clear that man could no longer depend on his personal courage or strength for victory or even survival; mechanization, the increased size of armies, the intensification of operations, and the scientific efficiency of long-distance weapons destroyed the very elements of human individuality: courage, hope, enterprise, and a sense of the heroic possibilities in moral and physical conflict. Needless to say, the old epic standards of heroic achievement have disappeared entirely or are invoked only as implicit points of bitterly ironic contrasts. The modern soldier is portrayed as a passive and often degraded victim of circumstances. Siegfried Sassoon's infantrymen, for example, succumb to hysteria ("Lamentations"), take their own lives ("Suicide in the Trenches"), or perish in an ill-conceived attack ("The General"). In "Third Ypres" Edmund Blunden's soldiers die ignominiously or, stunned and helpless, crouch amid the ruins of a shell-blasted pillbox. The weapons of modern warfare add new terrors to death: mutilation, dismemberment, the agony of poison gas (Wilfred Owen's "Dulce et Decorum Est"). In terms that reverse all idealistic conceptions of death in warfare, Isaac Rosenberg's "Dead Man's Dump" depicts the pitiable degradation of the slain. After the war a succession of novels confirmed or enlarged these earlier impressions of violence, horror, and brutality; personal narratives and autobiographical accounts, such as Edmund Blunden's *Undertones of War* (1928) and Robert Graves's *Good-bye to All That* (1929), corroborated the imaginative projections of the novel. Although all of these writers differ in their degrees of specification and emphasis, not even the most meditative can deal with his material without some reference to the demoralizing conditions of modern warfare. Amid such conditions a mood of bitter disillusionment was inevitable; this attitude, of course, provided the poetry of World War I with its major themes and materials. The generally negative character of modern war poetry thus contrasts directly with the positive, affirmative character of epic battle literature, with its proud sense of past glories and its total commitment to the imperatives of heroic action.

A further point of contrast bears more directly upon the development of certain less obvious attitudes and their effects on poetic technique. Unlike the epic poet, who usually wrote of the distant past and was thus able to enlarge and transform his subject imaginatively, the harassed soldier-poet was in the very midst of the events which he attempted to depict. He was confined to a historical reality well known—at least in its superficial aspects—to those who might read his verse; he could take no large imaginative liberties with the facts and phenomena of the struggle. The soldier-poet, indeed, was seldom inclined to take such liberties; he felt it his special role—even his obligation—to see and portray the war as a starkly contemporaneous event. His material was the reality of the war as personal experience revealed it to him, and the unadorned expression or communication of that reality was his urgent concern. If the function of the epic poet was to entertain his audience with tales of heroic adventure set in the distant past, the modern war poet presents his impressions of suffering and tragedy not as a matter for simple entertainment but as an implicit or explicit protest against the very aims and methods of that conflict in which he is engaged.

Doubtless the fact that the epic poets dealt with the distant past has some relation to the qualities of objectivity, proportion, and restraint that are characteristic of epic and heroic narrative. Well removed in time from the men and events of his tale, the epic poet could hardly be emotionally subject to the issues of a legendary past; divested of its urgency and immediacy, purified of all extraneous feeling, the drama of the epic narrative exists in a separate, self-sustaining dimension of its own. Modern war poetry, on the other hand, is deprived of the aesthetic advantages of temporal remoteness; it is inextricably involved in the whole physical and psychological complex of warfare and takes its particular spirit from a dedicated and often desperate representation of that complex. This situation is further intensified by the mood of disillusion and rejection, which lends particular animus to the presentation of the disagreeable aspects of modern warfare and raises special problems of selection and control.

In World War I the great mission of the poet who had some prospect of publishing his verse was to communicate his sense of the reality of war to the millions at home who would not or could not appreciate the magnitude of the experiences and sacrifices of the common soldier. Even the poet who had no ready public outlet for his verse seems to be aware of his mission as spokesman and his voice has nearly the same degree of urgency. Granting the imperative nature of that mission, the artistic virtues of objectivity, proportion, and restraint hardly seemed useful or even desirable. During the second winter of the war, when the true nature of the struggle was becoming apparent, poets began to react to the horrors around them with a directness almost unprecedented in verse. This literature of angry protest employed the weapons of satire, irony, and a savage realism, since realism seemed the only effective mode for depicting the disaster being enacted in France. As might have been expected, there were attacks upon civilian profiteering and indifference; upon official optimism; upon military incompetence and favoritism; and of course upon the continued prosecution of a war that had become particularly senseless to those who were fighting it. But most frequently of all, and most significantly from a literary point of view, we have accounts of the experiences of the common soldier amidst a new kind of warfare—a warfare that utilized to the maximum every species of concentrated scientific violence. As a partial and natural consequence, we have a tentative, episodic, disconnected, emotional kind of writing, a desperate insistence on the shocking facts of life and death, a compulsive focus on the obscene details of crude animal needs and reactions, on wounds, death, and decomposition. Never before in literature had war been described with this painful compression of action and incident, with this narrowing of focus, this fragmentation of reality, this obsessive emphasis on isolated and irrelevant sensory details. It is not really necessary to point out the almost incredible contrast between these tortured effects and the graceful, weightless songs of the Georgians. The "static lyric" had suddenly been forced to accommodate a flood of experience too vast for it to assess, too various for it to order, and too powerful for it to control.

If objectivity and restraint, selection and control are rare in modern war poetry, so also is that perspective which both orders and stabilizes the events of the present and unites them with a significant historical continuity. In the epic the distant past impinges upon and sometimes actually pervades the present narrative reality; depicted in the light of a compelling historical analogy or continuity, present events assume a special meaning and a particular force and depth. Most contemporary war poetry, on the other hand, is characterized by a sense of abrupt discontinuity with the past. The violence and intensity of mechanized warfare, the unprecedented scale of death and destruction, and the total national involvement all contributed to this feeling of complete historical severance. The war was seen, with some justice, as an absolutely unique event; it was hopeless to seek parallels in the past or to unite the shattering experiences of the present so that they would have some kind of relation to eras of past aspiration and endeavor. As we shall see, this lack of historical perspective in World War I poetry resulted in a lack of both temporal and moral depth, since any event ceases to have real significance unless it is in some way related to other events. Further, if an event seems to have no real significance, the physical phenomena of which it is composed are likely to be presented as erratic, disordered, and void of meaning. Giving both an impression of temporal depth and a thorough notation of particularized reality, the great epics never sacrifice moral or physical proportion to the demands of crude realism; the epic poet's sense of proportion always preserves the elementary distinctions between large and small, relevant and irrelevant, trivial and momentous, real and unreal. The war poets, however, obviously felt (in the words of one of their sympathetic successors) that they must "let the wrong cry out as raw as wounds," that the voice of the poet should be as direct and as spontaneous as the voice of anger or pain.

In addition to reducing the historical perspective and the sense of moral and physical proportion, the conditions of World

War I tended to obscure the very aims and ideals for which the struggle was being waged. In his brief critique of the war novel, Douglas Jerrold thus describes the factors which limited the soldier's conception of his role in the conflict:

"To the individual personally, all operations of war are meaningless and futile. He has no sense of personal contention with his enemies, not because they are not his enemies, not because the issue of the struggle is immaterial, but simply because the smallest fighting unit is, in modern national warfare, not the individual, the section or the company, not even the battalion, the regiment or the brigade, but the division. And that on rare occasions only. The movements which made history, which broke in succession the power of the Czar, the Turkish Empire, the Austro-Hungarian Empire and the German military bureaucracy, were the movements, the hammer blows, of Armies and Army groups. In relation to these movements, the agonies, the ardours, and the endurances of individuals assume a tragic and heroic dignity. Divorced from them, related not to the will of their Commanders, the moral, physical and economic resources of their nationals and the aims of their statesmen, but to the limited horizon of the individual soldier, the wanderings and sufferings of the squad, the platoon, or the company, not only appear to be, but are, utterly futile and without meaning."[1]

Though it is made with reference to the novel, Jerrold's analysis applies with equal accuracy to certain effects observable in modern war poetry. The epic, of course, dealt with a much smaller scale of conflict; during the heroic ages military organization had not yet developed to the stage of mass attack and maneuver, and the purposes of any military action were comparatively simple and direct. Furthermore, the epic was concerned only with aristocratic personages, the "leaders and lords" whose exercise of the heroic virtues constituted the major interest of the story. Unlike the epic, modern war poetry is

[1] *The Lie About the War* (London, 1930), pp. 22-23.

almost exclusively concerned with the experiences of the ordinary soldier; this figure, elevated by his obscurity, his sufferings, his patience and endurance, is the anonymous "hero" of contemporary poetry. He is, however, a passive rather than an active figure; as a mere unit in a vast military machine, he is controlled by directive intelligences remote from the field of battle. As the poet depicts him, he is a victim rather than a hero; what he does is not so important as what is done to him. Since the individual soldier can know little of the war outside his limited and generally passive experience of it, this fact—as the passage from Jerrold implies—contributes even further to the reduction of perspective and the consequent loss of temporal, moral, and physical proportion. If we had to depend upon World War I poetry for our knowledge of the causes and aims of the struggle, the ideals involved, and the military purposes which governed the fates of so many millions of men, our understanding of these matters would not only be meager but in some cases rather seriously distorted. Here, as with Georgian poetry, we have something of an index to the nature of the contemporary lyric as it sought to adjust itself to the demands of a reality that seemed almost retributive in its manifestations of savagery and chaotic violence. The "lies, and truths, and pain" vaguely sensed but ignored by Rupert Brooke and his contemporaries became the substance of daily existence for those who fought in the trenches. Having become brutal in its exposure of the lies and its revelation of the truths, poetry became all too human in its function as the voice of pain.

If it is obvious that the novel conditions of modern warfare strongly influenced the attitudes and techniques of World War I poetry, the effects of Georgian lyric practice are not so obvious—or at least these effects have not been very clearly designated or described. The literary discontinuity, like the historical, is so abrupt that we fail to notice the few important continuing strands that tend to support and confirm the patterns of the wartime lyric response.

William Butler Yeats, as editor of *The Oxford Book of Modern Verse* (1936), confessed "a distaste for certain poems written in the midst of the great war." He excluded all such poems from his anthology, remarking in his Introduction that "passive suffering is not a theme for poetry. . . . When man has withdrawn into the quicksilver at the back of the mirror no great event becomes luminous in his mind; it is no longer possible to write *The Persians, Agincourt, Chevy Chase*: some blunderer has driven his car on to the wrong side of the road—that is all." Yeats's judgment, though it refers in passing to a certain physical or historical effect—the theme of passive suffering—is really an aesthetic judgment; it may be applied, as Yeats's actual selections seem to indicate, to nearly the whole range of poetry directly inspired by the war. The intrusion of strong subjective elements into any work of poetic art, to the detriment of its necessary objective relationships, brings loss of perspective and ultimately loss of proportion and value; the real world exists only as it is partially and inaccurately reflected in the beholder's mind and is thus subject to his personal emotional reactions. The trivial or irrelevant detail thus becomes more important, through its emotional effect, than the general situation of which it is a part. The poet, "withdrawn into the quicksilver at the back of the mirror," becomes a mere sensorium and a transmitter of sensations which the reader must sort and assess for himself.

Functioning largely as the exercise of personal sensibility, Georgian poetry failed to go beyond the limits of carefully chosen "poetic" situations—situations that evoked a predictable, somewhat self-conscious personal response to rural beauty. Whatever they lacked in vision or genius, the Georgians made up for by their comforting sense of numbers and by their illusory impression of a poetic "renaissance." With the war, therefore, came a vaguely idealistic reaction developed in highly personal, self-dramatizing terms—an emotionalized response which interpreted the conflict as an opportunity for the poet's own moral regeneration. Just as the Georgians had refused to venture outside their accustomed modes of thought and expression, so the early poets refused to go beyond the personal implications of their involvement in the war. Apparently oblivious of causes, issues, and practical effects, they exploited the "poetic" aspects of the situation and indulged themselves in romantic fantasies of honor, sacrifice, self-redemption, and immortality. These were safe, traditional themes which could provide numerous elegant variations; but they had nothing whatever to do with the objective historical reality, even when patriotism was the source of inspiration. No previous body of poetry in English literature, inspired by momentous national events, has been marked by such limited knowledge and by such an excess of self-contemplation.

"Above all I am not concerned with Poetry," wrote Wilfred Owen late in the war, signifying his dissociation from the earlier response. Knowledge had replaced ignorance, but even in the shift to more realistic attitudes we find evidence that the Georgian sensibility had not been totally transformed. The deliberately shocking techniques of the new realism may be seen, in part, as a frequently exaggerated reaction to Georgian blandness and decorum. Brought to life by its contact with living materials, the "static lyric" suddenly became dynamic, deriving its motive and effect not only from the physical conditions of the war but also from a consciously exercised contrast to the Georgian mode. However, the personal response, though intensified and liberated from self-consciousness, was no less personal in its depiction of experience; instead of a formal artistic principle of selection and control, we have an emotionalized sensibility offering glimpses, impressions, fragments. The external reality had changed, but there had been no fundamental enlargement of the lyric vision. Sill "withdrawn into the quicksilver at the back of the mirror," the poet could not present his experiences objectively, nor could he discriminate clearly with respect to experiential values. Even the emotions of anger and pity remain, in the end, personal reactions that fall far short of encompassing the reality of modern warfare. Though the vision of pity comprehends most of what the later soldier-poets were struggling to say, it interprets only one aspect of war—that of passive suffering—rather than embodying the broader reality of which that suffering is a part. Certain poets, as we shall see, rejected the Georgian inheritance and success-fully drew upon other resources, personal and traditional; these exceptions, together with the general effort to break away from the limitations of the personal response, simply accentuate the major tendencies we have been tracing.

Yeats's dictum concerning objectivity and proportion has an even more important corollary with respect to that tragic tone to which all serious art aspires. A tragic event which is under-stood only in terms of personal misadventure ceases to be tragic. Tragedy implies a relationship between the part and the whole, between man and the mysteries of the moral universe. Since the modern war poet can discern no significant relationships among the phenomena that confront him, he cannot positively relate his experiences to the moral whole of which they are necessarily a part. Of pity, grief, and fear there is much in World War I poetry, but these emotions rarely attain the nobility proper to genuinely tragic emotions. Although the war poet was fre-quently a witness to tragic situations, he never seems quite sure what these situations are worth; he deplores, pities, attacks, and rejects, but aside from the compassionate vision (as set forth in Wilfred Owen's "Strange Meeting"), he has no values to apply or standards to affirm. He functions as conscience, as sensibility, and as the voice of anger or pain; but he seldom rises above these functions and the aspects of ugliness or suffering upon which they are based. Enveloped in the tragedy of war, he sees only magnified particulars and details—no event becomes "luminous" in his mind. If it is a function of poetry, as Wordsworth claimed, to follow the effects of science on man's life, it may be that poetry deals with the phenomena of technological warfare at the sacrifice of values which alone can make events luminous—the values of the tragic or heroic vision. Yet it is impossible to believe, as we follow the developments of World War I verse to their culmination in the late 1930's, that either poetry or the particular vision that happens to animate it can succumb to forces which invariably provoke man's instinctive rebellion and encourage his reassertion of the values by which he lives.

Most of the British poets whose work is examined in the following chapters are of a group, even when not known to one another personally; their names remain firmly attached to the First World War, and their figures are inseparable from the circumstances that inspired the poetry by which—in most cases—they are best known. They rebelled as much against the literary falsities, reticences, and decorums which preceded them, as against the intolerable conditions of trench warfare in France; and their influence, especially in poetic technique, is still felt. But their failure to universalize their work, their inability to elevate it much beyond the level of vivid reportage, relegates them—with one or two notable exceptions—to that class of poets whose secondary position is attributable not to the lack of skill or integrity but to a failure in responding to a quickly changing relationship between matter and form. Perhaps the justice of that relegation cannot be challenged, but the particular nature of their response and their efforts to adjust that response to the conditions of modern warfare deserve thoughtful attention.

CHAPTER II · THE
EARLY POETS

As we look back to the "Great War" of 1914-1918, we begin to feel that it has ceased to be a part of contemporary history. Two decades of disillusionment with the results of that vast conflict have given way to two decades of rapidly fluctuating attitudes based on a much broader and more threatening set of historical circumstances; and our present disillusionments—accepted, perhaps, as inevitable consequents of modern war and peace—tend to absorb and diminish those of the immediate past.

It is difficult, therefore, to imagine the spirit with which the British people viewed the opening of that first great world conflict. When England declared war against Germany on the night of August 4, 1914, the nation was swept by a wave of popular enthusiasm that has few parallels in modern history. Germany's violation of the general European pledge to respect Belgian neutrality evoked an outburst which was partly righteous indignation, partly a sense of relief at being committed, after a long period of indecisive diplomatic maneuvering, to a clear course of action, and partly an emotional sense of solidarity in exerting the common will. The rather bitter internal dissension of the day was either postponed or forgotten; all Britain seemed to be electrified by a rare species of national moral challenge. No one could foresee, of course, either the nature or the duration of the conflict; no one could predict the long, hopeless stalemate of trench warfare that was to follow after the German invasion of France had lost its original impetus.

Stimulated by the moral issue of an invaded Belgium as well as by a pleasurable sense of release from the routines of daily life, the young men of England responded quickly to the necessity of reinforcing the battered Expeditionary Force, retreating slowly, in late August, before the assaults of General von Kluck's First Army. The hastily improvised machinery of military organization was strained to the breaking-point with volunteers, for whom adequate training facilities, and even uniforms, could not immediately be provided. European wars of the past—fought mostly by professional soldiers—afford only one or two analogies to the spirit that motivated hundreds of thousands of young men to join the "New Armies." C. E. Montague, in his perceptive account of the rise and fall of this phenomenal enthusiasm, thus depicts the prevailing attitude of 1914:

"Most of those volunteers of the prime were men of handsome and boundless illusions. Each of them quite seriously thought of himself as a molecule in the body of a nation that was really, and not just figuratively, 'straining every nerve' to discharge an obligation of honour. Honestly, there was about them as little as there could humanly be of the coxcombry of self-devotion. They only felt that they had got themselves happily placed on a rope at which everyone else, in some way or other, was tugging his best as well as they. All the air was ringing with rousing assurances. France to be saved, Belgium righted, freedom and civilization re-won, a sour, soiled, crooked old world to be rid of bullies and crooks and reclaimed for straightness, decency, good-nature, the ways of common men dealing with common men. What a chance! The plain recruit who had not the gift of a style said to himself that for once he had got right in on the ground-floor of a topping good thing, and he blessed the luck that had made him neither too old nor too young."[1]

Needless to say, the young university men who were largely destined to officer the New Armies, and from whose ranks most of the best-known poets of the war were to emerge, were animated by the same enthusiastic feeling. These young men did not consider themselves victims, robbed of their ordinary destinies in life by a cruel climax of nationalistic and economic

---

[1] *Disenchantment* (London, 1922), pp. 2-3.

rivalry; they were proud, as Montague indicates, to have been "chosen" for a sacrifice they made only too willingly. Behind this spiritual ardor was a sense of gratification at finding, in the midst of the drab commonplaces and monotonies of a commercialized world, an opportunity for selfless, heroic action. Also, in the varied biographical and autobiographical accounts concerned with the Edwardian-Georgian period, one often discovers something close to a sense of relief at the termination of an inherited and unmotivated leisure—a leisure assimilative rather than productive, and confined, of course, to members of the educated upper classes. The call, nonetheless, was unmistakable; a crusade was under way, a meaningful effort which involved not complacent abstractions or tired social doctrines but a direct moral challenge which affected both national and personal honor. To this challenge the aged Thomas Hardy responded in his "Men Who March Away" (published in the London *Times* of September 9, 1914), which perfectly expresses the righteous crusading spirit of the first few weeks of the war:

> What of the faith and fire within us
> Men who march away
> Ere the barn-cocks say
> Night is growing gray,
> To hazards whence no tears can win us;
> What of the faith and fire within us
> Men who march away?
>
> . . . .
>
> In our heart of hearts believing
> Victory crowns the just,
> And that braggarts must
> Surely bite the dust,
> Press we to the field ungrieving,
> In our heart of hearts believing
> Victory crowns the just.

If Hardy's philosophic reserve could be so affected by the crisis, certainly one could hardly expect the younger poets, for whom the crusade had more personal implications, to remain silent.

Among the young men who were later to be called war poets, at least one—Rupert Brooke—already enjoyed a moderate reputation; the verse of another, Siegfried Sassoon, was beginning to attract attention; others, such as Charles Sorley, Robert Nichols, Edmund Blunden, Isaac Rosenberg, Wilfred Owen, and Herbert Read, were not publicly known, but they had begun to write verse and in some cases had published their work in school magazines or in small privately printed collections. Whatever their individual poetic reputations or preoccupations may have been prior to August 1914, when the war broke out those who were immediately affected naturally turned to the brief lyric as the most convenient means of expressing their sense of participation in the national crisis. Considering the pressure of time, circumstances, and emotion, and, in most cases, their own youthful poetic practice, such a development is not surprising. Nor is it surprising that throughout the course of the war the soldier-poets continued to employ the contemporary lyric form. They used it for a remarkable variety of ends: patriotic, meditative, descriptive, satiric, and elegiac; what might be called the lyric response, moreover, permeated and influenced the character of all major narrative efforts. Again, the nature of the crisis, as it prolonged itself into months of bitter struggle and exacted unprecedented effort and suffering, seemed to demand the swift and urgent expression that only the lyric could afford.

The emergence, decline, and eventual reversal of the early idealistic attitude is perhaps the most obvious phenomenon of World War I poetry, and it may serve us here as a convenient means of reference and classification. Thus our immediate interests are determined by the character of the verse written by certain poets before July 1916, when, as a result of the costly and disappointing Somme Offensive, the war assumed a much grimmer aspect. The poets who had achieved their main response before 1916—Brooke, Grenfell, Nichols, and Sorley—thus form a group by virtue of their reaction to the initial psychological impact of the war.

I. RUPERT BROOKE

Even today the romantic figure of Rupert Brooke is established in the popular mind as representative of the hundreds of thousands of young men whose lives were tragically cut short by World War I. Handsome, intelligent, personable, universally admired, Brooke was something of a legend even during his lifetime; and his premature death in the Aegean in 1915 seemed, to those who knew him, a sad but somehow fitting and dramatic fulfillment of the prophecy made in his famous sonnet sequence, *1914*.

Son of a Rugby housemaster, Brooke attended that school, where he had a reputation as both a scholar and an athlete, and in 1906 proceeded to King's College, Cambridge. At King's he was regarded as one of the leading intellectuals of the day; he was absorbed in poetry, dramatics, and literary discussion, and he shared—perhaps not with complete inner conviction—the experimental social and political interests of his contemporaries. Brooke's first volume of poems was published in December 1911, and in 1912, with Edward Marsh, he originated the plan for the first edition of *Georgian Poetry*. These activities were interspersed with short visits to the Continent and a brief period of residence at the Old Vicarage, Grantchester, near Cambridge. In May 1913 he embarked on a long voyage to the South Seas (by way of the United States and Canada), which he described in letters published in the *Westminster Gazette*. From this extended sojourn the poet returned to England in June 1914 —on the very eve of the war.

During August, after hostilities began, Brooke seems to have been uncertain about his course of action. With Frederick Keeling and several other university friends, he joined the Artists' Rifles, but by August 24 he had dropped out, intending to seek a commission. In early September Winston Churchill (then First Lord of the Admiralty) offered him a post in the newly formed Royal Naval Division. Brooke joined the Anson Battalion on September 27 and was present at the unsuccessful attempt to save Antwerp. During this brief action, according to his own admission, Brooke was "barely even under fire," though he witnessed some spectacular effects of wartime havoc and disruption. The five sonnets of 1914, upon which he had been working during the autumn, were finished at Rugby during his Christmas leave. In February 1915, after a spell of influenza, he embarked with his unit for the Dardanelles, characteristically rejoicing over the romantic possibility of meeting the Turks "on the plains of Troy." The following April, in Egypt, he suffered a touch of sunstroke, but this did not prevent him from sailing with his battalion when it departed, one week later, for Gallipoli. It was at the island of Skyros, on April 20, that Brooke developed the symptoms of his fatal illness, which was diagnosed as acute blood-poisoning. He was moved to a French hospital ship which happened to be in the vicinity, and there, three days later, he died. The words of his friend Edward Marsh intentionally convey a number of significant associations:

"Here then, in the island where Theseus was buried, and whence the young Achilles and the young Pyrrhus were called to Troy, Rupert Brooke died and was buried on Friday, the 23rd of April, the day of Shakespeare and of St. George."[2]

It is not difficult to discover other contemporary tributes to Brooke. For Edward Thomas, he was "a golden young Apollo," and Siegfried Sassoon, who met Brooke only briefly in June

[2] *Rupert Brooke: A Memoir* (New York, 1918), p. 180.

1914, saw him as "a being singled out for some transplendent performance, some enshrined achievement." In the London *Times*, a few days after the poet's death, Winston Churchill wrote grandiloquently, "Joyous, fearless, versatile, deeply instructed, with classic symmetry of mind and body, ruled by high undoubting purpose, he was all that one would wish England's noblest sons to be. . . ." However, Frances Cornford's epigram, though meant as a gracious compliment to the living poet, has since revealed a number of unintentional ironies:

> A young Apollo, golden-haired,
>> Stands dreaming on the verge of strife,
> Magnificently unprepared
>> For the long littleness of life.

Edward Marsh, saddened by Brooke's death, found a bitter irony in the word "long"; postwar critical opinion, however, free from the emotionalism of 1914-1915 and suffused with the disillusionment of the twenties, found the irony elsewhere. Speaking of Brooke's Georgian pastoralism, F. R. Leavis writes: "He energized the Garden-Suburb ethos with a certain original talent and the vigour of a prolonged adolescence. His verse exhibits a genuine sensuousness rather like Keats's (though more energetic) and something that is rather like Keats's vulgarity with a Public School accent."[3] I. A. Richards was of the opinion that Brooke's poetry has "no inside," and Vivian de Sola Pinto, while admitting that Brooke was "a wonderfully accomplished versifier," charges that "his mind remained to the end that of a clever public schoolboy."[4] Speaking for the World War II generation in the Preface of Robert Nichols' collection of war poems, Julian Tennyson finds Brooke's war sonnets "beautiful, perhaps, but nonetheless a little silly, even school-girlish."[5]

[3] *New Bearings in English Poetry* (London, 1950 ed.), p. 63.
[4] *Crisis in English Poetry* (London, 1951), p. 132.
[5] *Anthology of War Poetry, 1914-1918* (London, 1943), p. 31.

The charges against the "adolescence" of Brooke's prewar verse are comprehensible in terms of the new social consciousness that poetry assumed in the twenties, after the publication of T. S. Eliot's *The Waste Land*. The effete pastoralism that was the characteristic element of Georgian poetry represented an attempt to escape from the realities of modern urban and industrial life. Brooke himself, the most talented of the Georgians, seems to have realized that his ruminations among the "haunts of ancient peace," his melodious Platonic speculations on life and death, and his witty "metaphysical" conceits (after the manner of Donne and Marvell) were far from constituting the whole substance of poetic reality; his occasional "ugly" verse is an unsuccessful attempt to break out of the daydream of an artificial and self-conscious "poetic" attitude. Brooke admitted, in a letter to his publisher, that there was much "unimportant prettiness" in his 1911 volume, which his "new and serious" verse was intended to offset.[6] The "new and serious" verse, however, instead of reflecting a maturing sensibility or even the slightest social comprehension, merely presents unpleasant and even disgusting minor effects, as in "A Channel Passage":

> Retchings twist and tie me,
> Old meat, good meals, brown gobbets, up I throw.

These were the effects at which Brooke would "grasp relievedly" after he had "beaten vain hands in the rosy mists of poets' experiences." In this casual explanation we have a glimpse of the meaningless dichotomy upon which Georgian values were based: the "poetic" or unreal on the one hand, and the unpoetic or "real" on the other. Most Georgian verse eschewed the real—the broad reality of contemporary life—and subsisted on rosy poetic mists; Brooke, its most admired exponent, hardly mani-

[6] See the passage quoted by Marsh, *Rupert Brooke*, p. 81.

fested any genuine inclination to escape from the attitudes and practices that have come to be identified with it. "Smiling over his own fancies," remarks T. Sturge Moore, "Brooke seems to have sat half abstracted at a pleasure party till the outbreak of war."[7]

We are here chiefly concerned, of course, with Brooke's war verse, which consists of the famous five sonnets, 1914,[8] and a negligible posthumous "Fragment." Upon these scanty productions, which happened to coincide with the national mood described by Montague, the legend of Brooke as spokesman and symbol has been perpetuated. In the Preface to his 1943 anthology of war poems, for instance, Robert Nichols comments on the unique "sensation of being gathered up and lifted," which was the result, on the part of the young men of 1914, of viewing the war as an opportunity to accept a rare moral challenge:

"Rupert Brooke's sonnets are full of that sensation of being gathered up. They are wonderful works of art and it is sad that they have come to be regarded by many with suspicion. For I wish to assure you with all the sincerity I can command that they seem to me now, as then, a just, dazzling and perfect expression of what we then felt."[9]

But were the attitudes of 1914 really in accord with the feelings of Montague's "plain recruit" who lacked "the gift of a style" and who was free from the "coxcombry of self-devotion"? In view of the specific sentiments expressed in the sonnets, Nichols—a product of Westminster and an Oxford undergraduate when the war began—must be assumed to be speaking for the young university volunteers whose upbringing, education,

[7] *Some Soldier Poets* (New York, 1920), p. 25.

[8] The sonnets first appeared in the fourth and final issue of *New Numbers* (December 1914); they did not receive much attention, however, until just before the poet's death, when Sonnet V was quoted and praised by Dean Inge in the course of an Easter sermon at St. Paul's. In June 1915 they were published in *1914 and Other Poems* (edited by Edward Marsh); a few months later they appeared separately as *1914*.

[9] *Anthology of War Poetry*, p. 35.

and literary tastes equipped them to appreciate those sentiments and their manner of presentation.

Elegant, melodious, rich in texture, decorous and dignified in tone, the 1914 sonnets do not deal with war; they reveal a sophisticated sensibility contemplating itself on the verge of war. Like Wordsworth's impassioned sonnets of 1802, Brooke's 1914 was inspired by a great moral and social crisis; but instead of defining that crisis, as Wordsworth does, in national and historical terms, Brooke merely presents its effects on his own rather specialized range of responses. Though the poet refers to himself only in Sonnets II and V (this fact has been adduced to disprove the charge of egocentricity), he could hardly have done otherwise without appearing ludicrously immodest and affected. Actually, the earnest, fervid, self-revelatory nature of the sequence and its progression to the eloquent intimacy of Sonnet V leave no doubt about the highly personal nature of the sentiments expressed therein.

In Sonnet I, "Peace," the poet is prayerfully thankful for the moral challenge afforded by the war; this challenge, however, is not seen in terms of an outward wrong to be righted but in terms of an opportunity for personal moral regeneration:

> Now, God be thanked Who has matched us with His
>   hour,
>   And caught our youth, and wakened us from sleeping,
> With hand made sure, clear eye, and sharpened power,
>   To turn, as swimmers into cleanness leaping,
> Glad from a world grown old and cold and weary,
>   Leave the sick hearts that honour could not move,
> And half-men, and their dirty songs and dreary,
>   And all the little emptiness of love!

Thus the volunteer can rejoice in his escape from a malaise that is related to the languid ills of the nineties rather than to any reality that Brooke had experienced. The sestet proceeds to round off a comforting paradox, emotional rather than intellectual in content: the sufferings of warfare bring a spiritual "peace"; in battle, "the worst friend and enemy is but Death." Sonnet II, "Safety"—with its echo of Donne's "The Anniversarie"—is also developed in terms of paradox; the moral crusade, by its very nobility, guarantees a kind of spiritual safety and immortality:

> We have gained a peace unshaken by pain for ever.
> War knows no power. Safe shall be my going,
>   Secretly armed against all death's endeavour;
> Safe though all safety's lost; safe where men fall;
> And if these poor limbs die, safest of all.

Thus the war is again viewed—all too vaguely and remotely—in terms of its personal effects on the poet. Though it is apparently in the nature of that war to provide a kind of moral regeneration for those who volunteer to fight it, the nature and the purpose of the struggle remain undefined: they exist as vast unspoken premises behind the rhetoric of self-revelation and the artful shifts of paradox. The attitude of world-weariness, the suggestion of personal disillusion in love, and the hint of past "shame," in Sonnet I, all impart a private confessional flavor that dramatizes both terms of a vague moral contrast: what the poet has been, and what he hopes to be.

The next three sonnets are concerned with the implications of death, not, however, as it is related to the purposes which justify the war or even on its own terms as a physical reality, but as a species of translation from physical life to a retrospective awareness as "a pulse in the eternal mind." This rather worn poetic conception involves a number of elements: the pathos of abruptly terminated hopes and joys; the inspirational effect of these sacrifices on the living; and the assurance that death in battle procures a remote contemplative peace. In the final sonnet, the poet, meditating on his own possible death, gives the cumulative emotional substance of these themes an explicit personal application.

Sonnet III, "The Dead," considers the selfless generosity of the young men who have fallen in battle:

> These laid the world away; poured out the red
> Sweet wine of youth; gave up the years to be
>   Of work and joy, and that unhoped serene,
>   That men call age; and those who would have
>   been,
>   Their sons, they gave, their immortality.

These sacrifices, however, bring compensation in the return of the "heritage" of youth—Holiness, Love, Pain, Honor, and Nobleness—all lost, apparently, amid the mean circumstances of modern life. The best poem of the sequence, Sonnet IV, also entitled "The Dead," is more properly elegiac in effect. The octave presents a summation of human experience on the sensuous and emotional level, though one must remember that the experiences seem to be those of the cultured young Georgian poet enjoying his patrimony of peaceful leisure:

> These hearts were woven of human joys and cares,
>   Washed marvellously with sorrow, swift to mirth.
> The years had given them kindness. Dawn was theirs,
>   And sunset, and the colours of the earth.
> These had seen movement, and heard music; known
>   Slumber and waking; loved; gone proudly friended;
> Felt the quick stir of wonder; sat alone;
>   Touched flowers and furs and cheeks. All this is ended.

Death, as the sestet pictures it, arrests these pleasurable activities; but it "gathers" and immortalizes rather than cancels the range of experience with which Brooke was familiar:

There are waters blown by changing winds to laughter
And lit by the rich skies, all day. And after,
    Frost, with a gesture, stays the waves that dance
And wandering loveliness. He leaves a white
    Unbroken glory, a gathered radiance,
A width, a shining peace, under the night.

The rich images and delicate music of this sonnet constitute something of an achievement in poetic technique, but that achievement is strangely out of contact with the actuality that inspired it. Even in terms of Brooke's elevated idealism, the symbol employed in the sestet is too consciously elegant, too ingenious in its development, to reflect or even suggest the implications of death in battle. These implications are in fact avoided throughout the sequence not because of ignorance or fear of the truth but because the poet felt compelled to elaborate a personal and "poetic" concept that would be understood and accepted by his contemporaries. Hence the inwardness, the reference to a common fund of experience, and the elaborate embroidery of a few obsolete poetic themes. Brooke knew that he had to abide by the established Georgian limits of the "poetic"; if he had ventured beyond, if he had hazarded a guess at the truth, he would have dissolved the fantasy and nullified the special terms of his appeal.

In Sonnet V, "The Soldier"—possibly the most famous single poem of the war—Brooke speaks in his own person. Despite the self-effacement implied in the first line, the poet is dramatizing the pathos of his own possible death and, in effect, writing his own elegy:

If I should die, think only this of me:
    That there's some corner of a foreign field
That is for ever England. There shall be
    In that rich earth a richer dust concealed;

A dust whom England bore, shaped, made aware,
　Gave, once, her flowers to love, her ways to roam,
A body of England's, breathing English air,
　Washed by the rivers, blest by suns of home.

The sestet completes the picture of the England that Brooke knew and loved so well—not the England of factories, slums, cities, farms, seaports, and mining towns, but the academic-pastoral world of "Beauty," "Certainty," and "Quiet kind" presented in "Grantchester":

And think, this heart, all evil shed away,
　A pulse in the eternal mind, no less
　　Gives somewhere back the thoughts by England given;
Her sights and sounds; dreams happy as her day;
　And laughter, learnt of friends; and gentleness,
　　In hearts at peace, under an English heaven.

As Brooke had turned to the "holy quiet" of Grantchester, before the war, to forget "the lies, and truths, and pain," so also he turns to his memory of it, in 1914, to find an acceptable poetic basis for his sacrifice. Though the particular significance of that source of inspiration is necessarily limited to the understanding of Brooke's class and kind, the poet attempts, for the first time, to establish a relationship between himself and the values of the world in which he moved. Brooke implies that his world, as he knows it, is worth dying for; but he does not say, nor should he be given credit for saying, that the values of his world are those of the nation, morally aroused and conscious, in a dim, inarticulate way, of historical necessity. The plain recruit, had he the gift of a style, perhaps could have voiced his small share of that national consciousness. Brooke, blessed with a style and many other things besides, could dwell only on a series of refined poetic fantasies pleasing to himself and his friends.

At least one of the educated young Englishmen for whom

Brooke was ostensibly speaking refused to join in the public ac-
claim granted *1914*. In a letter written a few days after Brooke's
death, Charles Sorley, a soldier and a poet himself, recorded a
few penetrating observations: "That last sonnet-sequence of
his . . . which has been so praised, I find (with the exception of
that beginning 'These hearts were woven of human joys and
cares, Washed marvellously with sorrow' which is not about
himself) overpraised. He is far too obsessed with his own sacrifice, regarding the going to war of himself (and others) as a
highly intense, remarkable and sacrificial exploit, whereas it is
merely the conduct demanded of him (and others) by the turn
of circumstances, where non-compliance with this demand would
have made life intolerable. It was not that 'they' gave up anything of that list he gives in one sonnet: but that the essence of
these things had been endangered by circumstances over which
he had no control, and he must fight to recapture them. He has
clothed his attitude in fine words: but he has taken the sentimental attitude."[10]

Sorley's criticism is acute and essentially correct. It touches
the heart of the situation for the volunteers of 1914, whereas
Brooke's sonnets convey only a limited—and even distorted—
aspect of that situation. The tenor of Sorley's remarks suggests
that he, at least, did not regard Brooke as the spokesman for
any general mood; the passage is a criticism of both Brooke's
lack of maturity and his artistic culpability in taking "the sentimental attitude"—an effect, as Sorley implies, of choice. But
Brooke was not really free to choose; his commitment to the
attitudes and techniques of Georgian lyricism was such that he
could hardly deal with the war in any other way. To have admitted fact or necessity or expedience among his spiritualized
motivations would have been to destroy a semi-private fantasy
of heroic self-sacrifice and moral regeneration. A hint of what
may have been his real feelings emerges unexpectedly, con-

[10] *The Letters of Charles Sorley* (Cambridge, 1919), p. 263.

sidering the positive sentiments of 1914, in an early account of his reaction to the first news of the war. "I'm so uneasy—subconsciously," he wrote. "All the vague perils of the time—the world seems so dark—and I'm vaguely frightened."[11] Perils, darkness, subconscious fears—these physical and emotional realities find no expression in 1914, though they surely menace the very values upon which the poet bases his appeal. It was Brooke's misfortune to be the originator of sentiments that were soon to be swallowed by a vast tide of uncompromising fact and fully materialized perils. After the idealistic mood had evaporated, the suspicion grew that the appearance of the innocent enthusiast of 1914, while possible in terms of "Poetry," was something of a reproach and an embarrassment in the harsher terms of history.

II. JULIAN GRENFELL

The war verse of Julian Grenfell exhibits the same attitude of joyous acceptance expressed in Brooke's sonnets, but the fervor is of a different order and is inspired by altogether different conceptions. In 1914 Brooke speaks as a half-soldier, dramatically poised on "the edge of strife," but unwilling to deal with the unpleasantness that strife would certainly bring. Grenfell, however, speaks as a professional soldier fully alive to the physical implications of his function as a "fighting man."

Wounded in the head by a shell-splinter near Ypres, Grenfell died in a hospital at Boulogne on May 26, 1915, a little more than a month after Brooke's death. He was the eldest son of William Henry Grenfell (later Baron Desborough), full of high spirits and a passionate devotion to physical activity, yet subject to spells of religious withdrawal and moments of mystical experience. At Oxford, according to his brother William, he exhibited a "war-whooping, sun-bathing, fearless ex-

[11] Marsh, *Rupert Brooke*, p. 146.

terior," underneath which lay an incongruous "mysticism and idealism" and a "strange streak of melancholy."[12] He was not a member of the Georgian fellowship, but he belonged to the brilliant Eton-Balliol group (c. 1908-1910) with whom Edward Marsh consorted on his week-end visits to Oxford;[13] had he remained in England, no doubt he would have become one of the dozens of talented young poets, painters, and musicians whom Marsh, as supreme patron of the Georgian arts, was busy introducing into the London literary and cultural world. However, having always had a strong desire for a military career, Grenfell in 1910 joined the Royal Dragoons, then stationed in India. In that country the young cavalryman indulged his passion for the gentlemanly sports of buck-stalking, pig-sticking, and polo. In 1911, when his regiment was moved to South Africa, he established a reputation as a skilled horseman and boxer and assiduously developed his proficiency as a soldier. "I'm so happy here," he wrote home. "I love the Profession of Arms, and I love my fellow officers and all my dogs and all my horses." When the war broke out, the Royal Dragoons were ordered to England, and in early October Grenfell found himself in France. His letters from Flanders express a rather boyish exultation in the dangerous new game of war:

"Here we are, in the burning centre of it all, and I would not be anywhere else for a million pounds and the Queen of Sheba. . . . I have never, never felt so well, or so happy, or enjoyed anything so much. It just suits my stolid health, and stolid nerves, and barbaric disposition. The fighting-excitement vitalizes everything, every sight and word and action."

Somewhat strangely, he adds: "One loves one's fellow-man so much more when one is bent on killing him"—a cryptic re-

[12] This and subsequent quotations with reference to Grenfell are from the brief memoir by Viola Meynell, *Julian Grenfell* (London, 1917).
[13] See Christopher Hassall, *A Biography of Edward Marsh* (New York, 1959), p. 143.

mark that is subject to a number of interpretations. When the Royal Dragoons were converted to infantrymen in the trenches, Grenfell, we are told, made a specialty of stalking German snipers, Indian-style, and shooting them at point-blank range. For these and similar deeds he was mentioned twice in dispatches, and by December he was wearing the D.S.O. ribbon. In May of 1915, a week or so before he was fatally wounded, Grenfell sent home the single poem by which he is known, "Into Battle." It was published in the London *Times* on May 27, the day his death was announced, and was immediately acclaimed as one of the finest poems of the war.

Although it is no longer referred to in those high terms, in certain respects "Into Battle" is still unique among the poetry of World War I. It is a paean celebrating the sensations and joys of the soldier about to enter combat; the figure depicted, however, is not that of the modern soldier, an encumbered cog in the machinery of military organization, but that of the warrior in his elemental simplicity and significance. The poet first presents the natural background, "bursting" with a warmth and beauty that are somehow organically related to the soldier who is preparing for his own fulfillment:

> The naked earth is warm with spring,
>   And with green grass and bursting trees
> Leans to the sun's gaze glorying,
>   And quivers in the sunny breeze;
> And life is colour and warmth and light,
>   And a striving evermore for these;
> And he is dead who will not fight;
>   And who dies fighting has increase.

For the soldier, whose virtues bear fruit only in the heat of battle, fighting is thus a process symbolically identified with the renewal of nature. To die as a soldier is to share nature's "increase" not because death is a sacrifice (as in 1914) but because death comes as an effect of fighting. The poet goes on to describe the relationships between the soldier and the particular powers and aspects of nature:

> The fighting man shall from the sun
> Take warmth, and life from the glowing earth;
> Speed with the light-foot winds to run,
> And with the trees to newer birth;
> And find, when fighting shall be done,
> Great rest, and fullness after dearth.

The next five stanzas elaborate this concept of the soldier as the recipient of nature's sympathies, warnings, and adjurations; the stars "hold him in their high comradeship"; the trees, stirred by the wind, "guide to valley and ridge's end"; the owl and kestrel "bid him be swift and keen as they." The poet can take higher inspiration not from his leaders or from his fellow-soldiers but from the horses who also await the battle:

> In dreary, doubtful, waiting hours,
> Before the brazen frenzy starts,
> The horses show him nobler powers;
> O patient eyes, courageous hearts!

Thus the soldier is seen as an embodiment of the various powers and virtues separately present in the natural world; he represents the gathered perfections of the instinctive life, and apparently any moral or national purpose which might be responsible for his being a soldier is irrelevant. To make the point more explicit, the next two stanzas anticipate the "brazen frenzy" of battle and the exclusion of all thoughts and emotions save an instinctive delight in aggressive physical action:

> And when the burning moment breaks,
> And all things else are out of mind,
> And only joy of battle takes
> Him by the throat, and makes him blind,

39

Through joy and blindness he shall know,
  Not caring much to know, that still
Nor lead nor steel shall reach him, so
  That it be not the Destined Will.

Seized by the "joy and blindness" of battle, the soldier exhibits
no more intellection than the animals whose sensory gifts have
been incorporated into his being. Like them, he reposes unconsciously in the "Destined Will," mysteriously protected by his
identification with the elemental forces of life:

The thundering line of battle stands,
  And in the air death moans and sings;
But Day shall clasp him with strong hands,
  And Night shall fold him in soft wings.

Though Grenfell's professional and temperamental delight
in the hazards of warfare owes something to the adventurous
character of the conflict in 1914 and early 1915, his enthusiasm
was unlike that of the early volunteers, whose dedication sprang
from a sense of common responsibility. For Grenfell the war
was a major opportunity for the fulfillment of all his training
and proclivities; war for the volunteer, on the other hand, was
a dangerous but challenging parenthesis which he entered both
willingly and fearfully. Grenfell's exuberant delight in combat
was due to a mixture of professional pride, a boyishly romantic
conception of warfare, and a susceptibility to the excitement of
violent physical activity; his "Into Battle" is an intensely lyrical
evocation of that delight. The emotions and attitudes expressed
in the poem—the soldierly *mystique*, the blind "joy of battle"
that seizes the fighting man, his confident fatalism, the idealiza-
tion of death—are not factitious; the poem communicates a
genuine intensity of feeling even if the reader does not happen
to share the attitudes of the poet. "His lips must have been
touched," said Rudyard Kipling of Grenfell; the young profes-

sional soldier had indeed captured an attitude that has seldom been so eloquently expressed. On reading the poem, Sir Walter Raleigh said, "It can't be done again."

Perhaps the chief reason why it could not be done again is that "Into Battle"—as we have suggested—is an extremely limited poem, and the changing nature of the war would not permit it to be done again. In 1914 Brooke had not visualized the war at all, except in terms of its effect on his class and kind; Grenfell, it is true, advances us to the edge of battle, but the war hardly assumes any more reality, physical or otherwise. It remains merely a vague turbulence—a "brazen frenzy"—which promises some kind of fulfillment to those who are prepared to enter it. Though his combat experience was considerable by the time "Into Battle" was written, Grenfell is more preoccupied with his conception of himself as a soldier than with the particular or general significance of the war. The lyric response here, as with Brooke, is self-regarding, self-revealing, oblivious of cause, meaning, event, or consequence.

In his essay on Grenfell, T. Sturge Moore has attempted to define the feeling of exhilaration so effectively communicated by "Into Battle": "Young Grenfell exults at fulfilling an inborn promise. At last he feels free to be what instinct and capacity make him; general consent and his own conscience permit him to kill and to die. The ecstasy is like that of married love: a fundamental instinct can be gratified untaxed by inward loss or damage and with the approval of mankind. Harmony between impulse and circumstance creates this joy; but not only is it more complex than that of the young male stag who attacks the leader of the herd, there is in it an element of quite a different order, a sense that wrong within can be defeated by braving evil abroad. The strain between worldly custom and that passion for good which begets spiritual insight, finds relief in fighting, looks for peace in death."[14]

[14] *Some Soldier Poets*, p. 15.

That the instinct to kill is "inborn" or "fundamental" is, of course, open to question, though we must admit that Grenfell —an aristocrat, a graduate of Eton and Oxford, and the heir to considerable wealth and social eminence—displays little reluctance in venturing beyond the bounds of civilized conduct usually prescribed by his class. Indeed—and here Moore's judgment is more seriously mistaken—the peculiar nature of the fighting man in "Into Battle" is due to the fact that he is presented apart from any social, moral, national, or even military consideration; sanctioned and upheld merely by natural forces, he functions very much on the level of the young male stag. Not only is there no sense of the "wrong within" or the "evil abroad" in the poem, there is no "spiritual insight" and no effort to envision the war as a universal event, meaningful, in the historical sense, as a human tragedy and as a significant experience in the lives of millions of other participants. The soldier, it is true, exists to fight; but this fact hinges on the premise that soldiering and fighting are not ends in themselves and that warfare—unlike boxing or polo—involves a moral principle, whether invoked or denied. If Brooke indulged himself in romantic fantasies which sentimentalized his own and others' motives, Grenfell, in attempting to sublimate his fighting instincts, is just as remote from the conditions of modern warfare. "Into Battle" may have little affinity with the more obvious modes of Georgian lyricism, but, like 1914, it is a specialized response and therefore embodies only limited values.

III. ROBERT NICHOLS

Unlike Brooke, Grenfell, and Sorley, Robert Nichols survived the war, but his active participation in combat was terminated relatively early. Born in 1893 at Shanklin, Isle of Wight, Nichols was a poet from early boyhood, responding with typical Georgian rapture to the beauties of field and grove. He attended

Winchester, and when the war broke out he was an under-graduate at Trinity College, Oxford, enthusiastically composing poetic dramas and romances. Nichols entered the army imme-diately, and in October 1914 he was commissioned as a second lieutenant in the Royal Field Artillery. In the autumn of 1915, after only a few weeks of front-line duty, he was disabled by shell-shock, and after five months in a hospital was invalided out of service in early 1916. Later in the war, sponsored by the British Ministry of Information, he undertook a lecture tour in the United States; his account of contemporary war literature helped popularize the names of Robert Graves and Siegfried Sassoon.

Nichols was one of the first young war poets to appear in print. In 1914 the London *Times* carried one of his poems, and in December 1915 he published a small collection called *Invocation: War Poems and Others.* Echoing the ideas of Brooke's 1914 and devoid of poetic merit, these effusions in-dicate to what depths of febrile self-concern the "sentimental attitude" could lead. "Diseased with double doubt and the abhorred/ Drugs of Self-will and Pity," the poet invokes the "courage born of Fire and Steel"; now that "Honour's way" is open, he can go forth "to slay the Giants of Wrath." Nichols' brief battle experiences are somewhat more convincingly ren-dered in his second volume, *Ardours and Endurances* (July 1917), which had been prepared for the press by Edward Marsh.[15] *Ardours and Endurances* sold quite well, and Nichols became the most popular soldier poet of the year, being lionized by fashionable London society.[16] He apparently became adept at the public readings to which he was constantly invited;

[15] Nichols sent Marsh a copy of *Invocation* in the spring of 1917. Marsh wrote "encouragingly" to the author, and the two met in late June or early July. See Hassall, *Edward Marsh*, p. 413.

[16] Of the fifty-two war poets represented in E. B. Osborn's anthology, *The Muse in Arms* (November 1917), Nichols' eleven poems far exceed any other poet's total.

Sassoon, in the third volume of his autobiography (*Siegfried's Journey*), amusingly describes such a reading, and Nichols' "emotional and histrionic" manner of delivery. Obviously Nichols did not mind reaping the popularity that the accidents of war had denied to others.

As a title, *Ardours and Endurances* indicates something of the stages through which early war poetry was progressing. The first stage, that of ardent romantic idealism, is visible in both of Nichols' volumes. The second stage, that of an as yet exuberant and uncritical response to the thrills, adventures, and horrors of warfare, is likewise clearly expressed. The "endurances," like the "ardours," are personal and psychological rather than general: they pertain to the loss of friends, a sense of duress, and the poet's eventual disability; but there is certainly no suggestion of the tone of desperate endurance so common in later poetry, after the war had settled into a bloody and apparently futile stalemate. Though the mature Nichols was able to reflect with some acumen (in the Preface to his *Anthology of War Poetry*) upon the psychology of the war generation, his own youthful verse displays little disposition to penetrate beyond the initial idealistic motivations of 1914 or beyond the external crudity and violence of battle action. In Nichols' work, nevertheless, there is an advance into a new range of physical experience; we have a palpable intensification of the lyric response and an attempt to enlarge and co-ordinate that response.

The thirty poems of *Ardours and Endurances* are arranged in sections and subsections which are roughly chronological in order ("The Summons," "Farewell to Place of Comfort," "The Approach," "Battle," "The Dead," "The Aftermath") and thus represent an interesting attempt to unify a series of separate and mainly lyric responses into a larger and more significant whole. This lyric sequence, united by chronology, point of view, and emotional tone, suggests the conception, at least, of a more complex work, the material of which was obviously in need of a broader and more comprehensive treatment than the individual lyric could afford. Although committed to the contemporary mode of personal lyric response, Nichols obscurely recognized the limitations thereof and attempted to organize his scattered experiences into a continuity with beginning, middle, and end. This continuity, however, is both loose and rudimentary, and the whole has no really significant reference outside the experiences depicted. Looking at the matter from a different point of view, we may see *Ardours and Endurances* as a series of subjectively visualized and tenuously co-ordinated fragments of a poetic whole for which a mode of complete expression simply did not exist.

The first section of *Ardours and Endurances*, "The Summons," presents the poet's state of mind at the outbreak of the war; apparently some profound emotional disturbance has inhibited his response to honor's call. Rejected by "Fame," "Passion," and "Love," the poet must avail himself of the final opportunity to prove his moral worth. The three poems of "The Summons" are followed by "Farewell to Place of Comfort," in which the poet recovers his peace of mind; contemplating the natural world he loves, he takes leave of the past and faces his uncertain future: "Happy now I go." Thus up to this point Nichols depicts the war, as did Brooke, only as it impinges on his personal life; exhausted, disillusioned, his spirit a "smouldered wick," Nichols approximates the mood in which the poet of 1914 turned disdainfully "from a world grown old and cold and weary."

The three poems of the next section, "The Approach," take us to the edge of the battlefield and reveal the poet's mixed emotions as he nears the "Vortex." With Grenfell, he anticipates the "joy of battle," if not with that soldier's professional delight then at least with the novice's thrill at the sound of the guns: "It is a terrible pleasure." In "The Day's March" he regards the conflict as a source of purification and renewal:

45

Heads forget heaviness,
Hearts forget spleen,
For by that mighty winnowing
Being is blown clean.

Light in the eyes again,
Strength in the hand,
A spirit dares, dies, forgives,
And can understand!

And, best! Love comes back again
After grief and shame,
And along the wind of death
Throws a clean flame.

Here Nichols is obviously repeating the themes and sentiments of 1914. The vague private references to "grief and shame," as well as the concepts of moral and physical regeneration, are almost identical; and there is no effort to define the nature of the conflict in terms larger than those of personal renewal.

Nichols' verse is even more self-conscious than Brooke's, but it is less artful, less sophisticated, less assured. He is altogether too ingenuously preoccupied with his own emotional fluctuations between joy, fear, exultation, sorrow; and there is little of that enlarged comprehension in his poems which would convince us that these emotions have any valid correlative. "Nearer," for instance, merely records the presence of emotion rather than giving a full experiential evocation of it:

Nearer and ever nearer. . . .
My body, tired but tense,
Hovers 'twixt vague pleasure
And tremulous confidence.

Other notations similarly reflect a consciousness too avidly contemplating itself: "Happy now I go"; "I do not fear: I re-

joice"; and "I lift my head and smile." As in the poems of the
preceding sections, the poet is so intent on his own emotional
reactions that the external reality of war hardly exists.

The eleven poems of "Battle," though they are arranged in a
rough sequence, embody only fragments of the reality they are
intended to represent; the only co-ordinating element is the
poet's consciousness. In all save two of these the poet speaks
in his own person and records his own emotions and thoughts;
"Comrades," a brief narrative, is the only poem in which Nichols
adopts the technique of objective presentation. Though a
number of the themes employed in "Battle" are quite common
in subsequent war poetry, the mood of elevated acceptance
is peculiar to the early response; at this early date (1915) there
is as yet no note of protest or horror, nor is there any questioning
of the basic motives and conduct of the war.

Most of the poems of "Battle" are short lyrics dealing with
such subjects as the poet's grief for the dead ("Behind the
Lines"), with his nostalgia for the English countryside ("At the
Wars"), with his love for his men ("Out of the Trenches"),
and with his willingness to die beside them ("The Last Morning"). The last poem of the section, "Fulfilment," deals more
explicitly with the poet's consciousness of fraternal love; but
in view of Wilfred Owen's later treatment of this theme,
Nichols' emotionalized outbursts are callow and unconvincing:

> Was there love once? I have forgotten her.
> Was there grief once? grief yet is mine.
> O loved, living, dying, heroic soldier,
> All, all, my joy, my grief, my love, are thine!

A somewhat longer poem, "Battery Moving Up," is perhaps
the best of the series. The poet, passing a village church on
the way to the front with his unit, hears the bell which signals
the consecration within; he is reminded of the Golgotha which

he and his comrades are approaching and silently entreats the prayers of the worshipping congregation:

> Turn hearts to us as we go by,
> Salute those about to die,
> Plead for them, the deep bell toll:
> Their sacrifice must soon be whole.
>
> Entreat you for such hearts as break
> With the premonitory ache
> Of bodies, whose feet, hands, and side,
> Must soon be torn, pierced, crucified.

The decorous immolation pictured by Brooke gives way here to something more real, more substantial in its sense of actual suffering and death. Nichols, however, was not able to sustain or enlarge such an insight; the consciousness of fraternal love may inform his themes, but it does not transform his vision or affect his techniques.

Nichols' individual lyrics deal with only one idea or emotion and their structure is simple. When he attempts the longer descriptive, reflective, or narrative poem, however, he finds it much more difficult to order the separate sensations and perceptions of which they are composed. "Night Bombardment," for instance, begins with a somber description of a rainy night at the front:

> Softly in the silence the evening rain descends. . . .
> The soft wind lifts the rain-mist, flurries it, and spends
> Its grief in mournful sighs, drifting from field
>   to field. . . .

In the darkness the poet imagines he hears the melancholy voices of the dead, strewn among the fields and hedges; then suddenly he begins to recount, with altered tone and tempo, the brisk action of an artillery unit:

>   With a terrible delight
> I hear far guns low like oxen at the night.
> Flames disrupt the sky.
>   The work is begun.
> "Action!" My guns crash, flame, rock and stun
> Again and again. Soon the soughing night
> Is loud with their clamour and leaps with
>   their light.
> The imperative chorus rises sonorous and fell:
> My heart glows lighted as by fires of hell.

These separate perceptions and emotions achieve no convincing
unity of presentation; they are lyric fragments—descriptive,
elegiac, reflective—arbitrarily joined on a slight narrative framework. They do not directly embody the reality suggested by the
title, but only the poet's dramatized consciousness of that
reality. When the poet is dealing with the complexities of wartime experience and insists on the importance of his own emotional reactions, his reliance upon the personal lyric response
only emphasizes the highly limited nature of those reactions
as far as the objective reality is concerned.

The defects of "Night Bombardment" are visible in a different form in "The Assault," which is an attempt to portray
the thoughts and sensations of a soldier in battle rather than
the battle itself. Here the basic progression is narrative; but we
follow the action only by means of hectic, intermittent notations, and such notations become less frequent as the action
grows more violent:

> Blindness a moment. Sick.
> There the men are!
> Bayonets ready: click!
> Time goes quick;
> A stumbled prayer . . . somehow a
>   **blazing star**

In a blue night . . . where?
Again prayer.
The tongue trips. Start:
How's time? Soon now. Two minutes
    or less.
The gun's fury mounting higher . . .

Finally we are following merely a series of fragmentary impressions, reported with such feverish incoherence that the narrative declines into simple onomatopoeia:

A wail.
Lights. Blurr.
Gone.
On, on. Lĕăd. Lĕăd. Hail.
Spatter. Whirr! Whirr!

Considering only the dignified accents of Brooke's 1914, it is difficult not to believe that Nichols hoped to gain an effect of shocking contrast to the smooth decorum of the typical Georgian lyric. At any rate, the attempt to portray psychological stress by means of fragmentary, impressionistic details lacks the novelty it may once have had; we are now conscious not of the bold literary effects of fragmentation but only of the fragmentation itself. Nichols, moreover, was not as original as he thought he was; his narrative, concerned almost exclusively with the participant's sensations, embodies the same limited point of view that characterizes 1914 and "Into Battle." Since "The Assault" deals directly with crude battle action rather than with manageable "poetic" sentiments and abstractions, the liabilities of the personal response are even more evident. The frenetic quality of the poem may be a literary reaction to the "static" Georgian lyric, but its fragmentary and incoherent nature is due to an extension of the personal lyric response to materials it could not control or interpret. We are brought, obviously, to a poetic effect quite opposite to that of the epic, the traditional medium for the narration of battle action. The primary substance of the epic narrative is objective reality; there is rarely any lapse from the straightforward depiction of what was said and what was done. In concerning itself with the narrator-participant's emotional reactions, however, "The Assault" loses contact with the external reality upon which it is based.

"Comrades," another brief narrative, depicts the sufferings of a mortally wounded officer in No Man's Land and his efforts to reach the safety of his trench. Although Nichols here employs a third-person presentation and maintains complete narrative control, the incident itself is visualized in terms of conventional heroics and stilted, theatrical pathos:

> The parapet was reached.
> He could not rise to it. A lookout screeched:
> "Mr. Gates!"
> Three figures in one breath
> Leaped up. Two figures fell in toppling death;
> And Gates was lifted in. "Who's hit?" said he.
> "Timmins and Jones." "Why did they that for me?—
> I'm gone already!" Gently they laid him prone
> And silently watched.
> He twitched. They heard him moan
> "Why for me?" His eyes roamed round, and none
>   replied.
> "I see it was alone I should have died."
> They shook their heads. Then, "Is the doctor here?"
> "He's coming, sir; he's hurryin', no fear."
> "No good. . . .
> Lift me." They lifted him.

> He smiled and held his arms out to the dim,
> And in a moment passed beyond their ken,
> Hearing him whisper, "O my men, my men!"

In "The Assault" Nichols fails because he merely transmits his experiences as they happen; there is no effort to evaluate these experiences or to present them in relation to any larger reality. In "Comrades," on the other hand, he is obviously too remote from the events he depicts; he attempts to evaluate those events not in their own terms but in terms of a situation contrived to celebrate popular notions of sacrifice and heroism. Hence the false pathos: "He smiled and held his arms out to the dim"—dying, as Sassoon would have said, "with due regard for decent taste." Thus when Nichols attempts to report the actual sensations of battle, his narrative is disordered and incoherent; when he attempts to enlarge imaginatively upon a battlefield incident, his story is banal and his presentation is conventional and sentimental. In either case the poet lacks the means to interpret his experience and to present it in appropriate poetic form.

The four poems of the next section, "The Dead," are all elegiac, and, though two of them were written in late 1916, they express no feeling of protest or bitterness. Indeed, "Boy" is a glorification of the soldier's profession and concludes with sentiments that are tinged with something of the original idealism:

> What need of comfort has the heroic soul?
> What soldier finds a soldier's grave is chill?

"Aftermath," the final sequence, describes the poet's feeling of loneliness and depletion after his combat experiences; the last poem, "Deliverance," records his eventual emergence "out of the night" as a "man among men." Although most of these poems are undated, they obviously were inspired during Nichols' convalescence in 1916. The sentiments of one elegiac sonnet, "Our Dead," reveal how little effect the war had on Nichols' apparently incurable romanticism:

> They have not gone from us. O no! they are
> The inmost essence of each thing that is
> Perfect for us; they flame in every star;
> The trees are emerald with their presences.

These consolatory lines, written after Nichols had experienced the reality of combat, reflect no deepened understanding of the war's significance and no effort to depart from the images and techniques of Georgian lyricism.

Wilfred Owen described Nichols' verse as "self-centered and vaniteux," but the nature of the early response would seem to indicate that personal temperament is only partially responsible for the type of poetry we have in *Ardours and Endurances*. Nichols was the heir of an attenuated lyric tradition that subsisted on sensibility and the manipulation of familiar ideas and emotions. Mere sensibility, however, could not cope with the materials of modern warfare, nor could the lyric provide a means for assimilating and interpreting the experiences of the individual soldier. Though Nichols sought to integrate his separate lyric responses, the result is a cluster of experiences unified only by chronology; conventional "poetic" visualizations alternate with spasms of hectic emotionalism. In *Ardours and Endurances* there is no spiritual center and no core of critical or evaluative intelligence; war and poetry touch, but they are not brought into any meaningful artistic relationship.

IV. CHARLES SORLEY

Though he was only twenty when he was killed, Charles Hamilton Sorley was perhaps the most intellectually brilliant and perceptive of the English war poets. Of Lowland Scottish descent, he was born in 1895 in Aberdeen, one of the twin sons of W. R. Sorley, then professor of philosophy at Aberdeen University. In 1900 the Sorleys moved to Cambridge, the father having been appointed professor at that university. Quick of understanding and cheerful in disposition, Charles attended King's College Choir School and in 1908 won a scholarship to Marlborough College. At Marlborough he became totally absorbed in all phases of school life; he delighted in his relationships with his fellow students and his masters; he participated in football, in the officers' training program, and in literary and debating activities. These social interests, however, were balanced by an equally strong tendency toward contemplation and self-communion; he loved to take long solitary walks or runs over the surrounding Wiltshire downs.

In December 1913 Sorley won a scholarship to University College, Oxford, but a brief period of study abroad was prescribed by his parents as a useful preliminary to university life. Accordingly, he spent three months in Schwerin, Germany, delighting in the novelty of language and custom, and in April 1914 moved on to the University of Jena. There he attended lectures in philosophy and economics and further developed his enthusiasm for certain aspects of German culture. A projected walking tour of the Moselle Valley was cut short by the imminent war; on August 2 Sorley and a companion were arrested and imprisoned in Trier. Released with orders to quit the country, Sorley returned to England only a few hours before the storm broke. He arrived home on the evening of August 6 and the next morning applied for a commission. When the commission was delayed, he determined to enlist as a private; but shortly afterwards he was assigned to the Suffolk Regiment as a second lieutenant. From September to May 1915 Sorley was in England, training with his regiment and chafing over the enforced mindlessness of military routine. He was sent to France in late May, however, and during the summer months of 1915 he served with his regiment in the trenches around Ploegsteert, being advanced to the rank of captain in August. On October 13, during the Battle of Loos, he was killed, shot in the head by a sniper as he led his company in an attack near Hulluch.

Two or three of Sorley's poems rank with any others inspired by the conflict, and, as specimens of the early response, they display a grasp of reality altogether beyond the talents of Brooke, Grenfell, or Nichols. It is chiefly through his letters, however, that Sorley's personality and convictions are known to us; the poems are collateral manifestations of an intellectual force and clarity which never had the opportunity to express themselves fully in verse. The *Letters*, which date from the latter half of Sorley's Marlborough days until his death (from December 1911 to October 1915), are a remarkable record of the growth of an original and independent mentality and demonstrate the incalculable effects of the war in tragically terminating the potentialities of the best minds of a whole generation.

Even at Marlborough Sorley evinced an unusually mature social outlook. He deplored the apparent uselessness of a classical education and seriously entertained the idea of becoming a teacher in a workingman's college. He sensed, too, the inadequacy of his middle-class intellectual background: "I often feel terribly unworthy and untried in that life has given me no troubles or difficulties at home, such as alone strengthen a man," he wrote in 1915. He soon came to resent the artificiality and complacency of English public school life; his love of Marlborough was largely a love of the downs and their rich historical associations. His youthful passion for the social realism of Masefield, which he swiftly outgrew, was due to a sympathy for the common man, whose long neglected heritage, Sorley thought, Masefield had championed. Sorley's dislike of Tennyson, Browning, Swinburne, and Pater was pronounced; he saw clearly into the spirit of post-Victorian romanticism: "The voice of our poets and men of letters is finely trained and sweet to hear; it teems with sharp saws and rich sentiment: it is a marvel of delicate technique: it pleases, it flatters, it charms, it soothes: it is a living lie."[17] This extraordinary judgment indicates the extent to which the young poet was at odds with the tendencies that marked the Georgian retreat into sentiment and sensibility.

It was in Germany, however, that Sorley's mind came to full maturity. In those few months of freedom and widened experience, his sense of objectivity and critical detachment was developed to a remarkable degree. His successive enthusiasms for Masefield, Hardy, Ibsen, and Goethe were gradually moderated, and he came to appreciate more fully the simpler and more profound insights of the *Iliad* and the *Odyssey*. When the war came with its upsurge of emotions, Sorley could assess the situation with calmness and wisdom. Though he had applied for a commission the day after his escape from the war zone, he remained a critical appraiser of the sentiments expressed by those who too quickly identified their own reactions with the national mood. Speaking of Hardy's *Satires of Circumstance* in a letter dated November 30, 1914, Sorley remarks: "Curiously enough, I think that 'Men who march away' is the most arid poem in the book, besides being untrue of the sentiments of the ranksman going to war: 'Victory crowns the just' is the worst line he ever wrote—filched from a leading article in *The Morning Post*, and unworthy of him who had always previously disdained to insult Justice by offering it a material crown like Victory."[18]

In the same letter Sorley goes on, significantly, to praise the comprehensiveness and objectivity of *The Dynasts*, the form of which prohibited Hardy from obtruding himself and his personal emotions: "It has a realism and true ring which 'Men who march away' lacks." Sorley was constantly suspicious of subjectivism and emotionalism because they seemed to him per-

[17] *Letters*, pp. 37-38.
[18] *Ibid.*, p. 246.

sonal imperfections as well as major artistic faults and were often closely allied with affectation or insincerity. His accurate penetration of Rupert Brooke's "sentimental attitude" toward the war is another instance of his critical acuteness and of his refusal to be swayed by the course of public admiration.

In practical life Sorley's detachment permitted him to view both England's and Germany's cause with superior understanding. Although his patriotism was beyond doubt, he distrusted the emotions aroused by "childish and primitive questions of national honour"; he could admire Germany's motives and singleness of purpose but deplore the viciousness of her methods. Sorley was quick to note the perversion of values brought about by the war: Britain's self-righteousness, the emphasis on dangerous abstractions like absolute "justice," and the increasingly pragmatic evaluation of spiritual virtues. He writes thus in September 1914: "For the joke of seeing an obviously just cause defeated, I hope Germany will win. It would do the world good and show that real faith is not that which says 'we *must* win for our cause is just,' but that which says 'our cause is just: therefore we can disregard defeat.' All outlooks are at present material, and the unseen value of justice as justice, independent entirely of results, is forgotten. It is looked upon merely as an agent for winning battles."[19]

In a subsequent letter (October 1914) Sorley touches again upon the current cheapening and exploitation of virtues that had always been taken for granted in time of war: "Though everything is eclipsed at present except material values, it is something novel. But I don't know that it's really good for the nation. It makes people think too much of the visible virtues —bravery, endurance and the obvious forms of self-sacrifice, which are noticed and given their reward of praise. It's a time of the glorification of the second-best."[20]

[19] *Ibid.*, pp. 227-28.
[20] *Ibid.*, p. 229.

Later (in July 1915), when the gulf had begun to widen between the Home Front and the men in the trenches, he attacks the distorted civilian impressions which Siegfried Sassoon was to scourge so effectively: "I hate the growing tendency to think that every man drops overboard his individuality between Folkestone and Boulogne, and becomes on landing either 'Tommy' with a character like a nice big fighting pet bear and an incurable yearning and whining for mouth-organs and cheap cigarettes: or the Young Officer with a face like a hero and a silly habit of giggling in the face of death."[21]

Sorley had written verse with facility since the age of ten, but of his mature work we have only some thirty-eight poems, and of these only nine are classified by his editor as poems "Of War and Death."[22] His early productions, which date from about his seventeenth year, reveal a surprising variety of themes and are exceptionally free from youthful romanticism and introspection. Something of the sterner qualities of his character is manifested in his love of the bleak and stormy aspects of the Wiltshire downs ("Rain," "The Song of the Ungirt Runners").[23] In "A Call to Action" he severely condemns the "curse of Inactivity," contrasting the sterility and decadence of the modern era with England's heroic past. In other poems like "Barbury Camp" and "If I Have Suffered Pain" he proposes the Carlylean remedy of action, toil, and suffering. Another aspect of Sorley's social consciousness—his sympathy for the obscure, the "scorned and rejected," the inarticulate—is expressed in "The Seekers" and "To Poets"; here we see the effects of his passing admiration for Masefield. The influence of Hardy—clearly visible in his later war poems—is first apparent in "The River," which depicts the "black inscrutability" of the forces of nature; man can

---

[21] *Ibid.,* p. 284.

[22] *Marlborough and Other Poems* (Cambridge, 1916; fourth ed., enlarged and rearranged, 1919).

[23] See Robert Graves's "Sorley's Weather," *Fairies and Fusiliers* (London, 1917).

attain the "strength that comes of unity" only by surrendering his mortal body to the "one great strength/That moves and cannot die." These pessimistic speculations are taken up again in the two poems entitled "Rooks," in which Sorley deals with the haunting transience and mystery of life: "We would live on, these birds and I," he cries.

> Yet how? since everything must pass
> At evening with the sinking sun,
> And Christ is gone, and Barabbas,
> Judas and Jesus, gone, clean gone,
> Then how shall I live on?

Although in "What You Will" (June 1913) Sorley explicitly rejects the "rod and rule" of doctrinal Christianity, his later religious poems embody ironies, ambiguities, and contradictions which testify to the complexity and subtlety of his spiritual questionings. "Whom Therefore We Ignorantly Worship" (September 1914) and "Deus Loquitur" (undated, but clearly a late production) deal with the tensions between man's desire for intellectual freedom and his bondage to "the first ultimate instinct": God. However, in "Expectans Expectavi" (May 1915) the poet has apparently yielded to this instinct and opened his soul to spiritual influences; but is this capitulation—clothed in the fervor of Christian devotional imagery—merely ironical?[24] His previous values and attitudes, his scepticism and his coldly evaluative intelligence, would seem to indicate that it is. Sorley hardly wrote enough poetry, however, to permit us to answer with any degree of certainty. His ideas evolved rapidly, and he did not live long enough to give them a poetic expression which would expand or at least clarify their tensions.

When hostilities began, Sorley was quick to adjust his faculties

[24] The "Two Sonnets" on death, written only a month after "Expectans Expectavi," contain neither Christian sentiments nor Christian imagery; but they do suggest profoundly ironic undertones. See below, pp. 65-69.

to the reality of war: by the end of September 1914, when the conflict was only eight weeks old, he had written three of his best war poems. Considering his youth—he was barely nineteen at the time—and the general atmosphere of patriotic excitement, these early poems reveal an unusual intellectual and emotional maturity. They also reveal a prophetic insight into the true nature of the war; unlike Brooke and Grenfell, Sorley had strong forebodings of the tragic proportions of the conflict.

The most striking of the early war poems, "All the Hills and Vales Along" (probably written in August 1914), ostensibly expresses the physical exaltation of purposefully marching men, but the note of joy is ironically counterpointed with the poet's grim *memento mori*:

> All the hills and vales along
> Earth is bursting into song,
> And the singers are the chaps
> Who are going to die perhaps.
> O sing, marching men,
> Till the valleys ring again.
> Give your gladness to earth's keeping,
> So be glad, when you are sleeping.

In Grenfell's "Into Battle" the world of nature sanctions and upholds the soldier, but Sorley sees young men marching to their deaths amid nature's mindless benevolence, which provides an ironic contrast to the tragic necessities implicit in all momentous human endeavor:

> Earth that never doubts nor fears,
> Earth that knows of death, not tears,
> Earth that bore with joyful ease
> Hemlock for Socrates,
> Earth that blossomed and was glad
> 'Neath the cross that Christ had,

Shall rejoice and blossom too
When the bullet reaches you.
Wherefore, men marching
On the road to death, sing!
Pour your gladness on earth's head,
So be merry, so be dead.

Georgian poetry was incapable of irony or ambivalence because it could not achieve any critical distance from its subject-matter; avoiding any complexity of attitude, it exercised emotion and sensibility, not the intellect. Sorley manages both an emotional identification with his singers and an ironic reserve that evokes the tragic context of their song. The final stanza of his poem echoes the very rhythm of marching men, whose intensified physical life and movement correspond briefly to the vitality present in the natural world:

From the hills and valleys earth
Shouts back the sound of mirth,
Tramp of feet and lilt of song
Ringing all the road along.
All the music of their going,
Ringing swinging glad song-throwing,
Earth will echo still, when foot
Lies numb and voice mute.
On, marching men, on
To the gates of death with song.
Sow your gladness for earth's reaping,
So you may be glad, though sleeping.
Strew your gladness on earth's bed,
So be merry, so be dead.

There is no inspirational appeal or celebration of the "visible virtues" here, nor is there any romantic self-contemplation. Fully conscious of the practical effects of the war, Sorley interweaves his recurring reminders of death throughout the rousing measures of a marching song, combining the pathos of youthful vitality with the irony of its swift extinction. Considering the temper of Sorley's mind and the nature of his poetic antipathies, the echo of Housman's Lyric XLIX is probably not accidental:

> Think no more, lad; laugh, be jolly:
>   Why should men make haste to die?
> Empty heads and tongues a-talking
> Make the rough road easy walking,
> And the feather pate of folly
>   Bears the falling sky.

Sorley's irony, however, reaches far beyond Housman's sardonic rejection of intellectual responsibility; "All the Hills and Vales Along" embodies the opposition between the human capacity for sentience, emotion, thought, and action, and the blind, perennial vitality of the life-force, which mocks the brevity of man's participation in that vitality.

In the sonnet "To Germany" (also written in the first weeks of the war) Sorley demonstrates an understanding of the historical significance of the crisis which was unique among the younger war poets. Although most Britons saw the war superficially in terms of popular catchwords and patriotic slogans, Sorley valued his experiences in Germany and tried to account for the human failures that lay behind the folly of nationalistic rivalry:

> You are blind like us. Your hurt no man
>   designed,
> And no man claimed the conquest of your land.
> But gropers both through fields of thought
>   confined
> We stumble and we do not understand.
> You only saw your future bigly planned,

And we, the tapering paths of our own mind,
And in each other's dearest ways we stand,
And hiss and hate. And the blind fight the
    blind.

Thus Sorley could measure the depths of a tragedy which Brooke
and Grenfell ignored and which his elders—the Kiplings, the
Newbolts, and the Watsons—interpreted only in external terms
of outraged national honor and retributive confrontation. The
spare, monosyllabic diction of "To Germany" (of the 68 words
in the octave only 10 are disyllables, only 2 trisyllables) is characteristic of Sorley's definitive habit of thought and expression;
his blunt, economical Anglo-Saxon phrasing contrasts directly
with Brooke's aureate vocabulary. Hardy, perhaps, is the only
other poet writing at the time who would not have balked at
the adverb "bigly"; and it is clearly Hardy's manner rather than
the Georgian that Sorley is following.

In another early poem, "A Hundred Thousand Million Mites
We Go" (written in September 1914), Sorley actually attains
something of the cosmic vision we find in Hardy's *The Dynasts*.
The imagery of blindness, applied to opposed national policies
in "To Germany," is now extended to include the mass of humanity and the Hardyesque "Vicissitude" who controls the fate
of mankind:

A hundred thousand million mites we go
Wheeling and tacking o'er the eternal plain,
Some black with death—and some are white
    with woe.
Who sent us forth? Who takes us home again?

And there is sound of hymns of praise—to whom?
And curses—on whom curses?—snap the air.
And there is hope goes hand in hand with gloom,
And blood and indignation and despair.

> And there is murmuring of the multitude
> And blindness and great blindness, until some
> Step forth and challenge blind Vicissitude
> Who tramples on them: so that fewer come.

Even at this early date Sorley can prophetically envision the conflict as a vast human catastrophe; his imagery suggests the ravaged battlefields of 1917 and the mood of bewilderment, frustration, and protest that characterized the later poetry of the war. This attempt to grasp something of the total import of the struggle may be contrasted with Brooke's self-regarding lyricism, which, in communicating a personal attitude, altogether neglects the significance of the whole. Brooke did not seem to realize that, when a tragic happening is conceived of only in personal terms, it ceases to be tragic and becomes merely the source of an individual and therefore limited reaction. In each of these three early poems, however, Sorley demonstrates the range of his interests and sympathies: he sees the war in terms of the young men who must fight it; he tries to account for the tragic element in the conflict of national interests; and he foresees the universal misery that conflict will eventually produce.

"Lost" (December 1914) is one of the most personal and moving of Sorley's poems; in it he again employs the imagery of blindness, this time applying it to his early poetic themes and materials:

> Across my past imaginings
>   Has dropped a blindness silent and slow.
> My eye is bent on other things
>   Than those it once did see and know.

In June 1915, shortly after he had arrived in France, the suggestion was made that he publish his verse. His reply (dated June 13) indicates something of the discrepancy he felt between his youthful "past imaginings" and the nature of the experiences he was about to undergo: ". . . this is no time for oliveyards and vineyards, more especially of the small-holdings type. For three years or the duration of the war, let be."[25] Although he continued to write poetry, Sorley obviously felt that the type of war verse then in vogue—Brooke's celebration of the "visible virtues," for instance—was unworthy of the tragic implications of the conflict, the vast dimensions of which he himself had foreseen in "A Hundred Thousand Million Mites We Go."

The above poems were written before Sorley knew the reality of combat. Despite the naturally disturbing experience of being under fire, he characteristically did not respond to the details of fighting in the trenches; even his letters are somewhat reticent on this point. Of his last six poems, written in the summer of 1915, "There Is Such Change in All Those Fields" deals with themes he had touched upon previously: man's need to assert his superiority over the dumb vitality of nature, his bondage to the "grindstone" of habit and custom, and his desire for freedom and self-realization. "I Have Not Brought My Odyssey" is a verse-epistle which expresses Sorley's appreciation of the heroic past and "tales of great war and strong hearts wrung." Although of necessity he employs the lyric mode in his war poetry, one feels that the qualities of his mind and imagination would have been fully activated only in terms of some larger and more comprehensive form—the epic drama, for instance, or even a modern heroic narrative.

It is in three sonnets, however, that Sorley voiced what were to be his final and most profound thoughts about the war. The "Two Sonnets" on death were written in June 1915; "When You See Millions of the Mouthless Dead" is undated, but the grave elegiac tone corresponds to that in "Two Sonnets." In the first of the "Two Sonnets" Sorley again speaks of the myriads who are fated to die; his prophetic imagination seems to have been

[25] *Letters*, p. 273.

obsessed not with the details of suffering but with the sheer mass of humanity that the war would consume. Against the enormity of this sacrifice and its meaningless inevitability he envisions a hereafter completely stripped of conventional spiritual comforts:

> Saints have adored the lofty soul of you.
> Poets have whitened at your high renown.
> We stand among the many millions who
> Do hourly wait to pass your pathway down.
> You, so familiar, once were strange: we tried
> To live as of your presence unaware.
> But now in every road on every side
> We see your straight and steadfast signpost there.
>
> I think it like that signpost in my land,
> Hoary and tall, which pointed me to go
> Upward, into the hills, on the right hand,
> Where the mists swim and the winds shriek and
>   blow,
> A homeless land and friendless, but a land
> I did not know and that I wished to know.

Death brings no consolation here; bleakness and solitude rule in a land far different from the hereafter contemplated by the saint or poet. But to follow the "steadfast signpost" is to discover the truth behind the illusions created by religion and the imagination. The bitterness of this truth is suggested by the ironies of the companion sonnet:

> Such, such is Death: no triumph: no defeat:
> Only an empty pail, a slate rubbed clean,
> A merciful putting away of what has been.
>
> And this we know: Death is not Life effete,
> Life crushed, the broken pail. We who have seen
> So marvellous things know well the end not yet.

Victor and vanquished are a-one in death:
Coward and brave: friend, foe. Ghosts do not say
"Come, what was your record when you drew breath?"
But a big blot has hid each yesterday
So poor, so manifestly incomplete.
And your bright Promise, withered long and sped,
Is touched, stirs, rises, opens and grows sweet
And blossoms and is you, when you are dead.

At this point it is necessary to recall a number of facts: Rupert
Brooke's death in April 1915, two months before the composition
of "Two Sonnets"; the sudden public "discovery" of the 1914
sonnets, the popularity of Brooke's consolatory elegiac sentiments, and the heightening of these sentiments by the poet's
death; and, in June, the first publication of the sonnets in book
form. We must also recall Sorley's dissent from the general
admiration accorded the 1914 sonnets, written a few days after
Brooke's death (see above, p. 35); his remarks about verse
of the "small-holdings type," made on June 13; and, finally,
the fact that Sorley himself was expressing an elegiac attitude
in the sonnet form. The "Two Sonnets," together with
"When You See Millions of the Mouthless Dead," may therefore be read as an attempt to present the obverse of what Sorley
had called the "sentimental attitude." Direct contrasts in both
attitude and technique, heightened by grimly ironic undertones,
provide further evidence that Sorley had Brooke's famous sonnets
in mind when he wrote the second of the "Two Sonnets" and
"When You See Millions of the Mouthless Dead."

Sorley's diction and imagery emphasize the contrasts he seeks
to establish between Brooke's romantic, self-conscious interpretation of death in battle and his own tragic intuitions, now
confirmed by his introduction to the realities of trench warfare.
As noted previously, Sorley's vocabulary tends to be denotative
rather than connotative; unlike Brooke, he is usually more intent

on the definition of an attitude than on the manipulation of a feeling or an emotion. Technically, Brooke is the better poet; but we must not forget Sorley's contempt for the "finely trained" Georgian voice and his admiration for Hardy and Masefield. Like Hardy, Sorley prefers a deliberate harshness ("But a big blot has hid each yesterday. . . .") to the mellifluence which characterizes Brooke's verse. The imagery of "Two Sonnets"—the signpost, the empty or broken pail, the clean slate— is particularly meager and cheerless, suggesting irrevocability and blank finality; this imagery contrasts directly with the wealth of radiant figures which Brooke employs to develop his notions of immortality. Brooke relies almost wholly on the romantic and emotional evocations of his imagery, whereas Sorley—pursuing entirely different interpretations of death in war—avoids words and images that have become attached to conventional, consolatory elegiac sentiments.

In the first of the "Two Sonnets" Sorley speaks not of personal honor or sacrifice but of the millions who are doomed to die; he then unfolds his coldly stoic attitude, an attitude that is elaborated, in the second sonnet and in "When You See Millions of the Mouthless Dead," in terms that contrast ironically with the visualizations of 1914. For Brooke death is a transformation into "a white unbroken glory" (Sonnet IV) or into "a pulse in the eternal mind" (Sonnet V) which gives back the thoughts and sensations "by England given." For Sorley, on the other hand, death is a complete and final severance from all aspects of physical life, "a slate rubbed clean,/ A merciful putting away of what has been." In language that ironically echoes Brooke's in Sonnet IV ("Washed marvellously with sorrow, swift to mirth. . . . All this is ended"), Sorley projects his own vision of death: "We who have seen/ So marvellous things know well the end not yet." Brooke's catalogue of sacrificed pleasures and joys is irrelevant to the soldier who must die; his "record" is forever blotted out, and his past—

"So poor, so manifestly incomplete"—comes to an ironically envisaged fruition, the "bright Promise" which "blossoms and is you, when you are dead." This fruition—amid the bleak and homeless hills described in the first sonnet—is obviously meant to contrast with Brooke's comfortable depictions of immortality in Sonnets IV and V. In a war that takes its toll in the millions, conventionally "poetic" ideas of spiritual survival and compensation constitute a mockery of death, especially when doubt exists concerning the motives and methods of that war.

In "When You See Millions of the Mouthless Dead" Sorley again speaks of the vast numbers who have died and of the finality of their passing, this time openly reproving the facile elegiac sentiments of 1914:

> When you see millions of the mouthless dead
> Across your dreams in pale battalions go,
> Say not soft things as other men have said,
> That you'll remember. For you need not so.
> Give them not praise. For, deaf, how should they know
> It is not curses heaped on each gashed head?
> Nor tears. Their blind eyes see not your tears flow.
> Nor honour. It is easy to be dead.

The haunted, visionary quality of the sonnet brings to mind Hardy's "The Souls of the Slain," wherein the victims of the Boer War, after their spectral visit to England's shores, plunge "to the fathomless regions/ Of myriads forgot." In Sorley's poem the restless dead march on in hallucination and nightmare; unlike those vague, hovering presences Brooke discerns in 1914, they exist as a reproach to the conscience and not as a comfort to the imagination. Sorley was the first of the war poets to perceive that the nature of modern warfare made it "easy to be dead," that in a conflict based on mere human attrition the loss of life bore a sacrificial aspect that could no longer be treated in conventional elegiac terms. The three last sonnets may have been part of a sequence deliberately planned as an ironic commentary on the elegiac moods and emotions current in the first year of the war. Brooke's sonnets were fresh in Sorley's mind; they inspired him to present his own stern vision of death, and they afforded a perfect opportunity for an expression of the scepticism visible in his attitude toward the Georgian "small-holdings" type of poetry.

In his few poems and in his letters, Sorley not only displays a grasp of the essential truths behind the early emotional response but unmistakably anticipates the bitter revelations which were to inspire Sassoon's satiric utterances as well as Wilfred Owen's visions of catastrophe. We are conscious not only of what Sorley wrote but what, with his amazing clarity of mind, he might have written. Young as he was, he was impervious to the fallacies and lures of the "sentimental attitude" and was always an enemy of the conventional and the commonplace. His faculties of independent critical judgment and his originality of thought were of such an order that, as Robert Nichols speculates, his influence would have been profound enough to change the course of postwar poetry. Though it is with Sorley's verse that the later tendencies of World War I poetry first reveal themselves, he himself displayed intellectual and imaginative powers that could have conceivably directed those tendencies, in the course of the war, to altogether different ends. Just as he rejected the undisciplined romanticism of Brooke, so he would have rejected the undisciplined realism of Sassoon. It is also likely that he would have found Owen's theme of pity both physically and intellectually restrictive, as well as inadequate for the broadly tragic implications he had discerned in modern warfare.

CHAPTER III · REALISM AND SATIRE: SIEGFRIED SASSOON

Considering the "faith and fire" of the men who marched away in 1914, the disillusion that characterized the last half of World War I was indeed profound. This lapse of the early patriotic fervor can be attributed to a number of obvious external factors: to disappointment in hopes for an early victory, to the peculiarly frustrating nature of stalemated trench warfare, and to the steadily mounting total of casualties which all too often resulted in only trifling gains. These factors, of course, were all related to what seemed an unsuccessful prosecution of the war by England's political and military leaders. As C. E. Montague demonstrates in his *Disenchantment*, other less visible but equally potent causes of disillusion and disaffection on the part of the British soldier were operating from the very beginning of hostilities; these causes were related to conditions antedating the war or to human nature itself rather than to external events. The tide of the original idealistic enthusiasm, as it came to an ebb in 1916 and then quickly reversed, combined its own flood of embitterment with accumulated feelings of disappointment and frustration to produce the negative attitude that so strongly marks the verse written in the later stages of the war.

For a few dramatic weeks in the spring and early summer of 1916, however, the doubts and suspicions which had troubled the mind of the volunteer were forgotten. The approach of England's strongest war effort, an effort that represented the ultimate concentration of her vast physical and moral resources, seemed to harmonize all discords and unify all expectations. Primarily a British operation, the Somme Offensive was the first great attempt to crash through the bristling fortifications that the Germans had constructed along the Western Front. On

the morning of July 1, 1916, after a week of artillery bombardment unprecedented in weight and intensity, the Allies launched
the grand attack for which they had prepared so long and for
which they held such high hopes. The sheer magnitude of that
attack, which promised to end the war within weeks, brought
a final resurgence of the enthusiasms of 1914. This spirit of renewed dedication is visible in W. N. Hodgson's "Before
Action,"[1] written two days before the opening of the offensive.
The poem is at once a prayer for courage and a premonition of
death, but the note of confident idealism does not fail:

> By beauty lavishly outpoured
>   And blessings carelessly received,
> By all the days that I have lived
>   Make me a soldier, Lord.

Though the end of sensuous life is doubly a loss for the young
poet, his only concern is to die honorably and well:

> I, that on my familiar hill
>   Saw with uncomprehending eyes
> A hundred of Thy sunsets spill
>   Their fresh and sanguine sacrifice,
> Ere the sun swings his noonday sword
>   Must say good-bye to all of this;—
> By all delights that I shall miss,
>   Help me to die, O Lord.

Hodgson's premonition proved correct, for he was killed on
July 1, the first day of the battle. His is one of the last voices
to speak with the accents of faith and enthusiasm; after the
summer of 1916 the war assumed an aspect which would no
longer permit such an attitude to be sustained.

The Somme Offensive, though it threateningly breached the

[1] Hodgson's work was collected in *Verse and Prose in Peace and War*
(London, 1916).

German front line, fell far short of expectations. After ten days of furious fighting, the British advance could be measured not in miles but in thousands of yards, won at an incredible toll of human lives and suffering; apparently only the enemy's first system of defense had been broken. The tactical plan of the battle was too rigid to permit the exploitation of local gains; and the attack settled down to a massive and intensified attrition, interspersed with costly and only partially successful assaults. The expected break-through never came, and the offensive gradually lost momentum until it was brought to a halt by the autumn mud. This terrible four months' struggle cost the British some 420,000 casualties; as Ypres had been the graveyard of the Regular Army in 1914, so the Somme battles swallowed "Kitchener's Army" of volunteer citizens in 1916.

The verse of Leslie Coulson,[2] like that of Hodgson, voices a final expression of the idealistic attitude. In "The Rainbow" (dated August 8, 1916), he reaffirms his faith, amid the horror and violence of the Somme fighting, in universal beauty:

> I watch the white dawn gleam,
>> To the thunder of hidden guns.
> I hear the hot shells scream
> Through skies as sweet as a dream
>> Where the silver dawnbreak runs.
> And stabbing of light
> Scorches the virginal white.
> But I feel in my being the old, high, sanctified thrill,
> And I thank the gods that the dawn is beautiful still.

In Coulson's last verses, however, the psychological impact of the Somme battles is strikingly apparent. In "Who Made the Law?", written only a few days before his death on October 7, 1916, the poet wrathfully indicts the senseless nature of the

[2] Collected in *From an Outpost and Other Poems* (London, 1917).

conflict and the unknown power whose ordinance permits it to continue:

> Who made the Law that men should die in meadows?
> Who spake the word that blood should splash in lanes?
> Who gave it forth that gardens should be boneyards?
> Who spread the hills with flesh, and blood, and brains?
> > Who made the Law?

The final stanzas rise to a climax of agonized and insistent questioning:

> But who made the Law? the Trees shall whisper
> > to him:
> "See, see the blood—the splashes on our bark!"
> Walking the meadows, he shall hear bones crackle,
> And fleshless mouths shall gibber in silent lanes at
> > dark.
> > > Who made the Law?

> Who made the Law? At noon upon the hillside
> His ears shall hear a moan, his cheeks shall feel a
> > breath,
> And all along the valleys, past gardens, croft,
> > and homesteads,
> He who made the Law,
> HE who made the Law,
> HE who made the Law shall walk alone with Death.
> > > WHO made the Law?

Perhaps Coulson's rather simple talents—here, at the end, seeking to express an urgency through sheer repetition and typographical emphasis—could never have been equal to the kind of poetry this abrupt reversal of attitude would suggest; at any rate he was killed before he could write more. Other poets who had also experienced the unparalleled ferocity of the Somme battles were to demonstrate, sooner or later, the same general reaction of shock and dismay; Coulson's "Who Made the Law?", however, strikes first and most clearly the keynote of protest and rejection that was to sound throughout the rest of the war. The tide of disaffection, now renewed by the apparently unavailing sacrifice of the New Armies at the Somme, was beginning to display itself in poetry.

Leslie Coulson had time to express only the initial shock of disillusion, and that only in the most general terms; other poets, reacting not against an apparently indifferent Lawgiver but against the nature and direction of the war itself, began to present the particulars of a more detailed and emphatic indictment. Considering the nature of the war and the direction it had taken, one can hardly wonder at the drastic transformation of attitude experienced by those who were fighting it. The poets who by some miracle managed to survive the bloody contests of 1916 and 1917, and who were sensitive to this transformation, felt an overwhelming obligation to voice the change and the conditions that had brought it about. The habit of mere personal expression, as exemplified in the verse of the early poets, was replaced by an effort to expand and intensify the lyric response, to purify it of a limiting subjectivism, and to animate it with a new purpose that was both communicative and curative. Realistic depiction of the scenes of war became a weapon against growing civilian complacency and indifference; satirical verse was employed to scourge the abuses that had long rankled in the heart of the common soldier. Another kind of poetry, of nobler and more dignified conceptions, articulated the profound camaraderie that, in Wilfred Owen's words, was "wound with war's hard wire"; it developed a more disciplined attitude toward the details of suffering and death; and, finally, it attained, through the sensitivity and compassion of poets like Owen, Isaac Rosenberg, and Edmund Blunden, a new insight into the tragedy of modern war.

Among the later war poets, Robert Graves's record of trench service, if intermittent, is unique in one respect: it began in May 1915 and extended through Loos, the Somme, and on to the early months of 1917—thus spanning the period of idealistic aspiration as well as the period of disillusion. His verse, however, does not seem to be strongly motivated by either of these two moods and usually fails to communicate any deep sense of involvement or spiritual stress.[3] Graves was seriously wounded during the Somme Offensive; while convalescing in England during the autumn of 1916, he produced a number of poems which appeared in *Fairies and Fusiliers* (November 1917). One of these poems, "A Dead Boche," helped to win Graves his reputation as an early realist:

> To you who'd read my songs of War
>   And only hear of blood and fame,
> I'll say (you've heard it said before)
>   "War's Hell!" and if you doubt the same,
> To-day I found in Mametz Wood
> A certain cure for lust of blood:
>
> Where, propped against a shattered trunk,
>   In a great mess of things unclean,
> Sat a dead Boche; he scowled and stunk
>   With clothes and face a sodden green,
> Big-bellied, spectacled, crop-haired,
> Dribbling black blood from nose and beard.

Although this poem happens not to be characteristic of Graves's general response to the war, it illustrates a significant shift in attitude, purpose, and poetic technique; it was written, moreover, at approximately the same time as Coulson's "Who Made the Law?"—a poem that openly questions the necessity of such

---

[3] Unlike his contemporaries who also survived the conflict, Graves has rigidly excluded his World War I poems from later collected editions of his verse.

horrors. Among the early poets, whose imaginations had been shaped by the Georgian habit of describing innocuous pastoral scenes, there seemed to be an unspoken agreement not to deal with the physical effects of battle; "A Dead Boche" happens to be among the first poems to violate this convention. Although it is doubtful whether the poem was inspired by any sudden disenchantment such as Leslie Coulson experienced, Graves is obviously voicing, if only half-consciously, a general change of attitude which necessarily involved alterations of poetic purpose and technique.

The change in attitude is clear: war *is* hell and not a colorful chivalric contest; men are killed, and their corpses afterwards smell unpleasant. The poet, in his function of myth-destroyer, must deal with these lower, undepicted aspects of human conflict rather than with the customary sentimental abstractions; "Death" in warfare has been reduced from a vague poetic figment to the loathsome particulars of "A Dead Boche." The Somme Offensive thus belatedly put an end to all quasi-chivalric notions about modern warfare and pointed the way to an equally important change in poetic purpose. Graves's intent is obviously curative; he is speaking not to his fellow-soldiers, to whom scenes of violent death were common enough, but to civilians and other non-combatants whose vaguely romantic ideas of war had been rendered even more hopelessly false by distorted newspaper accounts. The poet shows no great revulsion himself but offers his depiction as a specific for ignorance and complacency. Thus war poetry here begins to assume—rather clumsily—an unwonted corrective role, anticipating the fully purposive and more devastating realism of later verse.

In technique, too, "A Dead Boche" is innovational. Its deliberate focus on disagreeable details, its isolation of the obscene from all other aspects of war, and its crude graphic force represent a rejection of the decorous generalities and vague notations that had long hidden the reality known only to professional soldiers. But the rejection of vague generalities in favor of a shocking photographic close-up does not guarantee poetic truth; our point of view has shifted to the opposite end of the scale, but the radius of our vision has been constricted by a relentless focus on particulars. Graves's technique presents the reader with only a single aspect of war—an isolated glimpse of horror related neither to the general significance of the struggle nor to the aims and ideals of the men who are engaged in it. The epic poet may have described, briefly, the unpleasant details of battle, but such descriptions were only a part of a much larger and more important reality—that of heroic endeavor and achievement—and the details themselves are never dwelt upon or disproportionately enlarged. The modern war poet repudiated his immediate poetic heritage as well as the outmoded rhetorical conventions that governed the descriptions of wounds and death; but in narrowing his focus to mere unsavory particulars, as Graves does, he is as far as ever from the truth because he ignores the broad physical and moral context of those particulars.

Apart from these considerations, "A Dead Boche" is not a remarkable poem. Graves's presentation is so clumsy and his curative intent so obvious that even the effect of shock is largely dissipated. His protest against war, moreover, lacks the authentic emotional force of a mature and disciplined conviction and is expressed only intermittently in his other poems. It fell to the lot of a somewhat older poet—Siegfried Sassoon—to become the most articulate spokesman for the mood of protest and rejection that animates the later poetry of the war. Sassoon's aggressive realism constitutes a second stage in the development of World War I poetry, and the problems he confronted were the problems confronted by all the later poets as they sought to communicate some of the catastrophic effects of the struggle.

Rupert Brooke, Siegfried Sassoon, and Wilfred Owen have today become the names most quickly identified with World War I poetry, probably because surveys of modern literature dwell upon the obvious contrasts in outlook between Brooke and the two later poets. Sassoon, especially, is pictured as developing his bitter protest against the war as a disillusioned reaction to Brooke's confident idealism. It is not commonly emphasized that Sassoon was medically examined for the army on August 1, 1914, and was in uniform on the morning of August 5, the day after England declared war, whereas Brooke wavered and delayed for nearly two months before joining the Royal Naval Division. Sassoon was, in fact, the first poet to offer himself for military service, and his early war verse voices precisely the same spirit that animated Brooke.

Born at Matfield, Kent, in 1886, Sassoon was twenty-eight when the war began, a few years older than most of the poets we are considering. His father was the descendant of a wealthy Jewish family of bankers and merchants which, after three centuries of migration through Spain, Persia, and India, had finally settled in England. His mother, an artist, was the sister of Sir Hamo Thornycroft, the noted sculptor. In his early boyhood Sassoon had no formal schooling; from his ninth to his fourteenth year he was taught by tutors and a German governess. In 1902 he was sent to Marlborough (where, a few years later, Charles Sorley was to find his early poetic inspiration), but his education was interrupted by two long periods of illness. After a year at a "cramming school," Sassoon entered Clare College, Cambridge, in 1905; but his dreamy and unmethodical temperament was ill suited to the discipline of formal study, and he left the university without taking a degree.

Despite his uncertain health, Sassoon had long been devoted to the gentlemanly sports of fox-hunting and racing; he now indulged himself fully in these pleasures and in the furtherance of his vague poetic ambitions. Introspective and inclined to solitude, he had written verses as a child and was always sensitive to the beauties of the Kentish downs. In December 1906 he issued the first of a number of small, privately printed volumes of verse and thenceforward set about developing his skill as a poet. It was not until 1913, however, that he achieved a minor success with *The Daffodil Murderer*, a clever parody of Masefield's realistic narratives which somehow managed to be interesting and moving in its own right. Sassoon received encouragement from Edmund Gosse, a friend of the family, and from Edward Marsh, who persuaded the young poet to move to London in May 1914. It was through Marsh that Sassoon began his initiation into the Georgian literary and artistic world to which he had aspired. Soon, however, he found himself restive and unhappy. Though his few months in London were enlivened by visits to the ballet and the opera (and by a brief meeting with Rupert Brooke in June), he was troubled by money matters and haunted by a sense of futile dilettantism. When the war came, therefore, he greeted it almost with relief, since it immediately solved his most pressing personal problems.

Having enlisted on August 3, Sassoon began his training as a trooper in the Sussex Yeomanry, but a fall from his horse resulted in a badly broken arm, and in January 1915 he was sent home for two months to convalesce. He had already turned down two opportunities to be an officer (feeling himself incompetent as a soldier), but after his injury he applied for a commission in the infantry. In the spring the commission came through, and Sassoon proceeded to Liverpool for training as an infantry officer. It was not until November 1915 that he was sent to France, where he joined the First Battalion of the Royal Welch Fusiliers near Festubert. Shortly afterwards, he met Robert Graves, already a veteran of six months' trench fighting and an aspiring war poet; despite a disparity in age and temperament, a close friendship began. (In his fictionized autobiography, *The Memoirs of George Sherston*,[4] Sassoon portrays Graves

---

[4] Garden City, N.Y., 1937. This volume is a trilogy which includes *Memoirs of a Fox-Hunting Man* (London, 1928), *Memoirs of an Infantry Officer* (London, 1930), and *Sherston's Progress* (London, 1936).

in the person of David Cromlech, and Graves gives an account of Sassoon's trials and exploits in *Good-bye to All That*.)[5] Sassoon took over the duties of battalion transport officer, and in early 1916, when his unit was moved south to the Somme area, established something of a divisional reputation (according to Graves, he was known as "Mad Jack") for his voluntary night patrols in No Man's Land. For his heroism in bringing back the wounded after a raid opposite Mametz, he was awarded the Military Cross. During the great Somme battles in early July he performed another extraordinary exploit by occupying, singlehandedly, a whole section of enemy trench. Late in July, however, he was afflicted with gastric fever and was invalided home, glad enough to be reprieved from an effort which all too frequently was assuming the aspect of a hopeless slaughter.

Though he recovered quickly from his illness, Sassoon was granted three months' extended sick leave. He renewed his friendship with Robert Ross (the art critic), and in September visited Robert Graves in North Wales, where he occupied himself in revising and arranging the poems which were later to appear in *The Old Huntsman*.[6] More significantly, perhaps, he met the brilliant Lady Ottoline Morrell, wife of a Liberal M.P. who was noted for his strongly pacifist views. At Garsington, the Morrells' home, which was a haven for pacifists and conscientious objectors, Sassoon heard open criticism of the war for the first time and learned of the peace overtures that Germany was then advancing. Philip Morrell's parliamentary connections lent weight to his "judiciously expressed opinions" about the "unworthy motives" for which the war was now being fought. Sassoon, already angered by civilian ignorance and apathy, could not fail to be impressed by this hostility to the war, which seemed to support his own gradually developing suspicions. Meanwhile, Ross, who had been urging Sassoon to

[5] London, 1929.
[6] London, 1917.

express candidly his inner doubts about the war, succeeded in having Heinemann agree to publish *The Old Huntsman* and in having single poems printed in various literary journals, among them the pacifist *Cambridge Magazine*.

In December, a great deal more thoughtful about his role as a soldier, Sassoon reported back for active service and by the middle of February 1917 was in France again. In April he took part in the Battle of Arras and was wounded in the neck in an attack on the Hindenburg defences. Recovering from his wound in a London hospital and in a Sussex rest home, he was more than ever haunted by the nightmare of violence in which he had been involved. In June he began to feel it his duty to protest against the prolongation of a war, the aims of which could no longer justify the continued reckless sacrifice of human life. With the advice and encouragement of Lady Ottoline, Bertrand Russell (who had been dismissed from Cambridge for his pacifism), and Middleton Murry, Sassoon prepared a declaration of protest which was conceived as a deliberate act of defiance to military authority. When his convalescent leave had expired, on July 7, he mailed this statement to his commanding officer at Litherland. As a measure of publicity, Russell had arranged to have the declaration mentioned in the House of Commons. Though he had previously been offered a home service position, and though his act of insubordination was received with surprising tolerance by his immediate superiors, Sassoon persisted in his lonely rebellion. In a moment of exasperation over the apparent ineffectuality of his act, he flung his Military Cross ribbon into the Mersey. At this crisis Robert Graves arrived and persuaded the distraught Sassoon to appear before a medical board, which was influenced by Graves's testimony that his friend was a victim of shell-shock. Accordingly, Sassoon, with Graves as his escort, was assigned to the hospital for neurasthenics at Craiglockhart. The Under-Secretary for War informed the House of Commons that Sassoon had been suffering from a "nervous breakdown," and the incident was officially closed.

At Craiglockhart Sassoon was under the care of Dr. W. H. R. Rivers, the eminent neurologist and psychologist, who became his kindly guide and friend. It was in August, not long after Sassoon's arrival, that Wilfred Owen shyly introduced himself; he had been attracted by Sassoon's reputation as the author of *The Old Huntsman* (published the preceding May). Sassoon's friendly criticism and encouragement—especially his insistence on a "compassionate and challenging realism" in war poetry—had much to do with Owen's ultimate achievement. During the autumn of 1917 the two poets enjoyed a companionship that was fruitful for both. Sassoon, who had just read Henri Barbusse's *Le Feu*,[7] loaned it to Owen; the novel "set him alight as no other war book had done." Owen continued his experiments in verse technique, and Sassoon composed the poems which were to appear in *Counter-Attack*. In early November, however, Owen returned to active duty, and a few weeks later Sassoon's request for service abroad, which he had submitted as proof of his integrity and purity of motive, was approved by a Craiglockhart medical board.

After a short stay in Ireland, Sassoon was ordered to Egypt, where he arrived at the end of February 1918. He spent two largely uneventful months in Palestine before being sent back to France in May. The German spring offensive, meanwhile, had pushed the Allied armies back many miles; and when Sassoon entered the trenches again in June, it was at a point well to the rear of the areas won at such a tremendous cost in 1916-1917. On July 13, while out on a daylight patrol, Sassoon was wounded in the head, and his days as a fighting soldier were at an end. He arrived in a London hospital in time to read notices of the publication of *Counter-Attack*. "Some of the

[7] First published in December 1916; the English translation, *Under Fire*, appeared in July 1917.

reviewers," he notes wryly in *Siegfried's Journey*, "were pained and indignant at my insistence on the ugly aspects of war." In August he saw Wilfred Owen, who was on final leave before returning to the front; this proved to be the two poets' last meeting. Sassoon spent the remaining few weeks of the war at a rest home in Berwickshire and was walking along the river below Garsington, on the morning of November 11, when a peal of bells from the village church announced the Armistice.

The thirty-nine war poems of *The Old Huntsman* were written between the late spring of 1915, when Sassoon began his training as an officer, and early 1917, when he returned to France for the second time. Only two or three of these poems were written in 1915, before he had been to France; his later, more characteristic productions date from the early months of 1916 and reflect, in their widening scope and intensity of presentation, a gradually increasing awareness of the true nature of the conflict.

Like so many of the early soldier poets, Sassoon voiced the idealism of the first months of the war, but—considering the date of his enlistment—his response was somewhat belated and perfunctory. "Absolution," for instance, written in the early summer of 1915, shortly after Rupert Brooke's death, was admittedly influenced by that poet's famous sonnet sequence. In what he later called his "too nobly worded lines," Sassoon celebrates the moral transformation brought about by the war:

> The anguish of the earth absolves our eyes
> Till beauty shines in all that we can see.
> War is our scourge; yet war has made us wise,
> And, fighting for our freedom, we are free.
>
> Horror of wounds and anger at the foe,
> And loss of things desired; all these must pass.
> We are the happy legion, for we know
> Time's but a golden wind that shakes the grass.

84

In another early poem, "To My Brother" (written after the death of his younger brother at Gallipoli, in August 1915), Sassoon similarly expresses a sense of deliverance from the pre-war disquietude that had afflicted Brooke and Nichols:

> Give me your hand, my brother, search my face;
> Look in these eyes lest I should think of shame;
> For we have made an end of all things base.
> We are returning by the road we came.

These two poems merely range over the sentiments current in 1915 and display no remarkable originality of response or presentation. "To Victory," written after Sassoon had been in France for a few weeks, is likewise conventionally "poetic" and introspective in its expression of aesthetic distaste for the mono-chromes of war:

> Return to greet me, colours that were my joy,
> Not in the woeful crimson of men slain,
> But shining as a garden; come with the streaming
> Banners of dawn and sundown after rain.
>
> . . . .
>
> I am not sad; only I long for lustre.
> I am tired of the greys and browns and the leaf-
> less ash.
> I would have hours that move like a glitter of
> dancers
> Far from the angry guns that boom and flash.[8]

This poem, incidentally, was published in the London *Times* through the offices of Edmund Gosse; it elicited a letter of praise

---

[8] At this stage Sassoon preferred an easy rhyme to realistic accuracy. In January 1916 he wrote to Edward Marsh: "I put '*angry* guns that *boom* and *flash*' in my poem, but they really flash and *thud*—the flash comes first, and they only boom when very near and in some valley." Hassall, *Edward Marsh*, p. 380.

from Lady Ottoline Morrell, who later drew Sassoon into the pacifist atmosphere of Garsington.

The poems of 1915 embody no authentic inspirational force; their commonplace diction and sentiments do not derive from any really profound attitude toward the conflict. The more Sassoon saw of war, however, the less disposed he was to write about it merely as a Georgian in uniform. During his period of initiation into trench fighting he wrote no poems that voice any sudden disillusionment; the transition from naïve idealism to the realistic attitude that came to be identified with his work can be marked only by an uncertainty of approach and a tendency to retain the techniques of conventional literary description and narration.

In early 1916 Sassoon began to produce a few "genuine trench poems" which "aimed at impersonal description of front-line conditions, and could at least claim to be the first things of their kind." Among these early realistic poems are "Golgotha," "The Redeemer," and "A Working Party." Written from the point of view of an interested but not deeply affected spectator, "Golgotha" is a somewhat generalized description of light and sound at the front:

> Through darkness curves a spume of falling flares
> That flood the field with shallow, blanching light.
> > The huddled sentry stares
> > On gloom at war with white,
> > And white receding slow, submerged in gloom.
> > Guns into mimic thunder burst and boom,
> > And mirthless laughter rakes the whistling night.
> The sentry keeps his watch where no one stirs
> But the brown rats, the nimble scavengers.

Here Sassoon wavers between the literary conventionality of the guns' "mimic thunder" and "mirthless laughter," and the barely suggested horror of "the brown rats, the nimble scavengers." "The Redeemer" and "A Working Party" are brief narratives which voice a newly found compassion for the sufferings of the infantry soldier. Perhaps because he had employed the narrative form in his prewar verse, Sassoon is the first poet to manage the battle narrative with some degree of success; these short tales—clear, succinct, objective—are free from the chaotic, half-articulated impressionism that mars the narrative efforts of Robert Nichols. "The Redeemer," however, which identifies the common soldier with the suffering Christ, still proceeds calmly and prosaically enough in its narrative pace:

> Darkness: the rain sluiced down; the mire was
> deep;
> It was past twelve on a mid-winter night,
> When peaceful folk in beds lay snug asleep;
> There, with much work to do before the light,
> We lugged our clay-sucked boots as best we
> might
> Along the trench; sometimes a bullet sang,
> And droning shells burst with a hollow bang. . . .

The details of trench fighting are apparently still novel enough to merit a contrast to the normal routines of civilian life; the violence of the approaching Somme battles, however, was to widen the gap between the soldier and the civilian beyond the point of conventional contrast. "A Working Party" relates the ordeals and ignominious death of an ordinary soldier, one among the hundreds of thousands in France:

> He was a young man with a meagre wife
> And two small children in a Midland town;
> He showed their photographs to all his mates,
> And they considered him a decent chap
> Who did his work and hadn't much to say,
> And always laughed at other people's jokes
> Because he hadn't any of his own.

This young man, the "hero" of the tale, is of course a deliberate antithesis to the hero of song and story. The narrative emphasizes his low origin, his commonplace personality, his weary resignation, the tedious nature of his duties, and his sudden defenseless end:

> He pushed another bag along the top,
> Craning his body outward; then a flare
> Gave one white glimpse of No Man's Land and wire;
> And as he dropped his head the instant split
> His startled life with lead, and all went out.

Though "A Working Party" may have been effective in dissipating popular myths about the excitement and glory of warfare, the artistic possibilities of this type of narrative are seriously limited. Passive suffering, as Yeats observed, is not a theme for poetry. The protagonist of "A Working Party" merely endures without any clear conception of the struggle or of his part in it; he goes out with his fellows to perform some incomprehensible drudgery and is "carried back, a jolting lump/ Beyond all need of tenderness and care." The unrelieved pathos of his life as a soldier is naturally succeeded by the bathos of his death: "all went out." The effect of the poem is entirely negative; Sassoon has reversed the heroic theme to such an extent that he excludes the possibilities of tragic interpretation.

At this early period, however, Sassoon did not find that the war restricted his own opportunities for action and excitement. In the winter of 1916 he made a name for himself as a volunteer scout; doubtless "The Kiss"—a canticle devoted to the qualities of "Brother Lead and Sister Steel"—reflects the combative instincts of the aggressive young infantry officer.[9] But in his

---

[9] Robert Graves comments upon the odd duality of Sassoon's nature in *Good-bye to All That*: ". . . when I was in France I was never such a fire-eater as he was. The amount of Germans that I had killed or caused

capacity as censor of his men's letters he can sympathetically read the thoughts behind awkward assurances of good health. "This leaves me in the pink," a soldier lamely concludes a letter to his sweetheart . . .

> And then he thought: to-morrow night we trudge
> Up to the trenches, and my boots are rotten.
> Five miles of stodgy clay and freezing sludge,
> And everything but wretchedness forgotten.
> To-night he's in the pink; but soon he'll die.
> And still the war goes on—*he* don't know why.
> ("In the Pink")

When Sassoon first met Robert Graves, the preceding November, the younger poet had been secretly amused by the romanticism of Sassoon's early war verse, just as Sassoon had been disturbed by the nature of Graves's "realism"; by the spring of 1916, however, Sassoon's attitude and style had changed considerably, and he had tentatively embarked upon the kind of poetry which was to express most forcefully the emotional revulsion of the later war years. Another poem which more clearly anticipates Sassoon's later methods is "Stand-to: Good Friday Morning." Its somewhat blasphemous character differs sharply from the sacrificial motifs suggested in the earlier "Golgotha"

---

to be killed was negligible compared with his wholesale slaughter. The fact was that the direction of Siegfried's unconquerable idealism changed with his environment; he varied between happy warrior and bitter pacifist. His poem ["The Kiss"] . . . was originally written seriously, inspired by Colonel Campbell, V.C.'s bloodthirsty 'Spirit of the Bayonet' address at an army school. Later he offered it as a satire; and it is a poem that comes off whichever way you read it. I was both more consistent and less heroic than Siegfried" (p. 327). In *Siegfried's Journey* (the third volume of his autobiography) Sassoon confesses that, in the trenches, "One couldn't be 'above the battle' while engaged in it, and I had sometimes been able to resort to the emotional 'happy warrior' attitude which was so helpful in sustaining one's fortitude" (p. 73). It is interesting to contrast Sassoon's ambivalent disposition with Edmund Blunden's conception of his role in the war: "a harmless young shepherd in a soldier's coat" (*Undertones of War*, p. 266).

and "The Redeemer," and its colloquial tone establishes a medium of direct expression which Sassoon was to employ almost exclusively in his later satiric poems:

> Deep in water I splashed my way
> Up the trench to our bogged front line.
> Rain had fallen the whole damned night.
> O Jesus, send me a wound to-day,
> And I'll believe in Your bread and wine,
> And get my bloody old sins washed white!

Here Sassoon creates an effect of double shock: he measures the desperation of his experiences by the desperation of his unwilling recourse to prayer and the sacramental benefits, which he invokes not out of faith or hope but out of despair. Descriptive effects of squalor and suffering—easily weakened by repetition—are thus made more real in terms of their ironically presented relationship to accepted religious values. Owen was later to employ this same device, though with greater subtlety and poetic art than Sassoon.

In April Sassoon was relieved of his front-line duties in order to take a refresher course at Flixecourt. Here he was able to relax, and his leisure is reflected in the calm mood of "The Last Meeting" (an elegy for his friend David Thomas, who had been killed in March) and in the lighthearted tone of "A Letter Home." The tensions of the approaching Somme Offensive are visible, however, in "Before the Battle" (dated June 25, 1916), wherein Sassoon expresses something of the half-mystical, half-poetic emotion that sustained W. N. Hodgson and Leslie Coulson during the same crisis.

Incapacitated by gastric fever and shaken by his Somme ordeal, Sassoon was in England by early August and did not return to France until the following February. During these six months he had ample opportunity to reflect upon the significance of the war and to evaluate his own experiences. His private doubts about the struggle had been aroused by the same forces that had produced the general mood of disillusion among his fellow-soldiers in France; fresh disappointment followed the failure of the "Great Advance" on the Somme; in England he was exposed to civilian ignorance, frivolity, and apathy, and to the scepticism of the Morrell circle. Most of the poems of this period, therefore, reflect an increasingly wrathful sense of the discrepancy between the shameful euphoria of the people at home and the sufferings of the soldiers overseas.

Earliest among the post-Somme poems were "Died of Wounds," in which the war's horror echoes in the pathetic ravings of a dying man, and "Stretcher Case," which presents the clouded, groping consciousness of a soldier being brought home in a hospital train. There is an ironical disparity between the nature of his experiences in France and his first clear perceptions in England:

But was he back in Blighty? Slow he turned,
Till in his heart thanksgiving leapt and burned.
There shone the blue serene, the prosperous land,
Trees, cows and hedges; skipping these, he scanned
Large, friendly names, that change not with the year,
Lung Tonic, Mustard, Liver Pills and Beer.

The sudden turn of the last line—to which the reader has been unsuspectingly led—became a special device of Sassoon's for concentrating the force of his ironic contrasts. Unlike Sorley, whose subtle ironies are derived from a detached and essentially tragic outlook, Sassoon emphasizes external discrepancies obvious enough to any reader of the *Morning Post* or the *Daily Mail*. If Sorley's ironic methods indicate an objectivity and a complexity of attitude beyond the reach of Georgian writers, Sassoon's venture into ironic realism, however crude, represents the end of Georgian lyrical introversion and a renewal of social purpose in modern poetry.

The above two poems were written in August, while Sassoon was confined to an Oxford hospital. In September, appalled by the general civilian attitude toward the war, he wrote the first of a number of poems "deliberately devised to disturb complacency." "The One-Legged Man" depicts the musings of a discharged soldier enjoying the prospect of a return to normal life:

> . . . he'd come home again to find it more
> Desirable than ever it was before.
> How right it seemed that he should reach the span
> Of comfortable years allowed to man!
> Splendid to eat and sleep and choose a wife,
> Safe with his wound, a citizen of life.
> He hobbled blithely through the garden gate,
> And thought: "Thank God they had to amputate!"

The poet thus deals an effective blow to civilian misapprehensions about the spirit of the fighting soldier, whose cheerful confidence had become a theme of home-front propaganda. Again, the turn of the final line, like a whiplash, completes the ironic contrast.

Other notable satiric poems written in the autumn of 1916 were "The Hero," which explodes the journalistic fiction of universally courageous behavior on the part of the British soldier, and "The Tombstone-Maker," which strikes out at civilian selfishness and hypocrisy. Discovering himself possessed of a hitherto unemployed skill for "composing two or three harsh, peremptory, and colloquial stanzas with a knockout blow in the last line," Sassoon later acknowledged an inability to account for any possible literary influence, save a faint echo of Hardy's *Satires of Circumstance* in his longer poems. In October, encouraged by Robert Ross to continue in this satiric vein, Sassoon produced one of his most scathing poems. " 'They' " is an attack leveled directly at the fatuities and empty consolations of formal religion, whose representatives, for the most part, had dismally failed to gauge the physical and moral havoc wrought by the war. With unctuous rhetoric, the Bishop of " 'They' " declares that the nobility of the struggle against "Anti-Christ" will have an elevating effect on those who return: "They will not be the same."

> "We're none of us the same!" the boys reply.
> "For George lost both his legs; and Bill's stone
>   blind;
> "Poor Jim's shot through the lungs and like to
>   die;
> "And Bert's gone syphilitic: you'll not find
> "A chap who's served that hasn't found *some*
>   change."
> And the Bishop said: "The ways of God are
>   strange!"

This kind of writing proved almost too easy for Sassoon, for he seldom advances much beyond the brash satirical techniques encouraged by such obvious targets. Wilfred Owen's sense of the cruel irrelevance of conventional religious values emerges not as satire but as tragedy; the contrasts he observes deflate no pompous bishop but reveal the underlying ironies of mortality in war and peace.

The last poem of Sassoon's early satiric period was written in January 1917, just before he returned to France. " 'Blighters,' " inspired by a revue at the Hippodrome in Liverpool, is probably the bitterest of his early productions; it attacks the frivolous and vulgar jingoism of the music hall and the hectic approval of the audience:

> The House is crammed: tier beyond tier they grin
> And cackle at the Show, while prancing ranks

Of harlots shrill the chorus, drunk with din;
"We're sure the Kaiser loves our dear old Tanks!"

I'd like to see a Tank come down the stalls,
Lurching to rag-time tunes, or "Home, sweet Home,"
And there'd be no more jokes in Music-halls
To mock the riddled corpses round Bapaume.

The anger here is certainly excessive and without a worthy target. Satire that loses its sense of proportion becomes mere invective; but to Sassoon, on his way to France for the second time, the scene apparently epitomized the spirit of wartime England.

The most important war poems of *The Old Huntsman* thus represent the character of Sassoon's response during the course of a single year, from January 1916 to January 1917. That year was psychologically the most crucial of the entire war, and Sassoon's poetic growth clearly accompanies the growing disaffection of 1916. No greater contrast could be imagined than that between the self-indulgent aestheticism of "To Victory" and the cold wrath of " 'Blighters.' " Significantly, however, *The Old Huntsman*, when it was published in May 1917, was far outsold by Robert Nichols' *Ardours and Endurances*, which appeared at approximately the same time. Even at this late date Nichols' uncritical and romantic interpretation of the war was more in accord with current taste than Sassoon's unpalatable truths.

The thirty-nine poems of *Counter-Attack*,[10] for the most part inspired by Sassoon's experiences in the Battle of Arras, were written during his second period of convalescence in England. At this time he was undergoing the profound personal crisis which resulted in his protest against the war and his eventual assignment to Craiglockhart. The tormented state of mind

[10] London, 1918.

94

which provoked this difficult act of rebellion also produced the agonized poems of *Counter-Attack*. As in the case of the early volunteers, the urgency of the occasion had again combined poetry with the necessity for practical action; as Rupert Brooke's personal response had symbolized the initial enthusiastic acceptance of the war, so Sassoon's *Counter-Attack*, and the personal crisis out of which it arose, represented an uncompromising rejection of all the war had come to signify.

Published in July 1918, in a "blood-red and yellow paper cover," *Counter-Attack* was prefaced by a brief quotation from the final apocalyptic pages of Barbusse's *Le Feu*, one of the most powerful anti-war novels produced by World War I:

"Dans la trêve désolée de cette matinée, ces hommes qui avaient été tenaillés par la fatigue, fouettés par la pluie, bouleversés par toute une nuit de tonnerre, ces rescapés des volcans et de l'inondation entrevoyaient à quel point la guerre, aussi hideuse au moral qu'au physique, non seulement viole le bon sens, avilit les grandes idées, commande tous les crimes—mais ils se rappelaient combien elle avait développé en eux et autour d'eux tous les mauvais instincts sans en excepter un seul; la méchanceté jusqu'au sadisme, l'égoïsme jusqu'à la férocité, le besoin de jouir jusqu'à la folie."[11]

As he records in *Sherston's Progress*, Sassoon read *Le Feu* in the English translation during his first few weeks at Craiglockhart. Although he tells us that the novel acutely increased his exasperation and antagonism, it is not clear to what extent he was

---

[11] Here is Fitzwater Wray's translation in *Under Fire* (New York, 1917), pp. 343-44: "In their troubled truce of the morning, these men whom fatigue had tormented, whom rain had scourged, whom night-long lightning had convulsed, these survivors of volcanoes and flood began not only to see dimly how war, as hideous morally as physically, outrages common sense, debases noble ideas and dictates all kind of crime, but they remembered how it had enlarged in them and about them every evil instinct save none, mischief developed into lustful cruelty, selfishness into ferocity, the hunger for enjoyment into a mania."

artistically inspired or encouraged by Barbusse's indictment of the war. Beyond the inclusion of this prefatory quotation in *Counter-Attack*, Sassoon—invariably scrupulous in such matters —does not acknowledge any direct literary influence. The conclusions that both men reached were obvious and inevitable in 1917; Sassoon's use of the passage from *Le Feu* merely keynotes and confirms the main theme of *Counter-Attack*.

The poems of *The Old Huntsman* had dealt boldly and impressively enough with the phenomena of modern warfare, but the opening lines of the first poem in *Counter-Attack* ("Prelude: The Troops") reveal a stricken world whose inhabitants have been overwhelmed by some unspeakable disaster:

> Dim, gradual thinning of the shapeless gloom
> Shudders to drizzling daybreak that reveals
> Disconsolate men who stamp their sodden boots
> And turn dulled, sunken faces to the sky
> Haggard and hopeless.

Like the survivors of the deluge in *Le Feu*, these men seem paralyzed by the enormity of their common misfortune; the "sad, smoking, flat horizons" bound a nightmare of tedium and misery, of ruin and death. Edmund Blunden is more successful, perhaps, in evoking the sinister particulars of a war-ravaged landscape, but in his title poem Sassoon almost vengefully shifts his vision to the obscene details that more shockingly summarize the war's undepicted horror:

> The place was rotten with dead; green clumsy legs
> High-booted, sprawled and grovelled along the saps
> And trunks, face downward, in the sucking mud,
> Wallowed like trodden sand-bags loosely filled;
> And naked sodden buttocks, mats of hair,
> Bulged, clotted heads slept in the plastering slime.
> And then the rain began,—the jolly old rain!

Few other lines in World War I poetry can equal this passage —with Sassoon's characteristic ironic fillip at the end—in sheer graphic intensity. To the horrors of simple carnage are added the frantic, intermingled, struggling grotesqueries of violent death: the final degradation of the human body which made modern warfare such an intolerable outrage to the poets who first confronted its effects. It was from scenes like this that Sassoon returned to England in April, so distraught that, as he told Graves, he often "saw corpses lying about on the pavement." The poet's seriously obsessed mental state—visible even in his postwar verse—is depicted in his "Repression of War Experience":

> You're quiet and peaceful, summering safe at home;
> You'd never think there was a bloody war on! . . .
> O yes, you would . . . why, you can hear the guns.
> Hark! Thud, thud, thud,—quite soft . . . they
>   never cease—
> Those whispering guns—O Christ, I want to go out
> And screech at them to stop—I'm going crazy;
> I'm going stark, staring mad because of the guns.

It was in such an overwrought state of mind that "Counter-Attack" was probably composed. This brief narrative attempts to depict the chaotic effects of a British assault and an abortive enemy counter-attack, and, indeed, the poem powerfully conveys a sensation of irredeemable horror and confusion. Considered as a narrative, however, "Counter-Attack" is no more successful than Robert Nichols' "The Assault." The progression is crude and ill-adjusted, amounting to no more than a loose series of narrative and descriptive notations. Again, the point of view shifts from generalized narration to the consciousness of an individual soldier, and the action ends abruptly with the death of that soldier. Finally, the visual perspective narrows from a generalized narrative actuality to a grim and purposive description of the dead, then adjusts itself to the dazed perceptions of the soldier who unaccountably emerges in the second stanza as the protagonist. In "Counter-Attack" confusion of form attends confusion of matter because Sassoon, like Nichols, has neglected to distinguish between the haphazard continuity of actual experience and the progression demanded by the narrative mode. No communicative intent, however urgent, can justify the fallacy of imitative form. Urgency and chaos, by their very nature opposed to the formal element in art, require both the discipline of traditional forms and the unremitting exercise of the poet's intellectual and imaginative powers. Concerned only with communication, Sassoon relies upon the raw force of his materials and their impact upon his personal sensibilities.

Though Sassoon's description of the dead has an overwhelming graphic power, its gruesome particulars are not really relevant to the central action and serve no discernible function with regard to the perceptions or fate of the protagonist. It is the poet himself who halts to observe the "naked sodden buttocks" and the "bulged, clotted heads"; in his desire to communicate the shock of this ultimate atrocity, he forgets his obligations to the action he has initiated and resorts to the dubious techniques of photographic realism. His depiction is not only irrelevant, but objectionable on other artistic grounds. As Middleton Murry observes,[12] this scene of carnage "is horrible, but it does not produce the impression of horror." The appeal is to the senses and not to the imagination; such a method "numbs, not terrifies, the mind." Thus undisciplined realism, since it tends to concentrate narrowly on purely sensory aspects and details, can distort the reality of warfare as much as undisciplined romanticism.

The narrative movement of "Counter-Attack" is by turns

[12] "Mr. Sassoon's War Verses," *The Evolution of an Intellectual* (London, 1920), p. 72.

sluggish and frenetically abrupt; it terminates blankly with the last obscure sensations of the protagonist, who sinks to his death amid "a blurred confusion of yells and groans." "We are given the blurred confusion," writes Murry, "and just because this is the truth of the matter exactly rendered we can not apprehend it any more than the soldier who endures it can." The continued attempt to depict the shattering physical realities of warfare was obviously destined to failure unless the poet could exercise some kind of control over his material. As Murry further observes, "The experiences of battle, awful, inhuman, and intolerable as they are, can be comprehended only by the mind which is capable of bringing their horror and their inhumanity home to the imagination of others. Without the perspective that comes from intellectual remoteness there can be no comprehension, no order and no art." This dictum touches the artistic dilemma that afflicted many World War I poets, whose Georgian literary background had hardly encouraged the discipline of intellectual remoteness. Thoroughly saturated with the sights and sounds of war, their imaginations lacked the support of a living poetic tradition capable of assimilating new materials and dealing with the disorder and violence of warfare. Thus poetry was but a single step from action and reflected— sometimes too directly and too grossly—the physical extremities that inspired it.

A number of other poems in *Counter-Attack*, though not as graphically insistent and confused as the title poem, seem to be marked by the same agonized intensity of presentation. "The Rear-Guard," for example, deals with a frightful incident in a tunnel under the Hindenburg Line. The protagonist, exploring the darkness, stumbles over what he supposes to be the body of a sleeping soldier. The soldier, however, does not respond to his tugging or to his angry demands for guidance. The protagonist, nerves on edge, completely loses his temper:

Savage, he kicked a soft, unanswering heap,
And flashed his beam across the livid face
Terribly glaring up, whose eyes yet wore
Agony dying hard ten days before;
And fists of fingers clutched a blackening
    wound.

Alone he staggered on until he found
Dawn's ghost that filtered down a shafted stair
To the dazed, muttering creatures underground
Who hear the boom of shells in muffled sound.
At last, with sweat of horror in his hair,
He climbed through darkness to the twilight air,
Unloading hell behind him step by step.

It is worth while to contrast Sassoon's prose account of the same incident in *Memoirs of an Infantry Officer* (pp. 225-26), written after the war with a somewhat different artistic purpose in view: "Once, when I tripped and recovered myself by grabbing the wall, my tentative patch of brightness revealed somebody half hidden under a blanket. Not a very clever spot to be taking a nap, I thought, as I stooped to shake him by the shoulder. He refused to wake up, so I gave him a kick. 'God blast you, where's Battalion Headquarters?' My nerves were on edge; and what right had he to be having a good sleep, when I never seemed to get five minutes' rest? . . . Then my beam settled on the livid face of a dead German whose fingers still clutched the blackened gash on his neck. . . . Stumbling on, I could only mutter to myself that this was really a bit too thick. (That, however, was an exaggeration; there is nothing remarkable about a dead body in a European War, or a squashed beetle in a cellar.)"

Here, in the larger context of prose narration, the incident obviously could not be isolated and intensified; it is part of a narrative progression composed of many such incidents. Sassoon actually minimizes the experience and its effect on his sensibility, whereas in the poem he deliberately heightens its horrific aspects. The lyric medium, together with the curative purpose for which it was being utilized, thus encouraged a strained emphasis and insistence which afforded little opportunity for the exercise of selection, proportion, and control. There is, indeed, nothing remarkable about a dead body in a European war unless the war itself is depicted as a significant event. As Frederic Manning states in his Prefatory Note to *Her Privates We*,[13] "War is waged by men; not by beasts, or by gods. It is a peculiarly human activity. To call it a crime against mankind is to miss at least half its significance; it is also the punishment of a crime." These words, if applied to Sassoon's attitudes and techniques, have an artistic as well as a moral import. In his parenthetical afterthought about the Hindenburg tunnel incident, Sassoon seems to be admitting that his poetic version was based on simple emotional reactions rather than on an effort to evaluate his experience in its actual historical context.

Other poems in *Counter-Attack* both portray and embody the emotional intensities of combat. "Attack," for instance, depicts the terrible anxiety of men about to cross the parapets:

> Lines of grey, muttering faces, masked with fear,
> They leave their trenches, going over the top,
> While time ticks blank and busy on their wrists,
> And hope, with furtive eyes and grappling fists,
> Flounders in mud. O Jesus, make it stop!

The fellowship of suffering completes Sassoon's identification with the men he must lead "To the foul beast of war that bludgeons life." Unlike Owen, he describes the demoralizing psychological effects of battle more often than wounds or phys-

---

[13] London, 1930.

ical anguish, and for the first time poetry reveals what modern scientific violence can do to men's minds. Sassoon's soldiers are numb with fear or horror, or they break down completely under the prolonged emotional strain of trench fighting. He pays tribute, of course, to the courage and tenacity of his "brave brown companions," but he never makes that bravery the subject of a specific poem. If young Hughes, in "Wirers," exerts himself manfully in repairing the barbed-wire defences in No Man's Land, Sassoon gives the account a bitter twist that nullifies any heroism involved:

> Young Hughes was badly hit; I heard him carried
>   away,
> Moaning at every lurch; no doubt he'll die to-day.
> But *we* can say the front-line wire's been safely
>   mended.

One wonders how much positive action and achievement is excluded from *Counter-Attack* in the interest of thematic unity. As an anti-war propagandist, Sassoon could hardly depict a successful attack or even an incident representing individual heroism; he could hardly portray a soldier mastering his own emotional turmoil and responding to the imperatives of duty. To write about such things would have been to grant that the war had some positive moral or historical significance, and Sassoon was in no state of mind to make such an admission. His interest in psychopathological effects was no doubt renewed during his stay at Craiglockhart, where the phenomena of "shell-shock" and other war neuroses engaged the attention of medical science. His own ordeals, plus a deep sense of identification with the common soldier, produced the haunted mental condition described in "Repression of War Experience" (the title indicates familiarity with the then novel terms of psychoanalysis). Other poems written during Sassoon's period of convalescence at Craiglockhart—"The Dream," "Dead Musicians," "Sick Leave," and "Banishment"—all portray a mind obsessed with suffering and death. In "Sick Leave" the poet is reproached by ghostly forms that gather about his bed:

> "Why are you here with all your watches ended?
> From Ypres to Frise we sought you in the Line."
> In bitter safety I awake, unfriended;
> And while the dawn begins with slashing rain
> I think of the Battalion in the mud.
> "When are you going out to them again?
> Are they not still your brothers through our blood?"

"Banishment" eloquently summarizes the feeling which led to the poet's protest against the war and which eventually compelled him to forgo his "bitter safety" for the comradeship of the "patient men who fight":

> Love drove me to rebel.
> Love drives me back to grope with them through
> hell;
> And in their tortured eyes I stand forgiven.

If Sassoon is a compassionate observer of mental and spiritual stress among his fellow-soldiers, he also expresses his own strained sense of the opposition between his duty as a soldier and his obligations as a poet.

These spells of troubled remembrance apparently did not diminish Sassoon's capacity for trenchant critical commentary. Most of the critical poems of *Counter-Attack* have a bitterly satiric intent or at least a strong ironic turn, but a few express unadulterated anger and hatred. Among these, "Fight to a Finish," which attacks "Yellow Pressmen" and the "Junkers" in Parliament, is one of his most violent poems; the poet, in company with his "trusty bombers," imagines himself to be ruthlessly exterminating these groups after the war. "Suicide in the Trenches" wrathfully lashes out at civilian ignorance:

> You smug-faced crowds with kindling eye
> Who cheer when soldier lads march by,
> Sneak home and pray you'll never know
> The hell where youth and laughter go.

In "Glory of Women" the poet directs his scorn at woman's shallow ingenuousness and her inclination to accept the falsities of the romantic interpretation of war:

> You love us when we're heroes, home on leave,
> Or wounded in a mentionable place.
> You worship decorations; you believe
> That chivalry redeems the war's disgrace.
> You make us shells.

In the same vein, "Their Frailty" condemns woman's selfish incapacity to visualize the war in terms other than those that affect her son, lover, or husband. These attacks are rather immoderate and indiscriminatory; they reveal a mind harried by a vast injustice and therefore disposed to magnify aspects of the undeniable disparity between the sacrifices demanded of soldiers and those demanded of civilians.

Among the poems in which the ironical method is employed with best effect are "How to Die," "Lamentations," "Does it Matter?", and "Survivors." Each of these poems is concerned in some way with current attitudes toward death and suffering; Sassoon caricatures these attitudes with a decorous gravity that barely conceals his own underlying wrath. Thus "How to Die" mocks the popular conception of death in battle:

> You'd think, to hear some people talk,
>   That lads go West with sobs and curses,
> And sullen faces white as chalk,
>   Hankering for wreaths and tombs and hearses.
> But they've been taught the way to do it
>   Like Christian soldiers; not with haste

And shuddering groans; but passing through it
With due regard for decent taste.

"Lamentations" depicts the hysterical grief of a soldier for his
dead brother; "in my belief," remarks the poet, turning dis-
tastefully from the scene, "such men have lost all patriotic feeling." "Does it Matter?" similarly mocks the blithe consolations
that civilians afford the crippled ("people will always be kind")
and the sightless ("there's such splendid work for the blind").
Written at Craiglockhart in October, "Survivors" portrays the
afflicted state of those whose nerves had given way under the
stress of battle:

No doubt they'll soon get well; the shock and
    strain
Have caused their stammering, disconnected talk.
Of course they're "longing to go out again,"—
These boys with old, scared faces, learning to walk.

No other war poet can approach Sassoon's facility as an ironist,
and Sassoon himself is at his best as a poet when he finds a
legitimate target for this particular skill.

Occasionally, however, explicit satire replaces the oblique
ironic method. "Editorial Impressions," "The Fathers," "Base
Details," and "The General" are directed against types rather
than attitudes; their simplicity and singleness of effect resemble
that of the clever, hard-hitting political cartoon. For instance,
"Base Details"—with its equivocal title—attacks the pompous
Staff officers who were safely remote from the dangers of the
front line:

If I were fierce, and bald, and short of breath,
    I'd live with scarlet Majors at the Base,
And speed glum heroes up the line to death.

"The General" similarly indicts the military caste for the incompetence and lack of imagination that characterized British

staff work during most of the war. The smiling General reviews
his soldiers on their way to the line:

> "He's a cheery old card," grunted Harry to Jack
> As they slogged up to Arras with rifle and pack.
>
> .   .   .   .
>
> But he did for them both by his plan of attack.

Counter-Attack was very nearly suppressed before it was published; no doubt "The General"—which violated the rule against
criticism of the conduct of the war—was partially responsible for
this difficulty with the censor. These aggressive satires are indeed
essentially negative and destructive. They strike out at specific
targets, but in so doing indict the whole national military effort
without taking any stand that would honor the positives implicit
in that effort (and visible in Sassoon's own individual exploits
as a soldier). Sassoon abolished the romantic myth of war, as
Vivian de Sola Pinto observes, but he provided no new myth
to take its place. It is for this reason, perhaps, that he is seldom
mentioned as an influence on postwar verse. The younger poets
of the thirties—Auden, Spender, Day Lewis—could hardly have
been unaware of his reputation as a figure of angry revolt; but
the negative aspect of his work was such that it provided no
inspiration for poets who were dealing with broad social and
ideological issues.

"To Any Dead Officer," written in June 1917, while Sassoon
was still hospitalized with his throat wound, may be classed as
an elegy, though the poet's grief is partially concealed by a play-
ful colloquial tone, and interspersed with satiric thrusts. The
imagined telephone conversation thus concludes:

> Good-bye, old lad! Remember me to God,
>   And tell Him that our Politicians swear
> They won't give in till Prussian Rule's been trod
>   Under the Heel of England . . . Are you there? . . .
> Yes . . . and the War won't end for at least two years;

But we've got stacks of men . . . I'm blind with tears,
   Staring into the dark. Cheero!
I wish they'd killed you in a decent show.

The contrast between "To Any Dead Officer" and the dignified elegiac symbolism of Brooke's Sonnet IV is almost profound enough to have been deliberate. Sassoon's manner, furthermore, is directly opposed to the style of other consolatory and inspirational elegies—Laurence Binyon's "For the Fallen" was perhaps the best known—that found public favor during the later years of the war.

Sassoon's intentions in *Counter-Attack* are revealed in his ironically ambiguous title: he was at war not so much with the enemy as with war itself and the people who were for one reason or another insensible to its terrible import. In pursuing these intentions he produced a volume that has no rival in its revelation of terror, stupidity, selfishness, and suffering. Though Sassoon's techniques of realistic depiction are less sound artistically than his satiric methods, they constitute the first real attempt to present the truth of the war, and the effect of his break with the conventions and traditions of earlier war poetry can hardly be overestimated.

This break is especially obvious when one compares Sassoon's verse with that of Kipling, who is in some ways Sassoon's predecessor as a "soldiers' poet." Kipling celebrated his own martial themes with expansive energy and confident, resounding rhythms. His early verses helped to establish the popular conception of the British "Tommy"—competent, cheerful, and mindless—which Sassoon was to expose with a mixture of savagery and compassion. Kipling also helped to popularize the public school athletic-military code of honor (best expressed, perhaps, in Newbolt's "Vitaï Lampada"[14]) which lies, too

[14] The second stanza gives a good idea of the whole:
   The sand of the desert is sodden red,—
   Red with the wreck of a square that broke;—

obvious a mark for direct attack, behind much of Sassoon's satire. In a great deal of their work both Kipling and Sassoon were propagandists; their levels of appeal do not differ markedly. By means of techniques which would assure him a vast public audience—simple rhythms, simple notions, and simple colloquial language—Kipling created a legend around the professional soldiers who protected the Empire by their strength and vigilance. As a civilian soldier newly initiated into the effects of national conflict on a grand scale, Sassoon made war not only on war itself but also on many of the popular conceptions which Kipling was indirectly responsible for perpetuating; his techniques—basically as simple as Kipling's but shrill, abrupt, discordant, and shocking—were therefore calculated to be as unsettling as the older poet's were reassuring. Only twenty or thirty years separate Kipling's Indian and Boer War verse from Sassoon's *Counter-Attack*; the contrast in attitude and technique, however, reflects the astonishing rapidity and profundity of the changes with which we are dealing.

After Sassoon was wounded in July 1918 he spent a few weeks at the American Women's Hospital, Lancaster Gate, London. *Counter-Attack* had just been published and the poet had leisure to review his accomplishments and speculate about the future. Though he felt it was probable that the war would last another year, he was conscious of no obligation to return to France, and Dr. Rivers assured him that he need feel no such obligation. In *Siegfried's Journey* Sassoon thus summarizes his reflections at that time: ". . . in spite of my hatred of war and 'Empery's insatiate lust of power,' there was an awful attraction in its hold over my mind, which since childhood had shown a

---

The Gatling's jammed and the Colonel dead,
  And the regiment blind with dust and smoke.
The river of death has brimmed his banks,
  And England's far, and Honour a name,
But the voice of a schoolboy rallies the ranks:
  "Play up! play up! and play the game!"

tendency towards tragic emotions about human existence. While at Lancaster Gate I was disquieted by a craving to be back on the Western Front as an independent contemplator. No longer feeling any impulse to write bitterly, I imagined myself describing it in a comprehensive way, seeing it like a painter and imbuing my poetry with Whitmanesque humanity and amplitude. From the routine-restricted outlook of battalion sectors I had seen so little, and the physical conditions were a perpetual hindrance to detached and creative vision. But I had experienced enough to feel confident that I could now do something on a bigger scale, and I wanted to acquire further material which would broaden and vitalize what was already in my mind."[15]

Sassoon goes on to describe the nocturnal visions which haunted his sleepless hours and which brought him "a delusive sense of power to put them into words": "An army on the march moved across the darkness, its doom-destined columns backed by the pulsating glare of distant gunfire. . . . I saw the shapes of sentries, looming against the livid and sombre cloud-shoals of forlorn front-line daybreak. Or it seemed that I was looking down on a confusion of swarming figures in some battle-ravaged region—an idea derived, perhaps, from the scenic directions in Hardy's *Dynasts*." A page or so later, he continues in the same vein of artistic self-examination: ". . . I was developing a more controlled and subjective attitude towards the war. To remind people of its realities was still my main purpose, but I now preferred to depict it impersonally, and to be as much 'above the battle' as I could. Unconsciously, I was getting nearer to Wilfred Owen's method of approach. (For it was not until two years later, when I edited his poems, that I clearly apprehended the essentially compassionate significance of what he had been in process of communicating.)"[16]

[15] *Siegfried's Journey* (New York, 1946), pp. 104-105.
[16] *Ibid.*, pp. 106-107. Mr. Sassoon has confirmed the author's suspicion that *subjective* ("a more controlled and subjective attitude") is a misprint, in the American edition of *Siegfried's Journey*, for *objective*.

Two months after Sassoon's release from the Lancaster Gate hospital the war was over and he had no cause for returning to the front either as a soldier or an "independent contemplator." In 1919, however, he published *Picture Show*, which contains about a dozen war poems written during 1918 and 1919. Although these poems are generally elegiac in tone, one or two, like "Battalion-Relief" and "Memorial Tablet," embody the satirical animus of *Counter-Attack*. Some pieces, like "Memory" and "Aftermath" (dated March 1919), show how persistently memories of the war disturbed Sassoon's consciousness. "Have you forgotten yet?" he asks his fellow-soldiers. "Look down, and swear by the slain of the War that you'll never forget." Even poems which are not directly concerned with the conflict evince an obsession with the old themes: death, suffering, and grief. The war poems of *Picture Show* are clearly anti-climactic; Sassoon's role as a satirist had been brought to an end by the Armistice, and his moods of haunted reminiscence embody no new ideas or techniques.

The poems of *Counter-Attack*, though they were inspired by events that took place in the spring of 1917, were thus to be Sassoon's last effective commentary on the war. The two passages quoted above, therefore, refer to attitudes and techniques that the poet had no opportunity to realize in verse; in so doing, however, they offer an indirect but interesting appraisal of the kind of poetry upon which his reputation is based. Sassoon acknowledges the obvious physical disadvantages of writing as a soldier: the individual (as Douglas Jerrold points out) is limited to the operations of his own unit and knows little of the larger movements in which that unit is engaged. The trench poet's response, therefore, is restricted to the phenomena that fall within the range of his personal experience; within that range, moreover, he is inclined to respond to gross externalities rather than to the less shocking but more significant aspects of the struggle. His depictions, created purposefully to communicate the physical horrors of war, exist in themselves, without any reference to the larger military or historical context in which these aspects could assume their proper value.

Thus as an "independent contemplator" Sassoon hoped to eliminate the physical and psychological restrictions imposed on his poetry by the circumstances of its inspiration. It is significant that he also hoped to deal with the war "on a bigger scale," viewing it in a "comprehensive way" after the manner of the painter.[17] Sassoon apparently was beginning to understand the inadequacy of the brief lyric and narrative forms he had been employing. It is not clear just what new poetic form he had in mind. He may have intended to expand the scope of his visualizations within the lyric, as Sorley did in "A Hundred Thousand Million Mites We Go." Again, he may have intended to employ a longer, objectified narrative form in which he could order and arrange the visions that haunted him at Lancaster Gate. Sassoon's desire for a larger and more comprehensive medium (and his interesting reference to *The Dynasts*) indicates that he may have considered a modified epic form. At any rate, it is evident that he felt some dissatisfaction with the forms and techniques he had employed in *The Old Huntsman* and *Counter-Attack*. He is frank in confessing his belated recognition of Owen's accomplishment; the implied revaluation of his own satiric and realistic methods indicates to what extent those methods had failed, in his opinion, to voice the profounder aspects of the war.

[17] Sassoon may have had in mind the official war artists, who were free to explore the battle areas as "independent contemplators" and who worked within a more objective and disciplined art form. Both C. R. W. Nevinson and Paul Nash exhibited their war paintings in the Leicester Galleries. Sassoon was in or near London when Nevinson held his first Leicester Galleries exhibition in late 1916. He may have heard of Nash's May 1918 exhibition during his late summer convalescence at Lancaster Gate. See C. R. W. Nevinson, *Paint and Prejudice* (London, 1937); Anthony Bertram, *Paul Nash* (London, 1923); and Herbert Read, *The Philosophy of Modern Art*, Ch. X, "Paul Nash" (London, 1952).

Sassoon's consciousness of the need for a fuller, more objective visualization of the war is of prime significance, especially since his implicit dissatisfaction with the shorter lyric form was shared by other poets. Sorley, as we have seen, dismissed verse of the "small-holdings type"; Nichols attempted to arrange his separate lyric responses in a chronological sequence, hoping thereby to increase the scope of his presentation. Among the later poets, Isaac Rosenberg planned a symbolic drama as a framework for his lyric material; and Wilfred Owen, shortly before his death, was attempting to organize his poems in a more meaningful pattern. Almost every poet who wrote during the war sought to enlarge, objectify, and arrange the raw material of experiences for which the lyric afforded little means of development and control; and this artistic necessity, free from wartime restrictions and urgencies, clearly determines the forms chosen by two poets who later sought a more comprehensive and imaginative evocation of the truth of modern warfare.

CHAPTER IV · UNDERTONES:
EDMUND BLUNDEN

ᴡɪᴛʜ the possible exception of Wilfred Owen, no other World War I poet succeeded better than Siegfried Sassoon in depicting the ugly and shocking aspects of modern technological warfare; no other poet, at least, was so relentless in communicating his sense of outrage or in presenting the terrifying and disgusting details of a conflict which had been completely divested of its early idealistic motivations. In concentrating on the obviously unpleasant aspects of modern warfare, Sassoon tended, however, to ignore other sources of poetry which, if less immediately shocking, were perhaps more expressive of the general disruption and tragedy wrought by the conflict. Sassoon's poetry is almost completely dominated by his hatred of war and his desperately curative intentions; this negative attitude, of course, determined what he saw and what he chose to depict. Toward the end of the war, as we have seen, he recognized the limited nature of his approach and contemplated a "detached," "independent," and "comprehensive" presentation, free from personal emotions of bitterness and revulsion.

Although the verse of Edmund Blunden certainly embodies something of the physical and spiritual distress that informs Sassoon's productions, his range of visualization is much wider and his imagination is not as obsessed with the crude details of suffering and death. His poetry is not inspired by any purposefully curative intent, nor is it limited by the motives and techniques of disillusion. His eye ranges freely over the phenomena of war; he discovers poetry in the ravaged landscape, in broken homes and deserted farms, and in the broad aspects of nature (dawn, sunset, night, the seasons) which seem to reflect, in their variously altered qualities, man's hapless commitment to the destruction of all he has created. Like Sassoon, Blunden also finds poetry in the trenches and in the moral and physical crises of personal experience. His lyrical responses are more sensitive, more varied, and more controlled than Sassoon's; his emotional reactions are not predetermined by a strongly negative attitude but emerge spontaneously as a significant element of his depictions. Although some of Blunden's descriptive and reflective lyrics rank with the best inspired by the war, his narrative efforts suffer from the same defects of presentation that we have observed in the narratives of Nichols and Sassoon. Within the brief lyric form Blunden can suggest—often more effectively than Sassoon—the tragic import of the war; but when he attempts to extend and enlarge his experiences by means of the narrative form, he is apparently unable to discover a controlling principle that would unify the experiences he seeks to portray.

Like Graves and Sassoon, Blunden published a volume of recollections, *Undertones of War*.[1] Although this book is one of the most eloquent prose accounts of the conflict, it does not have the autobiographical scope or intent of *Good-bye to All That* or Sassoon's autobiographical trilogy. At once emotionally intimate and factually reticent, *Undertones of War* provides little information about Blunden as a practicing war poet. The circumstances of poetic inspiration may be inferred from the volume with a fair degree of certitude, but Blunden is silent about his conception of himself as a poet and about the effects of the war on his verse. *Undertones of War* may be viewed, in fact, as a sensitive prose elaboration of the materials contained in his wartime poetry rather than as an autobiographical effort. In Blunden's case, therefore, we do not have the wealth of personal commentary and self-criticism that we find in Sassoon's fictional and non-fictional autobiographical narratives. The poems as a whole afford their own commentary, for they embody

[1] London, 1928. Additional wartime recollections were published in *The Mind's Eye* (London, 1934).

a unified imaginative vision that seldom surrenders to the violence and disorder with which it deals.

When the war began, Blunden was not quite eighteen years old, one of the youngest of the future war poets. He was born in Yalding, Kent, near Maidstone, and attended Christ's Hospital, London. He had written verse since boyhood and at Christ's Hospital, according to one of his masters, he "lived for poetry." Some of his work was published in the school magazine and in two small collections which appeared in 1914. Early in 1915, a scholar-elect of Queen's College, Oxford, Blunden left Christ's Hospital to enter the army. In April of 1916 he published another small volume of verse, *Pastorals*, which revealed an unusual gift for interpreting the sights and sounds of the English countryside. By May, as a lieutenant in the 11th Royal Sussex Regiment, he was fighting in France. During the summer of 1916 his battalion was employed in the trenches north and south of Bethune, but in August it was shifted southward to take part in the great battles still raging in the Somme area. In the valley of the Ancre and around Thiepval Wood Blunden experienced some of the most violent fighting of the war. In November, however, his unit was moved north to the Ypres salient, where it remained for over a year. Although Blunden was recommended for a captaincy in the autumn of 1917, he was rejected, being considered too young for that rank by his commanding general. In the course of his combat service he was gassed (to the subsequent impairment of his health) and was awarded the Military Cross. A miraculous survivor of nearly two years of extremely hazardous trench fighting, he was transferred, in March 1918, to a training center in England. Although he twice applied for permission to return to France, he was found physically unfit for further combat duty and was discharged after a brief period of service with the postwar occupation forces.

Upon his release from the army, Blunden sent Siegfried

Sassoon—then an acknowledged "war poet" and the newly appointed literary editor of the London *Daily Herald*—one of the small collections of verse that he had issued privately in 1916. Opening the volume, Sassoon was "instantly startled by a felicitous line." His recognition of the unknown author's talent was swift: "Within five minutes I knew that I had discovered a poet. Here was someone writing about a Kentish barn in a way I had always felt but had never been able to put into verse. I forgot that I was in a newspaper office, for the barn was physically evoked, with its cobwebs and dust and sparkling sun, its smell of cattle-cake and apples stored in hay, the sound of the breeze singing in the shattered pane and sparrows squabbling on the roof. Here, too, was description of mill-wheel and weir, beautifully exact and affectionately felt, where authentic fishes basked in glades of drowsy sun."[2]

It is noteworthy that in this, his first bid for public recognition as a poet, Blunden offered not his war verse but the pastoral verse he had written at the age of eighteen, apparently feeling that nature was still the true source of his inspiration and achievement. Sassoon was instrumental in bringing critical attention to Blunden's work; and the young poet received encouragement from J. C. Squire, H. J. Massingham, Edward Marsh, and Robert Graves. *The Waggoner* appeared in 1920; *The Shepherd* was published in 1922, winning the Hawthornden Prize for that year and establishing Blunden's reputation as a pastoral poet of uncommon sensitivity. Although a few war poems were published in these two volumes, the emphasis, as the titles indicate, was on the rural scene. The majority of Blunden's war poems were not collected until 1928, when they were published as a supplement to *Undertones of War*. Since this volume was the first of his artistic efforts devoted entirely to the conflict, it is not difficult to understand why his war poetry

---

[2] *Siegfried's Journey*, p. 217.

has never been considered as seriously as that of Sassoon and Owen. During the war his name remained unknown; when a representative collection of his war verse became available, the reputations of his contemporaries had already become fairly well fixed.[3]

The most characteristic qualities of Blunden's poetry are derived from the themes and traditions of eighteenth-century pastoral verse. His delight in simple observation, his evocation of a wide range of rural scenes, his sensitivity to the rhythms and harmonies of nature—all these indicate his close kinship with Thomson, Young, Collins, Cowper, and Clare. It is John Clare, however, that Blunden admires most; he is "in some lights the best poet of Nature that this country and for all I know any other country ever produced."[4] Blunden's description of natural scenes, like Clare's, is fresh and spontaneous; his lyrical gift accommodates itself to the external reality rather than to romantic flights of imagination suggested by the reality. Blunden's diction, too, resembles Clare's; simple and unpretentious, it is often invigorated by the use of dialectal words that reflect the poet's effort to assimilate the language as well as the landscape of his native region.[5] The pastoralism of the Georgians was forced and artificial; as "week-end poets" they cultivated their sensibilities on a part-time basis as a means of escape from the ugliness and complexity of modern life. Blunden, however, combines an understanding of the deeply rooted English pastoral

[3] Blunden himself helped fix Owen's reputation with his 1931 edition of the *Poems*. He is also the author of a brief study, *War Poets: 1914-1918* (The British Council and The National Book League, 1958), in which he is naturally prohibited from discussing his own work.

[4] *Nature in English Literature* (New York, 1929), p. 51. In France, as he records in *Undertones of War*, Blunden occupied his spare moments by reading John Clare and Edward Young (*Night Thoughts*). Young's voice, "speaking out of a profound eighteenth century calm," helped to restore his equanimity in times of crisis.

[5] See Robert Bridges, "On the Dialectal Words in Edmund Blunden's Poems," *Society for Pure English*, Tract V (London, 1921).

tradition with a genuine love of the rural scenes out of which
that tradition slowly developed.

As a young poet Blunden was unusually productive, and
during the period of his service in France he seems to have
been writing verse regularly, especially during the summer of
1917. Unfortunately, as he confesses in the Preface to his collected *Poems*,[6] the work of that summer "vanished in the mud,"
a sacrifice to the exigencies of war. The collected *Poems*, however, preserves a considerable body of war verse, and in it we are
presented with aspects of the conflict which few other contemporary poets seem to have been disposed to portray.

Though there are hints of separation and foreboding in *Pastorals*, Blunden's earliest war verse dates from the spring of 1916,
when he experienced his first period of service in the trenches.
By this time, as we have seen, romantic idealism had nearly
spent itself as a motivating force for poetry, except for a final
resurgence just before the Somme battles. Blunden entered
the war too late to be affected by this once powerful influence,
to which, moreover, we may suspect he would not have been
temperamentally susceptible. Though rather young, and romantic in his own fashion, he was too reserved and too fully dedicated and developed as a nature poet to echo—as did Sassoon,
before he originated his own response—the high aspirations
of Rupert Brooke; and he was too intelligent to adopt a poetic
attitude that was, in 1916, no longer quite relevant to the character of the war. Blunden was at first likewise disinclined to
deal with the crude externalities of trench fighting. Graphic
realism, to which Sassoon was beginning to turn in the late
winter of 1916, was a mode unsuited to Blunden's talent for
rendering diffused, though poignant, emotional states; for it
implied a purposiveness that was foreign to his gentle, equable
disposition.

[6] London, 1930.

Blunden's verse, though it deals with disagreeable realities, nearly always confines itself not to the reality but to emotional "impacts" and quiet, ruminative perceptions, to the "under-tones" of war as they echo in the poet's mind and imagination. The poet sees the harmonies and beauties of nature, as well as the productions of man's patient industry, destroyed or defaced by the inhuman mechanism of war; the result is an alien and sinister world in which he can discern only pathetic vestiges of normality. Blunden thus found most of his poetry not in a base-less idealism nor in purposive realism, but in a humanely aesthet-ic sense of desecration. He is not, however, merely a nature poet transported to the wars; his unflinching eye and strength of phrase can cope with the most appalling of scenes; and when he occasionally depicts the trials and sufferings of the infantry soldier, he can convey, simply but powerfully, a sense of tragic necessity as compelling as the more easily aroused emotions of anger and pity.

As the work of a poet whose sensibility had already been formed by a love of the English countryside, Blunden's most characteristic verse deals with the cruelly altered aspects of nature in a region defiled by war. Fields, streams, and trees have suffered a violation that reflects the vast, helpless disharmony of human conflict. Now deformed by shell-fire and clogged with unwholesome debris, the streams of Belgium can do no more than recall, by contrast, the peaceful waters of Kent and Sussex:

> This conduit stream that's tangled here and there
> With rusted iron and shards of earthenware,
> And tawny-stained with ruin trolls across
> The tiny village battered into dross—
> This muddy water chuckling in its run
> Takes wefts of colour from the April sun,
> And paints for fancy's eye a glassy burn
> Ribanded through a brake of Kentish fern,

From some top spring beside a park's gray pale,
Guarding a shepherded and steepled dale,
Wherefrom the blue deep-coppiced uplands hear
The dim cool noise of waters at a weir.

                                    ("Zillebeke Brook")

Throughout the war Blunden maintained his ability to see things freshly and to describe them in terms of significant contrasts. In "The Unchangeable" (obviously written toward the end of his service in France) he can still meditate sadly on the transformation wrought by the war and measure it against his memory of more tranquil times:

Though I within these two last years of grace
Have seen bright Ancre scourged to brackish mire,
And meagre Belgian becks by dale and chace
Stamped into sloughs of death with battering fire—
Spite of all this, I sing you high and low,
My old loves, Waters, be you shoal or deep,
Waters whose lazy and continual flow
Learns at the drizzling weir the tongue of sleep.

Trees, in "Thiepval Wood," have undergone a transformation to which the poet is equally sensitive. All life, all "impulses" have been extinguished from the blackened stalks, which remain as sinister symbols of suffering and death:

The tired air groans as the heavies swing over, the
    river-hollows boom;
The shell-fountains leap from the swamps, and with
    wildfire and fume
    The shoulder of the chalkdown convulses.
Then jabbering echoes stampede in the slatting wood,
Ember-black the gibbet trees like bones or thorns
    protrude
    From the poisonous smoke—past all impulses.

To them these silvery dews can never again be dear,
Nor the blue javelin-flame of thunderous noons strike
   fear.

Thus the poet does more than provide a simple description of a ruined landscape; he suggests a contrast between the normally flourishing life of nature and the sterile desolation to which it has been reduced.

Though the war changed the themes and materials of his poetry, Blunden's style, language, and modes of visualization remained essentially the same. The first two poems quoted above embody the sensibility of the nature poet; the diction and phrasing clearly echo the manner of eighteenth-century pastoral verse: "And paints for fancy's eye a glassy burn/ Ribanded through a brake of Kentish fern. . . ." In "Thiepval Wood," however, the scene involves a radical transformation of vocabulary; instead of expressions that suggest the peace and beauty of the countryside ("dim cool noise," "lazy and continual flow," "drizzling weir"), we have phrases that vividly evoke the qualities of sinister violence: "jabbering echoes," "slatting wood," "gibbet trees," "poisonous smoke." The change in descriptive terms, however, does not entail any essential change in Blunden's diction or in his manner of visualization. When he describes the effects of violence and spiritual stress, his vocabulary naturally reflects the pressures appropriate to that kind of material; when he describes the beauties of nature, he relaxes, so to speak, in the conventions of pastoral diction. Thus in "Thiepval Wood" he concludes with the thought that, for the ruined trees, "these silvery dews can never again be dear"; both sentiment and phrasing are again those of the meditative pastoral poet. Unlike Sassoon, he did not feel it necessary to develop a special mode for the presentation of his experiences. His style and sensibility were developed to such a degree that he could accommodate most of these experiences without any fundamental change, and he never utilizes his verse as a medium of purposive communication.

Blunden often resorts to a practice common among romantic poets: he endows animate and inanimate nature with human sentience and emotions, thereby forcefully evoking the feelings with which he himself views the landscape. This technique is employed above in "Thiepval Wood"; it is also employed in "Trees on the Calais Road": the trees, mourning the dead, "groan for the slaughter and the desecration." In "The Zonnebeke Road" the poet vividly evokes the oppression and anguish that inform the landscape by objectifying his feelings in the details of his description:

> Look, how the snow-dust whisks along the road,
> Piteous and silly; the stones themselves must flinch
> In this east wind; the low sky like a load
> Hangs over—a dead-weight. But what a pain
> Must gnaw where its clay cheek
> Crushes the shell-chopped trees that fang the plain—
> The ice-bound throat gulps out a gargoyle shriek.
> The wretched wire before the village line
> Rattles like rusty brambles or dead bine,
> And then the daylight oozes into dun;
> Black pillars, those are trees where roadways run.

Blunden is especially responsive to the sinister and malignant aspects of front-line scenes, but he seeks effects of a different order than those of simple physical horror. In "Festubert: The Old German Line," for instance, he manages to suggest the presence of an evil more subtle and more significant than that commonly depicted by Sassoon:

> Sparse mists of moonlight hurt our eyes
> With gouged and scourged uncertainties
> Of soul and soil in agonies.

One derelict grim skeleton
That drench and dry had battened on
Still seemed to wish us malison;

Still zipped across the gouts of lead
Or cracked like whipcracks overhead;
The gray rags fluttered on the dead.

The reality is there, but instead of mere graphic reproduction
we have an imaginative enlargement of the scene and a transformation of the details into an ordered and poetically significant whole. Again, the full moon of deep winter, normally
a source of poetic delight, is visualized as an unholy spectre
presiding over the horrors of Ypres:

Vantaged snow on the gray pilasters
Gleams to the sight so wan and ghostly;
The wolfish shadows in the eerie places
    Sprawl in the mist-light.

Sharp-fanged searches the frost, and shackles
The sleeping water in broken cellars,
And calm and fierce the witch-moon watches,
    Curious of evil.
                    ("January Full Moon, Ypres")

Most war poets found their sensibilities harried and warped by
battlefield scenes; for them truth was no longer beauty but
ugliness, and ugliness was a truth that must be communicated
at all costs. Blunden, however, retains his intellectual and
imaginative poise; his senses are alert for beauty as well as
danger and horror. In "Illusions" the three are blended not with
an effect of meaningless incongruity but as part of the poet's
physical and imaginative experience:

Trenches in the moonlight, in the lulling moonlight
Have had their loveliness; when dancing dewy grasses

Caressed us passing along their earthy lanes;
When the crucifix hanging over was strangely
    illumined,
And one imagined music, one even heard the brave
    bird
In the sighing orchards flute above the weedy well.
There are such moments; forgive me that I note them,
Nor gloze that there comes soon the nemesis of
    beauty,
In the fluttering relics that at first glimmer wakened
Terror—the no-man's ditch suddenly forking:
There, the enemy's best with bombs and brains and
    courage!
—Softly, swiftly, at once be animal and angel—
But O no, no, they're Death's malkins dangling in
    the wire
    For the moon's interpretation.

Although the purpose of much World War I poetry is the urgent communication of truth, the war poet sometimes implies that his experiences are actually incommunicable and that the reader can never understand the soldier unless he shares with him the "sorrowful dark of hell." Blunden's calm assumption of the direct poet-reader relationship ("There are such moments; forgive me that I note them. . . .") illustrates an unshaken belief in the universality of human experience and in the poignant significance of harmony and discord amid the scenes of war.

Nature assumes her most poignant aspect, however, when soldiers are permitted brief interludes of rest in areas behind the front lines. Men's eyes hungrily scan the beauties of a landscape unmarred by war, and they instinctively rejoice in the ordered harmony of farm life ("Bleue Maison," "The Sentry's Mistake," "Battalion in Rest"); but the weary mind, sharpened again to apprehension by the insistent cannonade in the east, cannot altogether relax ("Mont de Cassel"). The best poem on this theme, "At Senlis Once," captures the pathetic intensity of life as experienced by those who know themselves under reprieve:

> Clad so cleanly, this remnant of poor wretches
> Picked up life like the hens in orchard ditches,
> Gazed on the mill-sails, heard the church-bell,
> Found an honest glass all manner of riches.
>
> How they crowded the barn with lusty laughter,
> Hailed the pierrots and shook each shadowy rafter,
> Even could ridicule their own sufferings,
> Sang as though nothing but joy came after!

With characteristic sympathy and insight, Blunden thus measures the harsh disruption of warfare in terms of the simplicities and trivialities of normal life. The disharmony implicit in war is not depicted merely in its own terms as a disagreeable phenomenon but as a significant departure from the ordered processes of nature and human life.

Structures that are the products and symbols of peace, civilization, and ordered routine—houses, farms, shrines, churches, and civic buildings—are subject, no less than the forms of nature, to the "senseless rage" of war; and Blunden's eye rests pityingly on these smashed relics. In "A House in Festubert" he notes the "blind eyes" and the "great wound" of an old home from which domestic peace has fled; beside its "mellow walls" squat "four lean guns," sinister symbols of an indiscriminately destructive war. In "A Farm near Zillebeke" he laments, to the point of tears, the doom of a useful structure and the interruption of homely, peaceful tasks:

> Black clouds hide the moon, the amazement is
> gone;
> The morning will come in weeping and rain;

The Line is all hushed—on a sudden anon
The fool bullets clack and guns mouth again.
I stood in the yard of a house that must die,
And still the black hame was stacked by the door,
And harness still hung there, and the dray
    waited by.
Black clouds hid the moon, tears blinded me
    more.

At a moment of fearful crisis, in "Preparations for Victory," Blunden calms himself by considering the intact house, "the yet unmurdered tree," and the "relics of dear homes that court the eye." "Les Halles d'Ypres" depicts the famous Cloth Hall, once a proud monument to a vanished order of life, but now a "tangle of iron rods and spluttered beams"; only the tower retains a trace of its venerable beauty. Civilian poets, at a safe distance, could become publicly wrathful or sentimental about Louvain, the Cloth Hall, or the Cathedral at Rheims; and most soldier-poets were too deeply immersed in their personal trials and emotions to take particular note of the destruction around them, except as a source of contrast to the peaceful landscapes of England. Blunden, however, was a close observer of the background of war; with the keen sympathy and sensitivity of the dedicated nature poet for the objects of imposed violence and distortion, he depicted disharmonies more meaningful, in a sense, than the clamor and confusion of battle.

Although Siegfried Sassoon dramatized the demoralizing effects of modern warfare on the human spirit, he failed to evoke the full context of that demoralization so that its significance could be measured in terms other than those of simple shock and horror. Enlarging upon the realism of Sassoon's war poetry, Middleton Murry remarks:

"There is a value in the direct transcription of plain, unvarnished fact; but there is another truth more valuable still. One

may convey the chaos of immediate sensation by a chaotic expression, as does Mr. Sassoon. But the unforgettable horror of
an inhuman experience can only be rightly rendered by rendering also its relation to the harmony and calm of the soul which
it shatters. In this context alone can it appear with that sudden
shock to the imagination which is overwhelming. The faintest
discord in a harmony has within it an infinity of disaster, which
no confusion of notes, however wild and various and loud, can
possibly suggest. It is on this that the wise saying that poetry is
emotion recollected in tranquillity is so firmly based, for the
quality of an experience can only be given by reference to the
ideal condition of the human consciousness which it disturbs
with pleasure or with pain. But in Mr. Sassoon's verses it is
we who are left to create for ourselves the harmony of which he
gives us only the moment of its annihilation. It is we who
must be the poets and the artists if anything enduring is to be
made of his work. He gives us only the data."[7]

It is precisely in his evocation of a shattered "harmony and
calm"—both of the soul and of the landscape from which the
nature poet normally seeks sustenance—that Blunden's poetry
may be said to surpass Sassoon's. Blunden's descriptive lyrics give
us not only the "data" but the emotional attitude of the observer,
who finds his poetry in the transformations wrought by warfare
and in their effects on his own sensibility. The "data" of warfare,
as expressed in verse, may provide the material for a candid
and compelling transcription of what the poet has seen and
wishes us to see. As Middleton Murry suggests, however, the
"data" of warfare have meaning only when they are presented
in a significant moral or emotional context. In Blunden's case
the emotional "undertones" imply a humane assessment of
war that is both moral and aesthetic. The observer is not limited
by a merely curative intent; his attitude is positive rather than

[7] "Mr. Sassoon's War Verses," *The Evolution of an Intellectual*, pp.
73-74.

negative, since every aspect of warfare has its legitimate claim to the poet's attention. Blunden "measures" these aspects by referring, implicitly or explicitly, to the tranquillity and order from which they so significantly depart and by indicating his own sympathetic sense of disharmony and loss.

In an early poem entitled "To Victory," it may be recalled, Sassoon expressed a somewhat affected distaste for the uniformly drab colors of the battlefield: "I am tired of the greys and browns and the leafless ash." Of course, he quickly outgrew this mood of escapism and moved on to the more realistic attitudes and techniques that were to make him famous. Blunden's work, however, evinces no similar transitional attitudes; from the beginning his poetry is grounded in objective reality and in its effect on the sensibilities and not in self-conscious or self-revealing emotionalism. The background of war—"the greys and browns and the leafless ash"—became the material of his poetry. Unlike Francis Ledwidge and Edward Thomas, who refused to let the conflict interfere with their nostalgic rural visions, Blunden successfully adapted his talent for unpretentious landscape description to the scenes of war. The ability to see significance in the violence done to nature and to the works of man is the source of his emotional balance as well as his imaginative freedom as a poet.

In the later stages of the war, as the consumption of human life increased in rapidity and desperation and as his own experiences grew more harrowing, a new sense of suffering and sacrifice penetrated Blunden's usually calm meditative mood. Certain poems, such as "Preparations for Victory," "Zero," and "The Zonnebeke Road," attain a somber intensity of personal anguish which simultaneously manages to evoke the tragic as well as the physical dimensions of the conflict.

The ironically titled "Preparations for Victory" is developed as an exhortation from the poet to his soul and body:

My soul, dread not the pestilence that hags
The valley; flinch not you, my body young,
At these great shouting smokes and snarling
    jags
Of fiery iron; as yet may not be flung
The dice that claims you. Manly move among
These ruins, and what you must do, do well;
Look, here are gardens, there mossed boughs
    are hung
With apples whose bright cheeks none might
    excel,
And there's a house as yet unshattered by a shell.

The physical "data" of battle are depicted not as the primary reality but as the background of the poet's desperate struggle to retain possession of himself. The significance of that struggle is emphasized by its orderly and almost conventional presentation; the poet clearly comprehends his experience and interprets it in terms of the inner divisions that afflict him in this moment of extremity. Vestiges of the normal peacetime world (the gardens, the apple tree, the intact house) are symbols of the mental and physical harmonies menaced by the war, and they bring the poet some degree of composure. Out of this inner struggle emerges an imperative for action that is not simple patriotism but a primal courage born of a sense of tragic necessity and a basic need to assert the human will in the face of intolerable violence and brutality: "The body, poor unpitied Calaban,/ Parches and sweats and grunts to win the name of Man." The final stanza depicts the vast panorama of war against which the poet's moral struggle is enacted. Amid these "preparations for victory" the sense of oppression and futility is overwhelming:

Days or eternities like swelling waves
Surge on, and still we drudge in this dark maze,

The bombs and coils and cans by strings of
    slaves
Are borne to serve the coming day of days;
Pale sleep in slimy cellars scarce allays
With its brief blank the burden. Look, we
    lose;
The sky is gone, the lightless drenching haze
Of rainstorm chills the bone; earth, air are foes,
The black fiend leaps brick-red as life's last
    picture goes.

Blunden has the unusual ability to present his lyric visualizations in terms of a temporal or cosmic whole; his descriptions frequently have a point of reference (the passage of time, the sky, the sun, the stars) from which they take an added dimension and significance. In the stanza quoted above, for instance, we have specific descriptive details, but these details amount to much more than a simple graphic representation; they are imaginatively ordered and related to the passage of time—time that moves inexorably toward the crisis, and time that suggests, through the sunset, the triumph of darkness over human life. Similarly, " 'Transport Up' at Ypres," which depicts the endless traffic of a front-line supply route, provides the scene with a perspective that is larger than history, larger even than any human measurement of time:

From silhouette to pitchy blur, beneath the bitter
    stars,
The interminable convoy streams of horses, vans,
    and cars.
They clamour through the cheerless night, the streets
    a slattern maze,
The sentries at the corners shout them on their
    different ways.

And so they go, night after night, and chance the
    shrapnel fire,
The sappers' waggons stowed with frames and
    concertina wire,
The ration-limbers for the line, the lorries for
    the guns:
While overhead with fleering light stare down those
    withered suns.

Few World War I poets had this capacity to enlarge their
descriptions beyond the range of immediate perceptions and
sensations. Gilbert Frankau, for instance, who was one of the
few soldier-poets to adopt Kipling's resounding verse techniques,
describes transport scenes similar to Blunden's; but he fails to
evoke any reality beyond that of mechanical military efficiency:

I am only a cog in a giant machine, a link of an
    endless chain:—
And the rounds are drawn, and the rounds are fired,
    and the empties return again;
Railroad, lorry, and limber, battery, column, and
    park;
To the shelf where the set fuze waits the breach,
    from the quay where the shells embark.[8]

Although Frankau's verse is full of lurid scenes and vivid images,
he deals only with externals, with the "data." Blunden, on the
other hand, does not consider the externals of warfare important
in themselves; he utilizes them as the source of more significant
visions and intuitions.

"The Zonnebeke Road" also reflects Blunden's deepening
sense of tragedy and suffering. The descriptive portion of this
poem has already been discussed with reference to Blunden's
ability to "animate" a landscape with human sensations and

[8] "Ammunition Column," from *The Guns* (London, 1916).

emotions. Other portions of the poem—the beginning and the end—deal with the emotions and attitudes of the soldiers who must live and fight in the midst of that anguished landscape. Weariness, pain, and fear are evoked in the following lines; the speaker's disconnected thoughts and his weak attempt at ironic humor effectively suggest the quiet desperation of daily trench life:

> Morning, if this late withered light can claim
> Some kindred with that merry flame
> Which the young day was wont to fling through
> space!
> Agony stares from each gray face.
> And yet the day is come; stand down! stand down!
> Your hands unclasp from rifles while you can,
> The frost has pierced them to the bended bone?
> Why, see old Stevens there, that iron man,
> Melting the ice to shave his grotesque chin:
> Go ask him, shall we win?
> I never liked this bay, some foolish fear
> Caught me the first time that I came in here;
> That dugout fallen in awakes, perhaps,
> Some formless haunting of some corpse's chaps.
> True, and wherever we have held the line,
> There were such corners, seeming-saturnine
> For no good cause.

Contemplation of the blasted landscape (see above, p. 122) seems, however, to focus the poet's wandering thoughts and shifting emotions. His hatred of war's infinite boredom, ugliness, and pain emerges, in the concluding lines of the poem, with a spontaneous and climactic force:

> Even Ypres now would warm our souls; fond fool,
> Our tour's but one night old, seven more to cool!
> O screaming dumbness, O dull clashing death,

Shreds of dead grass and willows, homes and men,
Watch as you will, men clench their chattering
   teeth
And freeze you back with that one hope, disdain.

Thus all aspirations, all values have been reduced to one bleak virtue, the key to endurance and survival. Here is depicted an extremity of human courage that suggests, in the force of its desperate avowal, the extremity of Byrhtwold at the conclusion of *The Battle of Maldon*: "Heart must be keener, courage the hardier,/ Bolder our mood as our band diminisheth." The parallel can, of course, be pursued no further because Byrhtwold sounded a noble rallying cry against the Viking invader, while the modern soldier defies not the enemy but the inhuman circumstances of war itself. Nevertheless, Blunden approximates, if only for an instant, the epic cry of defiance against insuperable odds.

Only a small minority of the World War I poets had the capacity—or, indeed, the opportunity—to envision the struggle, as Thomas Hardy envisioned the Napoleonic Wars, as a necessary and inevitable enactment subject to the designs of a superintending power. This "metaphysical" capacity is sometimes visible in Blunden's better poems; it is the source of his calm sympathy, his controlled presentation, and his occasionally tragic insights. But if the mixture of restraint and tenderness is reminiscent of Hardy's manner, the scale of the younger poet's tragic perceptions is clearly limited by the nature of the lyric form to which he is committed. "Zero,"[9] for instance, depicts the poet's state of mind just prior to a dawn attack. Filled with wonder at the "torrent splendour" of the rising sun, his preternaturally alert senses stunned by the multitude and violence of the impressions that affront him, the poet begins to doubt the fact of his own bodily presence:

[9] Titled "Come On, My Lucky Lads" in *Undertones of War*.

In what subnatural strange awaking
  Is this body, which seems mine?
These feet towards that blood-burst making,
   These ears which thunder, these hands
    which twine

On grotesque iron? Icy-clear
  The air of a mortal day shocks sense,
My shaking men pant after me here.
  The acid vapours hovering dense,

The fury whizzing in dozens down,
  The clattering rafters, clods calcined,
The blood in the flints and the trackway
   brown—
   I see I am clothed and in my right
    mind. . . .

The sight of a wounded soldier further confirms the reality
and steadies his wavering purpose; out of the chaos of sensation emerges a single certitude, the poet's final word on the
ordeal of war:

    Here limps poor Jock with a gash in the
      poll,
     His red blood now is the red I see,

    The swooning white of him, and that red!
     These bombs in boxes, the craunch of
      shells,
    The second-hand flitting round; ahead!
     It's plain we were born for this, naught
      else.

This last line of "Zero," an acknowledgment of the fierce necessity of the moment, reflects the desperate spiritual discipline
evoked by the later stages of the war. More importantly, Blunden

has done more than merely transmit the sensations or the "data" of a terrible experience; he has passed a judgment and related the sufferings of the struggle to a philosophic conception. The chaos of sensation can assume meaning only if it is interpreted by a mind capable of relating that chaos to a dominant conception of action and endeavor. However, the brevity of the lyric mode and its nature as a vehicle of personal expression prevent a satisfactory embodiment of Blunden's vision of tragic necessity. The full implications of tragedy can be developed only on a scale commensurate to the importance of the events depicted. The lyric can only suggest the individual's sense of disaster, his personal vision of chaos and suffering; the reality of war is not so much embodied as presented as a perception— brief, intense, full of tragic implications—but still a tragedy perceived, not a tragedy artistically objectified and extended to its full potentiality as a record of warfare.

If we accept Blunden's "Third Ypres" as a modern battle narrative in verse and contrast it to the heroic poem, certain significant differences become apparent. Heroic poetry, of course, narrates the deeds of a noble personage who triumphs over his enemies in such a way as to illustrate the heroic virtues. Action is the primary ingredient of the heroic poem, for it is through action that the hero achieves his being; it is through action, moreover, that the heroic poem justifies itself as a narrative of battle. "Third Ypres" is notable for a powerful evocation of anguish and horror, but its action is impeded by diffused perceptions and an emphasis on emotional undertones. Blunden's sensitivity to certain levels of meaning is here a liability, since it prevents a satisfactory narrative progression.[10] Though the poem embarks upon a series of events and inter-

[10] The lyrics appended to *Undertones of War* are entitled "A Supplement of Poetical Interpretations and Variations"—phrasing which seems to imply a distinction between the artistic possibilities of a controlled prose narrative and the partial and limited illuminations of the lyric form.

135

mittently refers to the passage of time and to change of circumstance, it does not tell a story but records the limited perceptions of a sensibility burdened almost beyond the point of human endurance. The impulse toward personal expression in verse is normally confined to the lyric, but Blunden utilizes a quasi-narrative form to prolong a series of subjective impressions and to give a credible objective reality to the source of the emotions he attempts to depict. He apparently recognized the insufficiency of the brief lyric form with respect to certain kinds of battle experience, and he tried in "Third Ypres" to justify and give fuller play to the pressures that were accumulating in that form. In a prefatory note to *Undertones of War*, Blunden describes the poem as "one of his most comprehensive and particular attempts to render war experience poetically." "Third Ypres" embodies a great many appalling particulars, but it is comprehensive neither with respect to the war nor to the battle upon which it is based.

A few facts about the Third Battle of Ypres (July-November 1917) may serve to put Blunden's poem in its proper temporal and emotional perspective. The campaign was undertaken as an effort to turn the right flank of the German defense system in the West. Although the British armies succeeded in breaking out of the old Ypres salient, the campaign was a strategic failure, since it fell far short of its ultimate purpose. The main attack was launched on the morning of July 31, but at noon on August 1 rain began to fall on an already soaked terrain, making progress difficult if not impossible. Rain continued to fall incessantly for four days and four nights, disrupting an intricate schedule of artillery barrage and infantry assault. In the succeeding weeks the British campaign bogged down in a sea of mud; and the battle, from which so much was hoped, became merely another unsuccessful British effort in the demoralizing war of attrition.

The events narrated in the poem obviously begin on the morning of August 1, when hope and expectation still run high after the success of the first major assault. Blunden opens, characteristically, with a reference to the rising sun; he then goes on to depict the half-incredulous anticipation of victory among those who have survived the first day of battle:

> Triumph! How strange, how strong had triumph
>   come
> On weary hate of foul and endless war
> When from its grey gravecloths awoke anew
> The summer day. Among the tumbled wreck
> Of fascined lines and mounds the light was
>   peering,
> Half-smiling upon us, and our newfound pride;
> The terror of the waiting night outlived,
> The time too crowded for the heart to count
> All the sharp cost in friends killed on the assault.
> No hook of all the octopus had held us,
> Here stood we trampling down the ancient tyrant.
> So shouting dug we among the monstrous pits.

These generalized perceptions relate to the progress of the battle as a whole—or at least to that part of it which is visible to the group of which the poet is a member. In employing the first-person plural Blunden registers not only his own reactions but the moods and emotions of his fellow-soldiers. These emotions begin to waver between doubt and joy as an unnatural silence settles over the battlefield:

> Amazing quiet fell upon the waste,
> Quiet intolerable to those who felt
> The hurrying batteries beyond the masking hills
> For their new parley setting themselves in array
> In crafty fourms unmapped.

> No, these, smiled
> faith,
> Are dumb for the reason of their overthrow.
> They move not back, they lie among the crews
> Twisted and choked, they'll never speak again.
> Only the copse where once might stand a shrine
> Still clacked and suddenly hissed its bullets by.
> The War would end, the Line was on the move,
> And at a bound the impassable was passed.
> We lay and waited with extravagant joy.

As the day progresses, however, it is apparent that this joy is ill-founded: no word comes back from the first wave of infantry ("'They're done,'" croak the "slow moments," "'they've all died on the entanglements. . . .'"); the rain begins; and the German artillery resumes firing. At this point the narrator speaks for the first time in his own person:

> And you,
> Poor signaller, you I passed by this emplacement,
> You whom I warned, poor daredevil, waving your
> flags,
> Amid this screeching I pass you again and shudder
> At the lean green flies upon the red flesh mad-
> ding.
> Runner, stand by a second. Your message.—He's
> gone,
> Falls on a knee, and his right hand uplifted
> Claws his last message from his ghostly enemy,
> Turns stone-like. Well I liked him, that young
> runner,
> But there's no time for that. O now for the word
> To order us flash from these drowning roaring
> traps

And even hurl upon that snarling wire?
Why are our guns so impotent?

Here the sensibility of the poet as an individual begins to take
over; the narrative (at least in this portion of the poem) does
not lose its chronological progression, nor does it wholly abandon
reference to objective reality; but the material becomes partially
restricted to the range of the poet's personal observations and
emotions.

The next thirty lines carry the action forward through the
night. The poet's unit, heretofore held in reserve, is called upon
to relieve the remnants of the broken first assault. Although
Blunden's brief notations of vanished symbols of peace (the
ploughman and his team) are characteristic, they anticipate
a more serious restriction of the narrative in later passages. The
sensibility of the poet rather than the significance of the action
is here confirmed as the unifying factor:

> The grey rain,
> Steady as the sand in an hourglass on this day,
> Where through the window the red lilac looks,
> And all's so still, the chair's odd click is noise—
> The rain is all heaven's answer, and with hearts
> Past reckoning we are carried into night
> And even sleep is nodding here and there.
>
> The second night steals through the shrouding rain.
> We in our numb thought crouching long have lost
> The mockery triumph, and in every runner
> Have urged the mind's eye see the triumph to come,
> The sweet relief, the straggling out of hell
> Into whatever burrows may be given
> For life's recall. Then the fierce destiny speaks.
> This was the calm, we shall look back for this.
> The hour is come; come, move to the relief!
> Dizzy we pass the mule-strewn track where once

The ploughman whistled as he loosed his team;
And where he turned home-hungry on the road,
The leaning pollard marks us hungrier turning.
We crawl to save the remnant who have torn
Back from the tentacled wire, those whom no
    shell
Has charred into black carcasses—Relief!
They grate their teeth until we take their room,
And through the churn of moonless night and mud
And flaming burst and sour gas we are huddled
Into the ditches where they bawl sense awake,
And in a frenzy that none could reason calm,
(Whimpering some, and calling on the dead)
They turn away: as in a dream they find
Strength in their feet to bear back that strange
    whim
Their body.

    The final and climactic section of "Third Ypres" concerns
events that happen during a vicious bombardment at noon on
the following day. "Huge and shattering salvoes" suddenly begin
to fall on the newly established front line; the general action
which the narrative has developed up to this point is virtually
abandoned, and the perspective dwindles to a presentation of
the poet's stunned perceptions and his desperately overwrought
emotional state:

                          This wrath's oncoming
Found four of us together in a pillbox,
Skirting the abyss of madness with light phrases,
White and blinking, in false smiles grimacing.
The demon grins to see the game, a moment
Passes, and—still the drum-tap dongs my brain
To a whirring void—through the great breach
    above me

The light comes in with icy shock and the rain
Horridly drops. Doctor, talk, talk! if dead
Or stunned I know not; the stinking powdered
    concrete,
The lyddite turns me sick—my hair's all full
Of this smashed concrete. O I'll drag you, friends,
Out of the sepulchre into the light of day,
For this is day, the pure and sacred day.
And while I squeak and gibber over you,
Look, from the wreck a score of field-mice nimble,
And tame and curious look about them; (these
Calmed me, on these depended my salvation).

The major individual concerns of survival and sanity thus gradually replace the larger narrative conceptions with which the poem began. As an observer and imminent participant Blunden can visualize, in the first part of the narrative, something of the progress of the battle and the hopes and fears of those who are engaged in it; as a participant, however, his range of reference diminishes, even within the scale of personal observation, to details (such as the unpleasant smell of powdered concrete and the incongruous appearance of the "tame and curious" field-mice) which the psychology of crisis forces upon his attention. As vivid and as intense as portions of "Third Ypres" are, the poem does not fulfill its original narrative promise; on the contrary, we gradually lose contact with the narrative reality until we are gazing, with the poet, at field-mice amid the smashed concrete of a pillbox. This is not to deny the truth of the poem as a depiction of personal suffering and anguish; the shift in purpose and the uncertainty of the point of view, however, are serious faults for which no lyrical intensity of presentation can compensate. Although Blunden's intent is not as obviously curative as Sassoon's intent in "Counter-Attack," "Third Ypres" fails for reasons that are basically the same: loss of objective projection and continuity. The brief lyric, of course, can achieve—especially in the hands of Blunden—a significance and an intensity without these qualities; but the verse narrative that comes to depend almost wholly upon a succession of subjective visualizations has lost contact with the larger reality upon which it is based.

We have observed the difference between "The Rear-Guard" and Sassoon's postwar prose account of the incident upon which his poem is based. The same contrasts in attitude and emphasis are discernible between Blunden's "Third Ypres" and portions of *Undertones of War* which deal with the poet's experiences in that battle. The following passage recounts the incidents described in the quotation given above:

"Presently the drizzle was thronging down mistily again, and shelling grew more regular and searching. There were a number of concrete shelters along the trench, and it was not hard to see that their dispossessed makers were determined to do them in. Our doctor, an Irishman named Gatchell, who seemed utterly to scorn such annoyances as Krupp, went out to find a much discussed bottle of whisky which he had left in his medical post. He returned, the bottle in his hand; 'Now, you toping rascals'— a thump like a thunderbolt stopped him. He fell mute, white, face down, the bottle still in his hand; 'Ginger' Lewis, the unshakable Adjutant, whose face I chanced to see particularly, went as chalky-white, and collapsed; the Colonel, shaking and staring, passed me as I stooped to pull the doctor out, and tottered, not knowing where he was going, along the trench. This was not surprising. Over my seat, at the entrance the direct hit had made a gash in the concrete, and the place was full of fragments and dust. The shell struck just over my head, and I suppose it was a 5.9. But we had escaped, and outside, scared from some shattered nook, a number of fieldmice were peeping and turning as though as puzzled as ourselves. A German listening-set with its delicate valves stood in the rain there, too, unfractured. But these details were perceived in a flash, and meanwhile shells were coming down remorselessly all along our alley. Other direct hits occurred. Men stood in the trench under their steel hats and capes, resigned to their fate. A veterinary surgeon, Gatfield, with his droll, sleepy, profoundly kind manner, filled the doctor's place, and attended as best he could to the doctor and the other wounded. The continuous and ponderous blasts of shells seemed to me to imply that an attack was to be made on us, and being now more or less the only headquarters officer operating, after an inconclusive conference with the Colonel, I sent the S.O.S. to the artillery; the telephone wire went almost immediately afterwards. Our wonderful artillery answered, and at length the pulverization of our place slackened, to the relief of the starting nerves. . . ."[11]

The prose narrator describes his three shell-stunned companions without the slightest hint of his own feelings and sensations, which must have been equally if not more strongly affected by the blast; he is as emotionally detached as it is possible for an observer-participant to be. In the poem Blunden obviously heightens and intensifies the subjective aspects of his experience; while in the prose narrative he develops only the external aspects, filling in many details and relating the action, in some degree, to the immediate military situation. Thus the prose narrator's experience is one with the objective physical context and falls into place amid the succession of incidents which make up the narrative action. The obligation of maintaining a straightforward narrative progression obviously excludes any departure into the inner realm of emotion and sensation. In the poem, however, we find ourselves at the static center of a gradually constricted range of sensibility; the observer has become the participant to such a degree that he is no longer capable of objectifying the action upon which his narrative is based.

[11] *Undertones of War*, pp. 219-20.

"Counter-Attack," it will be recalled, ends upon a note of chaos and blank futility; the wounded protagonist is "Lost in a blurred confusion of yells and groans . . .":

> Down, and down, and down, he sank and drowned,
> Bleeding to death. The counter-attack had failed.

The narrative thus terminates abruptly; there is no real action, only noise and confusion; there is no real hero, only a dying soldier. "Third Ypres" ends in the same abrupt and inconclusive fashion. To the poet, stunned in his pillbox, comes a frantic call for aid:

> "For God's sake send and help us,
> Here in a gunpit, all headquarters done for,
> Forty or more, the nine-inch came right through,
> All splashed with arms and legs, and I myself
> The only one not killed, not even wounded.
> You'll send—God bless you!"

From this horror the final eleven lines of the poem subside into anguished but generalized reflection:

> The more monstrous
>   fate
> Shadows our own, the mind swoons doubly
>   burdened,
> Taught how for miles our anguish groans and
>   bleeds,
> A whole sweet countryside amuck with murder;
> Each moment puffed into a year with death.
> Still swept the rain, roared guns,
> Still swooped into the swamps of flesh and
>   blood,
> All to the drabness of uncreation sunk,
> And all thought dwindled to a moan, Relieve!

> But who with what command can now relieve
> The dead men from that chaos, or my soul?

So "Third Ypres" comes to a close that is, in effect, the climactic revelation of a tortured and harassed sensibility rather than the culmination of the action that the poet has initiated. A pathetic appeal for relief concludes not the action of the battle but the poet's comprehension of the dire extremity which he and his comrades confront. The final two lines, as moving as they are, relate the catastrophe to the poet's desperately over-wrought soul rather than to terms that are amenable to extension and completion on a narrative plane. As a succession of primarily subjective visualizations, accordingly, "Third Ypres" can have no proper conclusion save an implicit "The attack had failed."

It is possible, of course, to maintain that the character of modern warfare rarely admits the opportunity of clear-cut action and heroic achievement wherein the individual, by a decisive act of the will, changes the course of some momentous enter-prise. H. V. Routh, writing not long after the conflict, com-mented on the serious artistic restrictions imposed on the poet not only by the extent of total national warfare but also by the very nature of the scientific violence employed: "At the end of a war, compared to which the siege of Troy would rank as a minor operation, those who review their experiences will find that however much they admire isolated acts of self-sacrifice, the predominant impression is one of human littleness. It is not merely that the numbers engaged were too vast to allow any single person, whatever his rank, to play a conspicuous part. It was rather that the science of destruction has developed to such a degree of ingenuity that human beings are left with nothing but a sense of annihilation. When the strongest and bravest warriors are either crushed and smashed to atoms, or suddenly felled by something which they can neither hear nor see, it is impossible to discover any grandeur in a modern battle and for that reason an epic can never be composed on the Great War."[12]

Positive heroic action does not consist of "isolated acts of self-sacrifice" nor of passive endurance, and narrative verse can hardly exist when men are prohibited from acting positively or significantly. In "Third Ypres" Blunden, at the expense of his narrative development, evokes a strained "sense of annihilation," and it is quite possible, therefore, that in a simple, transcriptive sense he is closer to the reality of the experience he depicts. Since in its later stages the war was deprived—in the mind of the infantry soldier, at least—of moral sanctions and even of clear military goals, it lacked background and perspective for meaningful action. Clear-cut, meaningful narrative, consequently, was difficult or impossible, especially for those poets —and they constituted the overwhelming majority—who from the beginning had depended in a large measure upon the personal lyric response. For the "truth" of the war these poets had come to rely upon the chaos of their own impressions and upon the intensity of their lyric visualizations.[13]

[12] *God, Man, and Epic Poetry* (Cambridge, 1927), I, 27.

[13] The whole problem of verse narration, as revealed in the work of Nichols, Sassoon, and Blunden, seems to indicate that the development of a controlled, objective narrative medium was a psychological or artistic impossibility, at least while the war was in progress. The verse of one poet, however, suggests that this fact can be attributed to the habitual practice of the lyric mode as well as to the special circumstances of the conflict. Although he is known as the author of *The Diary of a Dead Officer* (London, 1919), Arthur Graeme West is seldom listed even among the lesser poets of the war. Much earlier than Sassoon, and with something of Charles Sorley's critical independence of thought, this young Oxford graduate saw through mistaken ideals and popular emotionalisms; his *Diary* records the growing disillusionment that afflicted the members of his generation and class as they were forced to participate in a struggle which had lost its meaning.

Included among other verses in the last section of the *Diary*, "The Night Patrol" (dated March 1916) is one of the most balanced and objective verse narratives written during the war. The experience of three soldiers on a patrol in No Man's Land is related with almost complete detachment; there is no departure from the course of action initiated by the author, no distortion of outline or detail, and no loss of narrative control. From the

Within the range of the lyric response, however, Blunden produced some of the most effective poetry of the war. Although his characteristic work deals, as we have seen, with the disruption of harmony in the world of nature and civilized order, he sometimes dramatically captures the overwhelming sense of pity that distinguishes the verse of Wilfred Owen. "It's plain we were born for this, naught else," writes Blunden in "Zero"; but this bleak sense of necessity magnifies the consciousness of individual suffering to unbearable proportions in "Trench Raid near Hooge." The decorous literary image in the first stanza evokes a contrast between the conventional—but somehow humanely reassuring—poetic visualization of dawn and the brutal reality of a pre-dawn bombardment:

> At an hour before the rosy-fingered
>   Morning should come
> To wonder again what meant these sties,
> These wailing shots, these glaring eyes,
>   These moping mum,
>
> Through the black reached strange long rosy
>   fingers
>   All at one aim
> Protending, and bending: down they swept,
> Successions of similars after leapt
>   And bore red flame

point of view of technique, at least, the poem might be seen as a page from an unwritten epic of World War I. The total effect of unity and control, as contrasted with the disorganized effects of so impressive a work as "Third Ypres," is immediately obvious.

Apparently West did not think of himself as a war poet. He seems to have produced "The Night Patrol" merely as an experimental adjunct to his prose notations. During a period when the lyric mode was very nearly the sole means of poetic expression, West, despite an obvious need to communicate his hatred of the war, wrote—or at least preserved—no lyric poetry. For his opinion of those who wrote lyric poetry after the fashion set by Rupert Brooke see his "God! How I Hate You, You Young Cheerful Men!"

To one small ground of the eastern distance,
    And thunderous touched.
East then and west false dawns fan-flashed
And shut, and gaped; false thunders clashed.
    Who stood and watched

Caught piercing horror from the desperate pit
    Which with ten men
Was centre of this. The blood burnt, feeling
The fierce truth there and the last appealing,
    "Us? Us? Again?"

Nor rosy dawn at last appearing
    Through the icy shade
Might mark without trembling the new de-
    forming
Of earth that had seemed past further storming.
    Her fingers played,

One thought, with something of human pity
    On six or seven
Whose looks were hard to understand,
But that they ceased to care what hand
    Lit earth and heaven.

Thus the scene is presented not in terms of its mere physical effects but in terms of its tragic import and its shattering psychological and spiritual implications. The "fierce truth" of war can be captured only when these effects achieve some kind of extension in the soul of the poet who is capable of interpreting his own and others' suffering in the light of tragic experience. Blunden's sensitivity to suffering, as might be expected, is often independent of his own ordeals and exposures to hazard; in "Concert Party: Busseboom," for instance, he portrays the general high spirits induced by a soldiers' entertainment. The "maniac blast" of a far-off barrage, however, chills the hearts of the departing audience:

> To this new concert, white we stood;
> Cold certainty held our breath;
> While men in the tunnels below Larch Wood
> Were kicking men to death.

It is of such sympathetically imaginative yet realistic perceptions that Blunden's verse is largely composed.

As a soldier-poet, Sassoon felt profound anger and pity, and his verse is animated with the shocked indignation of a man who must speak out whatever the cost to poetry or the feelings of his readers. Implicit in the work of Blunden and Owen, however, is a sense of tragic necessity which raises their anger and pity above the level of the merely curative response. Though Blunden's poetry may be read as a protest against the violence and inhumanity of modern warfare, his conceptions do not derive their spirit from protest or rejection. War forces its harsh significance upon the poet, who must reap whatever meaning he can from revelations both bitter and sweet. If the poet's generation was "born for this, naught else," an attitude of mere rejection is ultimately superfluous and futile. Consequently there is no satire in Blunden's work. His occasional irony, moreover, has no curative intent; it is employed only to enforce the impact of some meaningful contrast, as in "Rural Economy." A delight in the simple satisfactions of daily life ("Clear Weather") and a gentle humor ("The Prophet") relieve the intensity of his more somber visions and reveal a mind still in possession of itself and capable of a surprising variety and range of response. "Pillbox," which briefly recounts an ironic episode of death in the trenches, is done in Sassoon's forceful, colloquial manner, whereas "E. W. T.: on the death of his Betty" is a gentle, perfectly formed elegy that manages to capture the grief of a personal loss amidst the larger, enveloping tragedy of war:

And she is gone, whom, dream or truth,
You lived for in this wreck of youth,
   And on your brow sits age,
   Who's quickly won his siege.

My friend, you will not wish a word
Of striven help in this worst gird
   Of fortune as she gets
   From us our race's debts.

I see you with this subtlest blow
Like a stunned man softly go;
   Then you, love-baffled boy,
   Smile with a mournful joy.

Thereat I read, you plainly know
The time draws near when the fierce foe
   Shall your poor body tear
   And mix with mud and air.

Your smile is borne in that foredoom,
Beaten, you see your victory bloom,
   And fortune cheats her end,
   And death draws nigh, a friend.

In the first sonnet of 1914 Rupert Brooke had written that in battle "the worst friend and enemy is but Death"; a world of bitter experience, however, lies between Brooke's romantic visualization and Blunden's use of the same image as a measure of a soldier's quiet despair. To have so gracefully defined that despair, amid the gross shocks and hazards of war, is an achievement that demonstrates Blunden's balanced sensibility and his undiminished capacity to discern and respond to poetic material not directly related to the physical details of battle.

Blunden is the most lighthearted of the World War I poets; yet the strain of the war seems to have affected his consciousness nearly as much as it affected Sassoon's. Several postwar poems, elegiac in mood, testify to a sense of artistic debility and evince a haunted state of mind. In "1916 seen from 1921," for instance, Blunden portrays himself as troubled by vivid memories and the "lost intensities" of emotions he cannot forget:

> Tired with dull grief, grown old before my day,
> I sit in solitude and only hear
> Long silent laughters, murmurings of dismay,
> The lost intensities of hope and fear;
> In those old marshes yet the rifles lie,
> On the thin breastwork flutter the grey rags,
> The very books I read are there—and I
> Dead as the men I loved, wait while life drags
>
> Its wounded length from those sad streets of war
> Into green places here, that were my own;
> But now what once was mine is mine no more,
> I seek such neighbours here and I find none.

A number of other poems, like "La Quinque Rue," "The Ancre at Hamel: Afterwards," and "Another Journey from Bethune to Cuinchy," were inspired by visits to old battlefields and take their themes from various moods of troubled reminiscence. A moving elegy, "Their Very Memory"—the title is a phrase from Vaughan's "Departed Friends"—is one of the war's best tributes to the peculiar intimacy of soldierly friendship:

> Hear, O hear,
> They were as the welling waters,
> Sound, swift, clear,
> They were all the running waters'
> Music down the greenest valley.
>
> Might words tell
> What an echo sung within me?
> What proud bell

Clangs a note of what within me
  Pealed to be with those enlisted?

When they smiled,
Earth's inferno changed and melted
  Greenwood mild;
Every village where they halted
  Shone with them through square and alley.

Now my mind
Faint and few records their showings,
  Brave, strong, kind—
I'd unlock you all their doings
  But the keys are lost and twisted.

This still grows,
Through my land or dull or dazzling
  Their spring flows;
But to think of them's a fountain,
  Tears of joy and music's rally.

Despite the intricate stanzaic and metrical pattern, the poem depends upon words, images, and visualizations that are, in the literary sense of the term, conventional. The opening image, for instance, recalls the image employed by Rupert Brooke in the sestet of his Sonnet IV, "The Dead":

There are waters blown by changing winds
  to laughter
And lit by the rich skies, all day.

Brooke's elaborate metaphor seems even more facile, more over-wrought, when compared to the simplicity of Blunden's simile and the obvious sincerity with which it is developed. It is interesting, however, that Blunden chose the same figure to represent the vitality and spontaneity of young manhood in time of war. Except for his use of dialectal words (a practice probably inspired by John Clare's example), he attempts few visual or verbal innovations. His method, for the most part, is quiet and unpretentious; he does not venture outside the range of the established poetic response, as did Wilfred Owen. Although he sometimes employs a conventional visualization as a means of suggesting significant and occasionally ironic contrasts (as in "Trench Raid near Hooge"), he is a traditionalist, deliberately working within the norms and conventions of eighteenth-century pastoral verse.

The calm sense of an uninterrupted poetic vocation is perhaps Blunden's chief asset; he is a pastoral poet who has become, through harsh necessity, a soldier—not consciously a soldier-poet but a soldier who has the eyes and soul of a poet:

> War might make his worst grimace,
> And still my mind in armour good
> Turned aside in every place
> And saw bright day through the black wood:
> There the lyddite vapoured foul,
> But there I got myself a rose;
> By the shrapnelled lock I'd prowl
> To see below the proud pike doze.
>
> ("War Autobiography")

The more obvious and evanescent emotional forces of the war—romantic ardor, patriotism, and the anger of disillusion—affected neither his attitude nor his poetic technique; from these external influences, as well as from the stronger and more distracting effects of daily life in the trenches, Blunden was indeed protected by an "armour good": his fundamental dedication as a nature poet and the balanced sensibility which such a dedication encouraged. Within the range of the brief lyric form he developed a response that captured the larger disharmonies behind the crude and confusing (and often meaningless) data of warfare. To his awareness of the pity of suffering and death he occasionally brings a perception of the tragic necessity of such evils; the brevity and the essentially personal nature of the lyric response, however, prevent any extended realization of such perceptions. When Blunden attempts, through narrative means, to extend and objectify his sense of the war's reality, he is betrayed by the very qualities which make his lyrical poetry so effective. The intensity and truth of lyrical presentation cannot substitute for the order, progression, and completion of a narrative action; the mixture of lyric and narrative modes, especially under the pressure of heightened action and emotion common to warfare, results in an artistic hybrid that conveys little more than the desperate confusion of the events which inspired it. Blunden achieves his best poetry, therefore, within the "undertones" of the lyric range; and if we grant the limitations of the lyric with respect to the larger tragic vistas which every great conflict must suggest, his work stands as a remarkably sensitive record of personal experience, more sensitive and wider in scope than the productions of other war poets whose reputations have exceeded his own.

CHAPTER V · POETRY AND PITY: WILFRED OWEN

ALTHOUGH Blunden was extremely sensitive to the violence and ugliness of war, he seldom permits these evils to threaten his vision or disturb his poetic reserve. In some ways he fulfills Sassoon's conception of the "independent contemplator." His sense of suffering, though at times acute, does not permanently transform his sensibility or alter his response; only in a general way does his work follow the pattern of development we have discerned in the verse of other World War I poets. He seems to have deliberately restricted himself to a range of discord—the "undertones" of war—which he felt capable of controlling and interpreting. Although his verse is free from the turbulence of anger and the tensions of irony and satire, it fails to provide an encompassing vision in which the poet, as a participant, attempts to deal not so much with the discords themselves as with their deeper spiritual implications and effects.

Wilfred Owen, on the other hand, was far from being an "independent contemplator." He responded to the war in such a way that his whole outlook was profoundly affected; his sensibility, his perceptions, his attitudes, and his poetic technique all underwent a remarkable change. In him the roles of observer, participant, and poet are actively mingled. His poetry is conditioned by an inescapable awareness of himself as a participant and a spokesman; he felt it to be the duty of the "true poet" to disclose the truth of war—a truth compounded of ugliness and suffering, of brutality and horror, of ignominy and death. Although he was at first influenced by Sassoon's disillusioned realism, he quickly advanced beyond the negativism of anger and accusation. His poetry became an extraordinarily sensitive medium of the compassionate attitude—the only attitude, he felt, through which the tragedy of the war could be rightly revealed and interpreted. Unlike Blunden, he threw all of his resources into the struggle to express the deeper significance of the war. That struggle, if it did not bring him to full maturity as a poet, at least forced him to reappraise accepted poetic values and to alter—with compelling effect—the basic terms of his appeal.

In *Siegfried's Journey* Sassoon records his first meeting with the young poet whose later reputation was to equal and perhaps surpass his own:

"One morning at the beginning of August, when I had been at Craiglockhart War Hospital about a fortnight, there was a gentle knock on the door of my room and a young officer entered. Short, dark-haired, and shyly hesitant, he stood for a moment before coming across to the window. . . . A favourable first impression was made by the fact that he had under his arm several copies of *The Old Huntsman*. He had come, he said, hoping that I would be so gracious as to inscribe them for himself and some of his friends. He spoke with a slight stammer, which was no unusual thing in that neurosis-pervaded hospital. . . . He had a charming honest smile, and his manners—he stood at my elbow rather as though conferring with a superior officer—were modest and ingratiating. He gave me the names of his friends first. When it came to his own I found myself writing one that has since gained a notable place on the roll of English poets—Wilfred Owen."[1]

The ensuing period of friendship, though brief, provided just the touch of personal recognition and guidance that Owen apparently needed. In Sassoon—who already had some fame as the author of *The Old Huntsman*—Owen found a brother soldier-poet whose dark views seemed to give fuller sanction to his own feelings about the meaning of the conflict and his efforts to capture something of that meaning in verse. ". . . you

[1] *Siegfried's Journey*, pp. 86-87.

have *fixed* my Life—however short," wrote Owen to Sassoon in November 1917, after he had departed from Craiglockhart. "You did not light me: I was always a mad comet; but you have fixed me. I spun round you a satellite for a month, but I shall swing out soon, a dark star in the orbit where you will blaze."[2] Here is expressed a confidence, a certainty of poetic power and independence, that was not visible in the demeanor of the young autograph-seeker four months before. Henceforth he was to voice in his own way the tragic and compassionate intuitions that he had, until his meeting with Sassoon, only tentatively defined. A measure of his rapid poetic growth is suggested by Sassoon's modest admission that, despite this deep friendship, it was not until he came to edit Owen's verse in 1920 that he clearly understood "the essentially compassionate significance" of the younger poet's message. Owen's youth, his phenomenal poetic development, his proud but haunted sense of achievement, his tragically premature death—all these inevitably bring to mind the career of Keats, whose poetry Owen loved and with whom he seemed to be conscious of a personal as well as an artistic affinity.

In the absence of any full-length biography, the details of Owen's life are necessarily meager.[3] He was born in Oswestry, Shropshire, on March 18, 1893. His family background was not distinguished in any way. A deeply religious atmosphere apparently prevailed in the Owen home; the poet's mother and father always took an active part in the various Evangelical Church of England congregations to which they belonged, and

[2] From a letter quoted by Edmund Blunden in his prefatory Memoir to *The Poems of Wilfred Owen* (London, 1931). Unless otherwise indicated, the source of all further quotations from Owen's letters is Blunden's Memoir and the appended Notes.

[3] Harold Owen, the poet's brother, has completed the first volume of a projected trilogy, *Journey from Obscurity: Wilfred Owen 1893-1918* (London, 1963). Subtitled *Memoirs of the Owen Family*, this book is wider in scope than a biography. The first volume, *Childhood*, gives an account of the Owen family from the 1890's to 1911.

Owen's wartime poems and letters are those of a young man whose shocked imagination almost invariably sought Biblical parallels and allusions. The boy was educated at Birkenhead Institute, Liverpool, where the family had settled; but even Blunden's information about this phase of Owen's career is admittedly scant. By the age of fourteen Owen had developed a love of poetry and something of a studious bent; during two holiday trips to Brittany, between 1907-1909, he acquired an interest in the French language and an affection for the French people. At the age of sixteen or seventeen he began to write verse, with Keats as his prime model. In the early specimens that Blunden prints, we see the sensuousness of a youthful poet who is exploring the wealth of the romantic tradition and developing a style that might win the approval of his Georgian contemporaries. In 1912 Owen was living with the vicar of the small Oxfordshire village of Dunsden, where he taught Sunday school and attended classes at University College, Reading. In 1913, however, a serious illness forced him to seek a milder climate; he journeyed to Bordeaux, where he accepted a two-year engagement as a tutor in a French home. While in Bordeaux he met and enjoyed a close friendship with Laurent Tailhade, the symbolist poet and pacifist. Tailhade's pacifist tracts—*Lettre aux Conscrits* (1903) and *Pour la Paix* (1908)—must have been read and remembered by Owen, whose later ideas about war follow the French poet's too closely to be a coincidence.[4]

After the outbreak of the war Owen remained in France to fulfill the terms of his tutorial contract, returning to England in the summer of 1915. He joined the Artists' Rifles and spent the next sixteen months in infantry and officers' training, for it was not until early January 1917 that he was assigned to the Second Battalion of the Manchester Regiment, then on the Somme front. Pride and exuberance are expressed in a letter

[4] See D. S. R. Welland, *Wilfred Owen: A Critical Study* (London, 1960), pp. 89-92.

written home just before he left for the front: "There is a fine heroic feeling about being in France, and I am in perfect spirits. A tinge of excitement is about me, but excitement is always necessary to my happiness." His introduction to the ways of trench warfare was swift; in less than three weeks his mood had undergone a drastic change. On January 19 he wrote home as follows: "They want to call No Man's Land 'England' because we keep supremacy there. It is like the eternal place of gnashing of teeth; the Slough of Despond could be contained in one of its crater-holes; the fires of Sodom and Gomorrah could not light a candle to it—to find the way to Babylon the Fallen. It is pockmarked like a body of foulest disease, and its odour is the breath of cancer. . . . No Man's Land under snow is like the face of the moon, chaotic, crater-ridden, uninhabitable, awful, the abode of madness. . . . The people of England needn't hope. They must agitate. But they are not yet agitated even. Let them imagine 50 strong men trembling as with ague for 50 hours!"

During February Owen took a month's transport course at Amiens, returning to his battalion on March 1. Two weeks later he suffered a slight concussion as the result of a fall into a cellar, but he was able to return to the trenches after a few days of rest. The winter of 1916-1917 was especially severe; even April was a month of cold and snow, complicating the dangers of patrols, attacks, and intense shelling. In early May, after this ordeal, Owen was again in a hospital, suffering from headaches, fever, and a state of nerves—a condition diagnosed by his doctors as neurasthenia. On June 6 he was sent back to a general hospital, en route to England. In one of the letters written from this hospital he first defines the general attitude against war which was to inspire his later poetry: "Already I have comprehended a light which never will filter into the dogma of any national church: namely, that one of Christ's essential commands was: Passivity at any price! Suffer dishonour and disgrace, but never resort to arms. Be bullied, be outraged, be killed; but do not kill. It may be a chimerical and an ignominious principle, but there it is. It can only be ignored; and I think pulpit professionals are ignoring it very skilfully and successfully indeed. . . . And am I not myself a conscientious objector with a very seared conscience? . . . Christ is literally in 'no man's land.' There men often hear His voice: Greater love hath no man than this, that a man lay down his life for a friend. Is it spoken in English only and French? I do not believe so. Thus you see how pure Christianity will not fit in with pure patriotism." After a brief stay at the Welsh Hospital, Netley, Hampshire, Owen was sent on to the Craiglockhart War Hospital, where he arrived during the latter part of June. In early August, his open defiance of military authority having come to naught, Sassoon arrived; the meeting between the two poets occurred at about the middle of August.

Owen remained at Craiglockhart only four months, but these months constituted a crucial period in his poetic life. His outward activities, on the advice of his doctor, were many: he edited the fortnightly hospital magazine, *The Hydra*; he belonged to the debate club; he gave lectures at Tynecastle School; he was engaged in historical research at the Advocates' Library; he took lessons in German from Frank Nicholson, librarian of Edinburgh University; and he was an active member of the Field Club, to which he read at least one paper. These pleasantly varied undertakings were products of a leisure that also fostered activity on a different level. The meeting with Sassoon, the exchange of views about the war, the discussion of poetry, the older poet's advice and encouragement—all contributed to a strengthening of the poetic impulse along the lines previously indicated in his letters from France. With creditable candor, Sassoon has defined the nature and limits of his influence on Owen during the Craiglockhart period:

"It has been loosely assumed and stated that Wilfred

modelled his war poetry on mine. My only claimable influence was that I stimulated him towards writing with compassionate and challenging realism. His printed letters are evidence that the impulse was already strong in him before he had met me. . . . Up to a point my admonitions were helpful. My encouragement was opportune, and can claim to have given him a lively incentive during his rapid advance to self-revelation. Meanwhile I seem to hear him laughingly implore me to relax these expository generalizations and recover some of the luminous animation of our intimacy. How about my indirect influence on him? he inquires in his calm velvety voice. Have I forgotten our eager discussion of contemporary poets and the technical dodges which we were ourselves devising? Have I forgotten the simplifying suggestions which emanated from my unsophisticated poetic method? (For my technique was almost elementary compared with his innovating experiments.) Wasn't it after he got to know me that he first began to risk using the colloquialisms which were at that time so frequent in my verses? And didn't I lend him Barbusse's *Le Feu*, which set him alight as no other war book had done? It was indeed one of those situations where imperceptible effects are obtained by people mingling their minds at a favourable moment. Turning the pages of Wilfred's *Poems*, I am glad to think that there may have been occasions when some freely improvised remark of mine sent him away with a fruitful idea. And my humanized reportings of front-line episodes may have contributed something to his controlled vision of what he had seen for himself."[5]

Sassoon's criticism seems to have been directed mainly at the "over-luscious" writing which characterizes Owen's early verse. "There was an almost embarrassing sweetness in the sentiment of some of his work, though it showed skill in rich and melodious combinations of words."[6] This judgment, however, could have

[5] *Siegfried's Journey*, pp. 89-90.
[6] *Ibid.*, p. 88.

been applied to much of the early verse of the soldier-poets whose youthful sympathies were in accord with the spirit that produced the fragile music of the Georgians. Owen's weaknesses were common enough at a time when the debilitated romantic tradition had turned to prettiness and favor, disguising an inner lack for which no finely tuned sensibility could compensate. However, the Owen manuscripts give evidence of the poet's painstaking efforts to exclude romantic grandiloquence and sentiment from his work.[7] Unlike Charles Sorley, Owen did not possess an active critical intelligence; and it is in the stimulation of Owen's capacity for self-criticism that Sassoon probably performed his most valuable service.

In early November Owen left Craiglockhart and was assigned to light duty at a Scarborough military hotel. On the night of December 31, writing thoughtfully to his mother, he professed a calm confidence in his maturing artistic powers: "I go out of this year a poet, my dear mother, as which I did not enter it. I am held peer by the Georgians; I am a poet's poet. I am started. The tugs have left me; I feel the great swelling of the open sea taking my galleon." Owen's apparently ingenuous remark about being "held peer by the Georgians" may have been merely a way of indicating to his mother a sense of pride in Sassoon's friendship and assistance. His concluding figure, like the "dark star" metaphor in his letter to Sassoon, surely suggests a belief that his individual poetic destiny was to be achieved on terms far different from the communal Georgian response.

As a soldier, however, Owen was caught up in the slow but fateful process that eventually was to take him back to France. During the spring and early summer of 1918 he was an instructor in a training camp. A letter written to Osbert Sitwell during

[7] See D. S. R. Welland, "Wilfred Owen's Manuscripts," *TLS*, June 15, 1956, p. 368, and June 22, 1956, p. 384. The Owen manuscripts are now in the British Museum.

this period reveals his attitude toward the soldiers he was help-
ing to prepare for the front; his mixture of military and sacrificial
imagery is not whimsical but profoundly expressive of a troubled
conscience in his conflicting roles of leader and betrayer:

"For 14 hours yesterday I was at work—teaching Christ to
lift his cross by numbers, and how to adjust his crown; and not
to imagine he thirst till after the last halt; I attended his Supper
to see that there were no complaints; and inspected his feet that
they should be worthy of the nails. I see to it that he is dumb
and stands at attention before his accusers. With a piece of
silver I buy him every day, and with maps I make him familiar
with the topography of Golgotha."[8]

In early August, having been judged fit for the trenches, he
wrote: "I am glad. That is I am much gladder to be going out
again than afraid. I shall be better able to cry my outcry, playing
my part." On August 31 he embarked for France and within a
short time had rejoined his old battalion at Corbie, on the
River Ancre.

Owen's famous Preface to his projected volume of war verse
is sometimes referred to as a product of his last weeks in France.
It is quite probable, however, that the poet formulated the
Preface and attempted to arrange the accompanying Table of
Contents (which Blunden reproduces, with its "perplexities")
before he left England. Three important poems known to have
been completed in September are not included in the Table of
Contents, and the summing-up such a statement as the Preface
would require could have been more effectively undertaken in
England than in the trenches. The manuscript of the Preface
is in some places almost indecipherably revised; hence Blunden's
version, below, differs slightly from Sassoon's.

This book is not about heroes. English Poetry is not yet fit
to speak of them.

[8] Osbert Sitwell, *Noble Essences* (Boston, 1950), p. 120.

Nor is it about deeds, or lands, nor anything about glory, honour, might, majesty, dominion, or power, except War.

Above all I am not concerned with Poetry.

My subject is War, and the pity of War.

The Poetry is in the pity.

Yet these elegies are to this generation in no sense consolatory. They may be to the next. All a poet can do to-day is warn. That is why the true Poets must be truthful.

(If I thought the letter of this book would last, I might have used proper names; but if the spirit of it survives—survives Prussia—my ambition and those names will have achieved themselves fresher fields than Flanders . . .).

Whatever else may be deduced from still other arrangements of these well-known words, it is clear that Owen is distinguishing between "Poetry" (a specific, pejorative term) and the truth of the compassionate vision. If "English Poetry" (a generic term) is to be worthy of heroes, the "true Poets" must abandon their preoccupation with "Poetry," which by implication is either false or irrelevant to the present historical situation. Thus Owen is concerned not only with war poetry (somehow we feel that the term would not have meant much to him) but with poetry as a whole; he sensed a radical shifting of the historical and social values which determine the artist's response to his milieu. The nineteenth-century poetic tradition had run its course with respect to the sources of its original vitality; and the contemporary Georgian movement—isolated from human concerns and incapable, therefore, of dealing with the crisis—symbolized not a beginning, as Edward Marsh and others thought, but the end of an era. At Craiglockhart Owen read a biography of Tennyson and contrasted that poet's "unhappiness"—amidst "fame, wealth, and domestic serenity"—with the effects of his own bitter experiences. "Tennyson, it seems, was always a great child," he concluded. "So should I have been, but for Beaumont Hamel." This distinction between innocence and experience has artistic as well as personal or psychological implications; in conjunction with the Preface, it illustrates the difference that Owen was beginning to perceive between "Poetry" as the thoughtless pursuit of beauty and poetry as the product of the "true Poets" who, in being faithful to their actual experience of life, painfully renew and rejustify the terms of their art. Owen's year of convalescence in England and his contact with Sassoon certainly encouraged much reflection on these matters; the prospect of returning to France must have prompted the attempt to outline his ideas and to arrange his poems so that they would more effectively depict the evil violence to which he would again be exposed.

The war was in its final stages when Owen once more heard the sound of the guns; his regiment sustained heavy casualties in the fighting of late September and early October. After one difficult and costly attack there were only two officers left in Owen's company, and he became acting company commander. It was during this attack that he won the Military Cross for "having taken a few machine guns." His nerves, he wrote, remained in "perfect order," though he confessed to a paralysis of his emotions and perceptions: "My senses are charred." In one of his last letters he tells his mother, "I came out in order to help these boys—directly by leading them as well as an officer can, indirectly by watching their sufferings that I may speak of them as well as a pleader can." On the morning of November 4, one week before the Armistice, he was attempting to maneuver his company over the Sambre Canal near the village of Ors. Heavy machine gun and artillery fire blocked the crossing, and Owen felt it necessary to help with the construction of a makeshift bridge. It was while engaged in this task that he was struck and killed.

Any close criticism of Owen's work must be conditioned by the fact that only four of his poems were published during his lifetime;[9] his habit of continuous revision has therefore created a number of textual problems not entirely laid to rest by the Blunden edition. Again, less than half of the sixty-odd poems printed by Blunden can be dated with respect to the month of composition. Fortunately, however, most of the essential poems have dates or can be inferentially dated with some degree of certitude. With regard to these, a rough division, based on Owen's contact with Sassoon, is helpful. Thus the verse written or apparently written before August 1917 can be examined apart from the effects of Sassoon's personal influence. To Owen's great creative period—extending from August 1917 to September 1918—belongs the verse that makes up the second and larger part of our division; these poems can be examined with respect to the broader themes and attitudes developed during that period.

In August 1914 Owen was in Bordeaux and probably out of touch with the surge of patriotic emotion that swept over England when war was declared. At any rate, if he greeted the outbreak of hostilities with sentiments similar to those voiced by his contemporaries, he did not capture or preserve those sentiments in verse. His temperament and poetic practice were such that he might easily have responded in the fashion of Rupert Brooke; but in 1914 he possessed neither Brooke's confidence as a Georgian spokesman nor Sorley's individualized and ironically evaluative mental powers. Thus his first attempt to deal with the war, a sonnet entitled "The Seed" (probably written in August 1914), is somewhat remote and rhetorical, taking its theme from history rather than from any sense of direct personal involvement:

> War broke. And now the winter of the world
> With perishing great darkness closes in.

[9] "Songs of Songs," *The Hydra*, September 1917; "Miners," *The Nation*, January 16, 1918; "Futility" and "Hospital Barge at Cérisy," *The Nation*, June 15, 1918.

The cyclone of the pressure on Berlin
Is over all the width of Europe whirled,
Rending the sails of progress. Rent or furled
Are all art's ensigns. Verse moans. Now begin
Famines of thought and feeling. Love's wine's thin.
The grain of earth's great autumn rots, down-hurled.

Although Owen goes on to contrast the catastrophic abruptness of this "exigent winter" with the "slow grand age" of Greece and Rome, the generalized nature of the treatment as well as the absence of any compelling emotion suggest that he had not yet considered the war in terms of its full human impact. The Hardyesque imagery of the first four lines may reflect a recent reading of *The Dynasts*—a work which a thoughtful young poet would be most likely to remember during the crisis of late 1914.

Another early poem, "Ballad of Purchase Moneys," was written before Owen joined the Artists' Rifles. Here he adopts both his theme and his manner from Housman, whose depictions of submissive or sacrificial heroism appear intermittently in *A Shropshire Lad.*[10]

> The Sun is sweet on rose and wheat
>   And on the eyes of children;
> Quiet the street for old men's feet
>   And gardens for the children.
>
> The soil is safe, for widow and waif,
>   And for the soul of England,
> Because their bodies men vouchsafe
>   To save the soul of England.
>
> Fair days are yet left for the old,
>   And children's cheeks are ruddy,

[10] See Lyrics I, III, XXII, XXXIV, XXXV, and LVI. Owen, of course, was originally a "Shropshire lad."

> Because the good lads' limbs lie cold
> And their brave cheeks are bloody.

Owen was to enlarge this theme to more significant proportions in his mature poems; here, however, he does not go beyond Housman's melodiously sardonic manner in revealing what is merely an unpleasant paradox. The first poem in which Owen expresses a deeply felt reaction to the war is the sonnet entitled "Happiness," which was not written until January 1917, the month of his arrival in France. Here the poet contrasts the innocent happiness of boyhood with the deeper joys and sorrows of experience—in this case the morally dubious experience of war. As he wrote from Craiglockhart on August 8, 1917, "Not before January 1917 did I write the *only* lines of mine that carry the stamp of maturity—these:

> But the old happiness is unreturning,
> Boys have no grief as grievous as youth's yearning;
> Boys have no sadness sadder than our hope."

But maturity is a relative thing: here—a few days before his meeting with Sassoon—Owen significantly cites lines dealing with the loss of youthful innocence rather than earlier lines in the same poem that refer to the guilt of "sick and sorrowful wrongs"—a much more important theme and one to which he obviously had not yet devoted his full imaginative powers.

"Exposure," Owen's first important war poem, seems to be a particularization of the transforming experiences only hinted at in "Happiness." "Exposure" was written in February 1917, but according to Sassoon it was extensively revised after Owen had been "set alight" by Barbusse's *Le Feu* at Craiglockhart.[11] The first few stanzas describe the winter landscape of No Man's Land and recall the vivid (but somewhat more consciously rhetorical) depiction of the scene in the poet's letter of January

[11] See Welland, "Wilfred Owen's Manuscripts" and *Wilfred Owen*, p. 114.

19. The impression of agonized minds and bodies, of intolerable cold and desolation, also recalls Blunden's "The Zonnebeke Road," which likewise portrays the terrible effects of winter trench warfare.

Our brains ache, in the merciless iced east winds
    that knive us . . .
Wearied we keep awake because the night is silent . . .
Low, drooping flares confuse our memory of the
    salient . . .
Worried by silence, sentries whisper, curious, nervous,
        But nothing happens.

Watching, we hear the mad gusts tugging on the wire,
Like twitching agonies of men among its brambles.
Northward, incessantly, the flickering gunnery rumbles,
Far off, like a dull rumour of some other war.
        What are we doing here?

J. Loiseau has pointed out how the opening lines echo, with a directly opposite effect, Keats's "Ode to a Nightingale":[12] "My heart aches, and a drowsy numbness pains/ My sense . . ." The peculiar blankness of the refrain ("But nothing happens") also suggests a contrast between the range of positive experience that Keats explores (with its richly varied possibilities and alternatives) and the essentially negative experience of war, which draws the senses taut with misery and apprehension. The feeling of tension, monotony, and defeated expectation is reinforced by the device of pararhyme, which Owen here uses for the first time in a war poem. He had experimented with the effects of this device in a prewar poem entitled "From My Diary, July 1914":

Leaves
    Murmuring by myriads in the shimmering trees.

[12] "A Reading of Wilfred Owen's Poems," *ES*, XXI (1939), 97-108.

Lives
   Wakening with wonder in the Pyrenees.
Birds
   Cheerily chirping in the early day.
Bards
   Singing of summer scything thro' the hay.
Bees
   Shaking the heavy dews from bloom and frond.
Boys
   Bursting the surface of the ebony pond.
Flashes
   Of swimmers carving thro' the sparkling cold.
Fleshes
   Gleaming with wetness to the morning gold.

The effect here is one of pleasingly modulated variety, which reflects the variety of the sensuous experiences involved without disturbing the tonal unity of the poem; the words themselves are as euphonious as those which provide the conventional end-rhyme. The pararhymes of "Exposure," however, deliberately create painful discords. The words themselves are without poetic associations and therefore, unlike the words in "From My Diary," have a negative or neutral connotative value; the half-rhymed combinations vex the hearing with ugly discords which remain unresolved. Blunden has described the effects of Owen's pararhyme as those of "remoteness, darkness, emptiness, shock, echo, the last word."[13] As the contrast between "From My Diary" and "Exposure" indicates, these effects are gained through a reversal of conventional tonal and connotative values; instead of a pattern of modulated verbal harmonies, we have an atonal texture devoid of imaginative or auditory resonance.[14] In his earlier war verse Owen had not seriously departed from

[13] *Poems*, p. 29.
[14] For a fuller discussion, see Welland, "Half-Rhyme in Wilfred Owen: Its Derivation and Use," *RES*, 1 (n.s.), 3 (July 1950), 226-41.

his prewar poetic practice. In "Exposure," however, he seeks a new medium which would embody, in form as well as in theme, the terrible experiences he was undergoing. His dissonant echoes of Keats and use of discordant, non-connotative half-rhymes indicate—in a poet so sensitive to the musical and imaginative qualities of words—an abrupt and radical transformation of technique. This transformation foreshadows, in Owen's later verse, a more subtle use of the forms and themes of romantic poetry to suggest meanings far different from those they ordinarily convey.

The first four stanzas of "Exposure" depict the numbing wretchedness of a winter night in the trenches. In the fifth stanza, however, the descriptive focus shifts. Overwhelmed by tedium and misery, the soldiers fall into a trancelike state (perhaps another reminiscence of Keats's "Ode"); they dream first of spring, then of the warmth and peace of home. These blessings, the poet then reflects, can be re-won only through a penitential sacrifice which his own generation seems fated to offer. Spring (the blessings of life) can come only if errant man learns to love God anew:

> Slowly our ghosts drag home: glimpsing the sunk
>   fires, glozed
> With crusted dark-red jewels; crickets jingle there;
> For hours the innocent mice rejoice: the house
>   is theirs;
> Shutters and doors, all closed: on us the doors
>   are closed,—
>   We turn back to our dying.
>
> Since we believe not otherwise can kind fires burn;
> Nor ever suns smile true on child, or field, or fruit.
> For God's invincible spring our love is made afraid;
> Therefore, not loath, we lie out here; therefore
>   were born,
>   For love of God seems dying.

Here the shift in descriptive focus brings a corresponding shift in verbal technique; both words and images are rich in musical and connotative values appropriate to the scenes of peaceful harmony remembered by the poet. The melodious consonance of "the sunk fires, glozed/ With crusted dark-red jewels" contrasts with the sharp dissonance of its opposite conception, "the merciless iced east winds that knive us." The clashing half-rhymes of the first two stanzas (knive us/ nervous, brambles/ rumbles) are resolved into rhyme (glozed/ closed) or into a mild variation (burn/ born).

The final stanza of "Exposure" brings the physical ordeal into relation with the penitential concept; thus the soldiers' suffering—apparently futile and meaningless on a political level—is endowed with moral significance:

> To-night, His frost will fasten on this mud and us,
> Shrivelling many hands, puckering foreheads crisp.
> The burying-party, picks and shovels in their
>   shaking grasp,
> Pause over half-known faces. All their eyes are ice,
>   But nothing happens.

The empty refrain returns us to the waiting, the watching, and the dying: "not otherwise can kind fires burn." There is also a suggestion, in the grammatical relationships of the last sentence, that the enormity of the sacrifice can bring no perceptible consequence, no relief, no sign: "nothing happens." The poem ends as it began. It is, as Owen was later to say of his poetry in general, "in no sense consolatory."

The theme of "Exposure" is the same as that of "Ballad of Purchase Moneys"; both poems are developed in terms of a parodox. "Exposure," however, is far above the level of a merely sardonic notation. The force of personal experience and awakened perception is visible in both form and content. Owen is no longer the observer, as he is in "The Seed"; he is a participant who seeks some meaning for his own and others' suffering. He finds that meaning, apparently, in the orthodox Christian concept of penance and expiation; but there is a tentative note in the poem—"For God's invincible spring our love is made afraid"—which anticipates the uneasy tensions and doubts that haunt some of his later poems. "Exposure," in the light of these later poems, seems to be an effort to reconcile the disparity between the unredeemed evil of war and the positives inherent in Christian doctrine.

At least two minor poems—"To My Friend" (March 1917) and "The Fates" (June 1917)—were written between the first draft of "Exposure" and Owen's arrival at Craiglockhart; but these, with their rhetorical flourishes and references to Time, Fame, Chance, and Beauty, are as remote from the author's actual experiences as "The Seed." Other poems may have been conceived and even drafted before August 1917, but the number and quality of the poems produced during and after that month make it evident that Owen had finally found his true inspiration, as well as an underlying stimulation in the practical advice and encouragement of Sassoon. The poems written during and after August 1917, accordingly, may be divided into two groups: one group shows obvious affinities with the style and temper of Sassoon's verse; the other group is characterized by a more profound and tragic attitude—the attitude Owen first defined in "Exposure."

Sassoon's *The Old Huntsman* was, of course, well known to Owen; we are certain, furthermore, that he saw some of the *Counter-Attack* poems that Sassoon was writing in the fall of 1917, since the older poet asserts that during the composition of those poems "Wilfred's praises heartened and helped me."[15] Owen therefore had the advantage of seeing poems that were inspired by the same desperate conditions (between January and April 1917) which were providing his own materials and

[15] *Siegfried's Journey*, pp. 95-96.

inspirations. The angry poems of *Counter-Attack* were not to have their full public impact until July 1918; we may, however, imagine their personal impact on Owen, who was seeking, during the late summer and fall of 1917, some appropriate mode for the interpretation of his own experiences in the trenches.

Two poems written in August demonstrate that Owen was experimenting with the attitudes and techniques that Sassoon had employed so successfully. The negative, cynical attitude of "Dulce et Decorum Est," however, together with its emphasis on shockingly realistic details, represents an element in Owen's verse that is not really natural to it. He is sincere, of course, but neither cynicism nor purposive realism is a major factor in his true poetic vision. In "Dulce et Decorum Est" the reader is merely invited to share the poet's experience in watching the agonies of a gassed and dying soldier:

> If in some smothering dreams, you too could pace
> Behind the wagon that we flung him in,
> And watch the white eyes writhing in his face,
> His hanging face, like a devil's sick of sin;
> If you could hear, at every jolt, the blood
> Come gargling from the froth-corrupted lungs,
> Bitter as the cud
> Of vile, incurable sores on innocent tongues,—
> My friend, you would not tell with such high zest
> To children ardent for some desperate glory,
> The old Lie: Dulce et decorum est
> Pro patria mori.

The purpose here is one with the purpose that led Owen to carry photographs of maimed and wounded men in his pocket, ready for display to overzealous patriots. If he had continued to write solely on this communicative or curative level, he would probably be viewed today as a talented imitator of

Sassoon. Perhaps the younger poet, in the capacity (as he later put it) of a "pleader," was only exploring the immediate potentialities of this kind of writing. At any rate, the four pieces he published during his stay in England were not narrowly cynical or realistic poems; two of these, in fact ("Miners" and "Futility"), evince an ability to see far beyond the urgent but limited issues developed by Sassoon.

The other August poem, "The Dead-Beat," depicts a soldier whose mind and will have been broken by the war; suspected of malingering by his fellows, he dies unwounded, unmarked—a victim, apparently, of forces more sinister than shells or bullets. The poem has affinities with Sassoon's "Lamentations" and "Suicide in the Trenches," both of which portray the effects of utter personal demoralization. More importantly, however, we see Owen employing for the first time a blunt colloquial style, a style in obvious contrast to the rich musical and imaginative texture of his more eloquent productions. This colloquial style Owen continued to use in such minor poems as "The Chances" and "Inspection"; it is visible, to a less obvious degree, in more important poems such as "A Terre" and "The Sentry." Put on his guard against romantic luxuriousness by Sassoon, Owen doubtless felt that the colloquial manner afforded an antidote to this type of verbal excess, or at least an appreciable counterweight to his more deliberately poetic efforts. Speaking of his "Spring Offensive," part of which he sent to Sassoon on September 22, 1918, he asked, "Is this worth going on with? I don't want to write anything to which a soldier would say *No Compris!*" Usually, however, the poems employing the colloquial manner turn upon some minor ironic revelation and do not attain any remarkable power or insight.

Much more in Owen's natural poetic vein than "The Dead-Beat" is "Anthem for Doomed Youth," which was probably composed between August and October 1917. The grave elegiac tone of this sonnet differs markedly from the open discords of

"Exposure," yet the carefully modulated music of the poem embodies a deeper and more subtle sense of disharmony:

What passing-bells for these who die as cattle?
 Only the monstrous anger of the guns.
 Only the stuttering rifles' rapid rattle
Can patter out their hasty orisons.
No mockeries for them from prayers or bells,
 Nor any voice of mourning save the choirs,—
The shrill, demented choirs of wailing shells;
 And bugles calling for them from sad shires.

What candles may be held to speed them all?
 Not in the hands of boys, but in their eyes
Shall shine the holy glimmers of good-byes.
 The pallor of girls' brows shall be their pall;
Their flowers the tenderness of silent minds,
And each slow dusk a drawing-down of blinds.

Like Sorley, Owen perceived the terrible discrepancy between the patriotic-religious elegiac attitude and the sacrifices that it sanctioned and commemorated. The magnitude of those sacrifices caused Sorley to reject all elegiac sentiments: "Say only this, 'They are dead.'" Owen, on the other hand, balances the consolatory rituals of Christian burial against the degradation of those "who die as cattle." Bells, orisons, prayers, choirs, candles, pall, and flowers—these formalities constitute a visible and audible commemoration of death; they mitigate grief by interpreting life and death in Christian terms. But what religious formalities can encompass the enormity of life and death in modern warfare? This question implies an indictment of formal religion that follows logically from Owen's understanding of the "greater love." Owen suggests that Christianity, which had betrayed itself by failing to condemn the evils of war, is no longer equal to the universal principles which it invokes; since it had ignored one of "Christ's essential commands," it could hardly be called upon to sanctify the effects of murderous violence. The Christian attitude was not merely irrelevant—this would have been a somewhat different conclusion—but tragically inadequate. Indeed, one of Owen's major themes is the inadequacy of all traditional evaluations within certain vital areas of human experience, and in illustrating this inadequacy he created his finest and most impressive poetry. The finely integrated imagery of "Anthem for Doomed Youth" indicates how far Owen had progressed beyond the slack and superficial art of the Georgians. The poem gains its force through a carefully developed pattern of contrasting images. The externals of Christian ritual are suggested by images rich in religious and imaginative significance; they evoke impressions of dignity, solemnity, circumstance. In the octave, auditory images are paired with opposed images that evoke contrary impressions of anger, haste, impersonality; only the bugles—contrasted to the bells and choirs—seem to be capable of expressing the actuality of human loss. In the sestet, however, the opposed images are merged. Candles, pall, flowers, and closed blinds—symbols of a grief they can no longer adequately represent—suggest analogies that communicate a sorrow far beyond formal representation. The primary theme of the poem is thus developed in terms of contrasted images and associations; beyond the meanings developed within this pattern, however, is the inescapable suggestion that Christianity has lost contact with the very reality it is called upon to interpret.

Although it is undated, "Asleep" has close thematic affinities with "Anthem for Doomed Youth" and probably belongs to the same period. Both poems are elegies, yet they derive their primary effect from conflicting elegiac attitudes rather than from a particularized elegiac emotion. In the second part of "Asleep" Owen depicts a vague but comfortable hereafter which embodies both the truth of the Christian promise and its convention-

alization in religious art and poetry; he then contrasts that hereafter with the poignant physical actuality, the truth that embodies its own compelling but contrary suggestions:

> Whether his deeper sleep lie shaded by the shaking
> Of great wings, and the thoughts that hung the stars,
> High-pillowed on calm pillows of God's making
> Above these clouds, these rains, these sleets of lead,
> And these winds' scimitars;
> —Or whether yet his thin and sodden head
> Confuses more and more with the low mould,
> His hair being one with the grey grass
> And finished fields of autumns that are old . . .

The conflict leaves the poet—cold, weary, and mindful of his
own pain—in a state of suspended indifference; that very indifference, however, clearly favors the naturalistic attitude,
which has the force of an experienced reality behind it:

> Who knows? Who hopes? Who troubles? Let it pass!
> He sleeps. He sleeps less tremulous, less cold,
> Than we who must awake, and waking, say Alas!

Although the poem ends on a note of deep pessimism, Owen
does not completely reject the Christian attitude. It is true
that he invests it with unreality and inadequacy, but the attitude
itself hovers somewhat ambiguously between the externals and
the essentials of Christian faith. Thus, though his unanswered
questions are used to dramatize his own point of view, the poet's
indifference is not poised between two equally valid alternatives.
This difficulty is perhaps due to the unifying image of sleep,
which is applied to both alternatives but which suggests, in the
Christian alternative, a deliberately conventionalized interpretation of life after death. In "Anthem for Doomed Youth" the
contrasts, together with the varied images that represent them,
are equal; they involve external rituals which in turn suggest

deeper levels of meaning. In "Asleep," however, the contrasts are unequal—and therefore less poetically effective—because they are based on disparate evocations.

Another poem certainly conceived during the Craiglockhart period, "Apologia pro Poemate Meo" (dated November 1917), represents an interesting transitional stage in Owen's poetic development. As a statement of personal artistic belief, "Apologia" is related to the Preface and "Strange Meeting"; but in the autumn of 1917 Owen was more preoccupied with the suddenly altered terms of his art than with his function as a poet. As his title suggests, he is defending the experiential basis of perceptions totally different from those that had provided the substance of traditional poetry. Battlefield experience, for example, may be the source of unexpected revelations:

I, too, saw God through mud,—
    The mud that cracked on cheeks when wretches smiled.

Again, the experience of killing may produce strange moral and psychological effects:

Merry it was to laugh there—
    Where death becomes absurd and life absurder.
    For power was on us as we slashed bones bare
    Not to feel sickness or remorse of murder.

Also transformed are the poet's aesthetic sensibilities, which are now keyed to a new range of perception:

I have perceived much beauty
    In the hoarse oaths that kept our courage straight;
    Heard music in the silentness of duty;
    Found peace where shell-storms spouted reddest
        spate.

Utilizing traditional and richly associative imagery, Owen contrasts the fragile fictions of romantic love to the deep camara-

derie of the trenches—again emphasizing the experiential basis
of the stronger and more durable bond:

> I have made fellowships—
>> Untold of happy lovers in old song.
>> For love is not the binding of fair lips
>> With the soft silk of eyes that look and long,
>
> By Joy, whose ribbon slips,—
>> But wound with war's hard wire whose stakes are
>>> strong;
>> Bound with the bandage of the arm that drips;
>> Knit in the webbing of the rifle-thong.

Thus Owen purposefully illustrates a radical shift in poetic
values which is visible not only in these altered perceptions but
also in his efforts to create a new poetic technique. In
"Apologia," however, he is thinking primarily of the uninitiated
reader, whose understanding of these transformations is likely
to be limited:

> Nevertheless, except you share
>> With them in hell the sorrowful dark of hell,
>> Whose world is but the trembling of a flare,
>> And heaven but as the highway for a shell,
>
> You shall not hear their mirth:
>> You shall not come to think them well content
>> By any jest of mine. These men are worth
>> Your tears. You are not worth their merriment.

Edmund Blunden deals with moral and aesthetic disharmonies
in a way that assumes the universal human appreciation of
beauty and goodness; his poetic appeal is based on the reader's
recognition of evil and his sympathetic response to the effects
of violence. In "Apologia," however, Owen dwells upon the
exclusive nature of his experiences as soldier and poet. The new

experiential basis of his poetry really becomes an experiential bias which, though it seems to invite pity, coldly forbids sympathy and understanding. Of course Owen could not observe these limitations without surrendering his motives as a poet. His later appeals, based on compassion and the "greater love," could hardly have had any validity if he had maintained the attitude he expresses in "Apologia." Blunden, whose sensibilities were rather firmly grounded in the pastoral tradition, does not display this experiential bias; his imaginative processes could accommodate the new reality in terms of its departure from the old. Owen deals with the old and the new not in terms of an imaginative accommodation but in terms of abrupt contrast and ironic reversal. At this stage of his development he was gradually disengaging himself from a tradition that could no longer be directly invoked to express what he had seen and felt in the trenches, for its values had faded in the harsh light of a personally experienced reality.

To the Craiglockhart period may also be assigned "À Terre," since another version of this poem, "Wild with All Regrets," is dated December 5, 1917, and is dedicated to Sassoon. In "À Terre," death for the soldier becomes a Shelleyan absorption into nature; the maimed speaker—"blind, and three parts shell" —considers his precarious hold on life and how his condition is mocked by lesser but more durable forms of animal and vegetable existence:

> Dead men may envy living mites in cheese,
> Or good germs even. Microbes have their joys,
> And subdivide, and never come to death.
> Certainly flowers have the easiest time on earth.
> "I shall be one with nature, herb, and stone,"
> Shelley would tell me. Shelley would be stunned:
> The dullest Tommy hugs that fancy now.

"À Terre"—the subtitle is "Being the Philosophy of Many Soldiers"—is one of a half-dozen poems which have been interpreted by some critics as indicating Owen's abandonment of orthodox Christianity. In view of the nature of the war—and especially the unseemly attitude of the churches toward the war—it is not extraordinary to encounter a disillusion with the formal doctrines of Christianity or a rejection of Christianity itself.[16] As both his letters and his later poems indicate, Owen was profoundly sensitive to the implications of "pure Christianity," especially the concept of the "greater love." The religious attitudes expressed in some of his poems, however, are weighted with doubts that are not voiced in his letters to his mother. In two early poems—"The Unreturning" and "To Eros"—there are hints of spiritual disillusionment and a rejection of Christianity; in "Exposure" his quest for a solution to the problem of suffering ends on an ambivalent note; and in "Anthem for Doomed Youth" he implies that death in modern warfare is beyond the scope of Christian ceremony. Although Owen implies that the forms and perhaps the essential spirit of Christianity are unequal to the crisis, his attitude does not become negative in the sense that Christianity is rejected as a source of poetic reference. Instead, he draws a number of subtle ironies out of the failure of the "greater love" ideal, first with respect to its exercise on the human level. In grimmer and less orthodox moments he can see the "greater love" practiced by the soldier but not by an apparently indifferent God. As a poet, Owen extracts a whole range of ironic significance from a situation naturally replete with contrast and paradox; questions of personal orthodoxy must await the sympathetic biographer.

"Miners," which was printed in *The Nation* of January 16,

---

[16] See C. E. Montague, *Disenchantment*, Ch. V, on the role of the churches during the war. See also Robert Graves, *Good-bye to All That*, pp. 230-32.

1918, must have been composed very quickly, for the Halmerend colliery explosion which inspired it occurred on January 12.[17] In this poem we have Owen's most explicit and moving statement of the theme of pity, which is worked out in terms of a highly imaginative analogy. Just as the bones of forgotten miners are figuratively mixed with the coal burning in the poet's comfortable hearth, so the sacrifices of the equally obscure soldiers who die in the trenches insure the comfort and security of future generations:

> I thought of some who worked dark pits
>   Of war, and died
> Digging the rock where Death reputes
>   Peace lies indeed.
>
> Comforted years will sit soft-chaired
>   In rooms of amber;
> The years will stretch their hands, well-cheered
>   By our lives' ember.
>
> The centuries will burn rich loads
>   With which we groaned,
> Whose warmth shall lull their dreaming lids
>   While songs are crooned.
> But they will not dream of us poor lads
>   Lost in the ground.

Owen had employed the same image some ten months before in "Exposure": "We turn back to our dying," he wrote, "Since we believe not otherwise can kind fires burn." In "Miners," however, the aspect of voluntary sacrifice for attainable ends has vanished; now the sacrifice is passive, and the benefits are so remote that those who enjoy them are oblivious of their source.

---

[17] Nearly 150 miners were entombed in this disaster; the fact that most of the victims were young men and boys must have appealed powerfully to Owen's imagination.

A voluntary sacrifice for worthy ends usually arouses admiration as well as a degree of pity; those who willingly sacrifice themselves are heroes, not victims. A passive sacrifice for ends so remote that they cannot be identified as a product of the sacrifice can arouse only pity; those who are sacrificed are victims, not heroes. The poetry of modern warfare may be in the pity, but neither pity nor self-pity in themselves can inspire great poetry. If the poet simply contemplates his own involvement in passive suffering, he is entertaining an attitude not much different from that of Rupert Brooke, who merely dramatized the pathos of his own voluntary sacrifice. Aside from Owen's disillusioned tone and the passive nature of the sacrifice he envisions, there is a real affinity between the attitude of "Miners" and that of Brooke's 1914 sonnets. The subdued pathos of Owen's final stanzas recalls Sonnet III, "The Dead," which elaborates upon the personal aspects of the sacrifice rather than upon its larger temporal aspects. In both poems, however, the plea for recognition is the same. If Owen's poetic temperament could be imagined as a composite, certainly a romantic self-consciousness similar to Brooke's would figure as a minor but never quite eradicable element; Sassoon's force and bluntness would also be clearly visible. Owen's own characteristic qualities would be seen as an element between the two, occasionally blending with one or the other and occasionally manifesting themselves apart from any lesser elements. In "Miners," however, the larger vision of the war that Owen was in the process of developing is unfortunately combined with a self-consciousness that is not compatible with the poetic truth that inspired the poem. Perhaps the fact that it was hastily written and published made it impossible for the poet to exercise any care in excluding that self-consciousness.

In the closing weeks of 1917 Owen twice indicated that he was strongly aware of his artistic maturity and independence. To the period between January and August 1918, therefore, may be assigned a number of undated poems which bear the mark of his full poetic power. A few of these—"Mental Cases," "The Calls," "And I Must Go"—may be dated with some certitude; others may be dated only by inference or conjecture, through kinship in substance and theme with poems of a more firmly established date.

In May 1918 Owen wrote to his mother from Scarborough, "I've been busy this evening with my terrific poem (at present) called 'The Deranged.'" This poem—the title was later changed to "Mental Cases"—was obviously inspired by Owen's stay at Craiglockhart. Sassoon had dealt with the same subject in "Survivors" (dated October 1917), and the two poems afford an interesting contrast in attitude and technique. Sassoon's sarcasm is aimed at those who were too obtuse to understand the terrible mental and spiritual effects of the war on individual soldiers:

> No doubt they'll soon get well; the shock and strain
> Have caused their stammering, disconnected talk.
> Of course they're "longing to go out again,"—
> These boys with old, scared faces, learning to walk.

Owen's treatment, modeled after Dante's rhetorical method, is much more impressive because of the parallel that method suggests:

> Who are these? Why sit they here in twilight?
> Wherefore rock they, purgatorial shadows,
> Drooping tongues from jaws that slob their relish,
> Baring teeth that leer like skulls' teeth wicked? . . .
>
> —These are men whose minds the Dead have ravished.
> Memory fingers in their hair of murders,
> Multitudinous murders they once witnessed. . . .

Sassoon deals with a contemporary public attitude toward the incapacitated, whereas Owen enlarges upon the tortures of the mad as the effect of sin and guilt—an effect that constitutes a broad moral condemnation of those who still approved of the aims and methods of the war.

Three other poems that deal with incapacitated soldiers may indicate a close temporal connection with "Mental Cases." The best of these, "Futility," appeared in *The Nation* of June 15, 1918; another, "Disabled," was sent to Osbert Sitwell in July or early August 1918; the third, "Conscious," cannot be dated, but it has close affinities with "Disabled." "Conscious," which recalls Sassoon's "Stretcher Case," depicts the puzzled gropings of a soldier regaining consciousness in a hospital bed, while "Disabled" presents the reflections of a youthful triple amputee who had volunteered while half-drunk simply "to please his Meg":

> There was an artist silly for his face,
> For it was younger than his youth, last year.
> Now, he is old; his back will never brace;
> He's lost his colour very far from here,
> Poured it down shell-holes till the veins ran dry,
> And half his lifetime lapsed in the hot race,
> And leap of purple spurted from his thigh.

The young soldier's maimed condition effects a permanent sexual incapacity which broadens the implications of the title; the war not only strikes down the individual but also destroys the procreative principle:

> Now he will never feel again how slim
> Girls' waists are, or how warm their subtle hands;
> All of them touch him like some queer disease.

The theme of the poem—the pathetic destruction of youth, beauty, and strength—is an ironic reversal of Housman's theme in "To an Athlete Dying Young," which develops the idea that a premature death is a desirable termination of life's sorrows and disappointments. Although Owen employs the colloquial manner, his phrasing occasionally echoes Housman's poem: "One time he liked a blood-smear down his leg,/ After the matches, carried shoulder-high"; "Some cheered him home, but not as crowds cheer Goal." The background of poignant, irreparable physical loss sharpens Owen's sarcastic jibe at the obtuseness of a visiting clergyman: ". . . a solemn man who brought him fruits/ *Thanked* him; and then inquired about his soul." Housman's athlete, "smart lad," slips away from the uncertainties and discouragements of life; but Owen's soldier is condemned to the horror of an immobilized existence in hospital wards:

> Now, he will spend a few sick years in Institutes,
> And do what things the rules consider wise,
> And take whatever pity they may dole.
> To-night he noticed how the women's eyes
> Passed from him to the strong men that were whole.
> How cold and late it is! Why don't they come
> And put him into bed? Why don't they come?

The anguished voice of the cripple rounds off a picture that contrasts not only with Rupert Brooke's vision of decorous immolation but with the conventional concept of heroic death in action.

"Futility" goes far beyond the attitude of reproach implied in "Mental Cases" and "Disabled." Here, as he views a piece of the human wreckage of war, the poet considers the sun as the source of warmth and life, of vitality and awakened consciousness. In the body of the dying soldier, however, the principle of vitality is destroyed by the negative principle of war, which robs life—and the processes ultimately responsible for life—of purpose and meaning:

> Move him into the sun—
> Gently its touch awoke him once,

At home, whispering of fields unsown.
Always it woke him, even in France,
Until this morning and this snow.
If anything might rouse him now
The kind old sun will know.

Think how it wakes the seeds,—
Woke, once, the clays of a cold star.
Are limbs, so dear-achieved, are sides,
Full-nerved—still warm—too hard to
    stir?
Was it for this the clay grew tall?
—O what made fatuous sunbeams toil
To break earth's sleep at all?

The final question implies a disillusionment far more profound than that associated with the reactions of the idealists and the humanitarians. The nature of that disillusionment reveals how deeply Owen had considered the problem of evil and its demands on both flesh and spirit. In "Exposure" he had attempted to justify those demands through the Christian concept of penance and expiation; in "Futility," however, he implies that the forces of evil can neither be reconciled with the principle of creativity nor interpreted in terms of Christian providence. For Owen the war is not merely a military struggle between Germany and England but a manifestation of the fundamental forces that shape or destroy human life.

Such poems as "The Show," "Arms and the Boy," and "Insensibility" (all undated, but probably composed at Scarborough) illustrate Owen's unusually wide range of visualization as well as the unity of imaginative perception behind it. Most war poets restricted themselves—as did Blunden—to apparently adventitious phases of personal experience, but Owen seemed to be occupied in filling out a picture of the war that would represent as many different aspects as possible. "The Show" presents a terrible panorama of the battlefields of western Europe; we see below us a landscape like an evil dream, a scene of sadness, desolation, and horror:

> My soul looked down from a vague height with Death,
> As unremembering how I rose or why,
> And saw a sad land, weak with sweats of dearth,
> Gray, cratered like the moon with hollow woe,
> And pitted with great pocks and scabs of plagues.

When Owen writes of the physical effects of the war on human beings, much of his imagery deals with parts of the body, especially the parts in which masculine beauty and strength are manifest. War cripples, maims, distorts, and corrupts; these are the penalties exacted of flesh and bone. When Owen notes the smile "Faint, and exceeding small/ On a boy's murdered mouth" (in the fragment "It Is Not Death"), he vividly focuses our attention on the detail which captures both innocence and the effects of evil. "The Show," however, is devoid of any human reference. Men have become loathsome caterpillars, writhing and dying amid the scabrous landscape. The details of this scene reflect an imagination torturing itself to the point of collapse:

> On dithering feet upgathered, more and more,
> Brown strings, towards strings of gray, with bristling
>   spines,
> All migrants from green fields, intent on mire.
>
> Those that were gray, of more abundant spawns,
> Ramped on the rest and ate them and were eaten.
>
> I saw their bitten backs curve, loop, and straighten,
> I watched those agonies curl, lift, and flatten.

The climax comes when the poet discovers that he himself had been among the crawling mass; the head of one caterpillar, "the fresh-severed head of it," is his own; its feet are "the feet of many men." The poem thus departs radically from Owen's usual mode of complex, evocative contrasts; it is almost masochistic in its direct appeal to the senses, in its blend of nausea and anguish. Owen obviously could go no further in this direction without sacrificing some of the most important qualities of his poetry.

In "Arms and the Boy" Owen's focus shifts to the individual soldier, and we have a portrait of youthful innocence confronting the mysteries of the bullet and the bayonet. But can this innocence—depicted, characteristically, in terms of masculine beauty—withstand the sinister suggestions from malicious steel and "blind, blunt bullet-heads"? The terrible transformation described in "The Show" indicates, perhaps, that innocence is not immune to other transformations and that the poet's statement of his faith is really a statement of his fear:

> . . . his teeth seem for laughing round an apple.
> There lurk no claws behind his fingers supple;
> And God will grow no talons at his heels,
> Nor antlers through the thickness of his curls.

Exposure to evil and to the "sharpness of grief and death" destroys youthful innocence and with it, in many cases, the capacity for feeling. This loss of elemental human sympathy Owen treats in "Insensibility":

> Happy are men who yet before they are killed
> Can let their veins run cold.
> Whom no compassion fleers
> Or makes their feet
> Sore on the alleys cobbled with their brothers.

Experience may bring an increased sensitivity to evil or a willful disregard of the bond of suffering created by the war—the fellowship that is "wound with war's hard wire." The boys

who wonderingly caress the "blind, blunt bullet-heads" may be
transformed into the "dullards whom no cannon stuns":

> Wretched are they, and mean
> With paucity that never was simplicity.
> By choice they made themselves immune
> To pity and whatever moans in man
> Before the last sea and the hapless stars;
> Whatever mourns when many leave these shores;
> Whatever shares
> The eternal reciprocity of tears.

Thus Owen ranges from the large-scale vision of catastrophe,
repulsive in its details, to the tender glance at the youth whom
pain and grief have not yet touched; he turns from innocence to
the cold callousness that is encouraged by experience; and,
echoing Virgil's most eloquent line, he rises above the issues
of the war to lament the tragedy that is inherent in the varied
sorrows that experience must bring to man.

Most World War I poets dealt only with material that was
subjectively or experientially important, since their purposes
ranged from that of simple self-dramatization to that of shocking the British public out of its ignorance and apathy. Owen,
however, seemed to realize the limitations of a narrowly subjective or experiential approach; the numerous revisions in the
British Museum manuscripts, according to D. S. R. Welland,
reveal a "progressive movement toward impersonality in the
gradual elimination of pronouns in the first and second person
in favor of less personal constructions."[18] By controlling the
subjective element in his verse, Owen sought a greater freedom
in exploring the larger moral and spiritual aspects of the conflict. His rapid poetic growth during the Scarborough period is
also visible in his gradual mastery of an individualized lyric
technique that embodied the discords of modern warfare and

---

[18] "Wilfred Owen's Manuscripts."

in his rejection of the rather narrow experiential bias implicit in "Apologia pro Poemate Meo." Instead of insisting upon the exclusive nature of the soldier's experience, Owen was henceforth to dwell upon its universality.

Although Owen's "Greater Love" is undated, its relationship to other poems indicates that it was composed in the spring or summer of 1918. The theme of pity touched upon in "Apologia pro Poemate Meo" (November 1917) and fully developed in "Miners" (January 1918) is here combined with Owen's most eloquent statement of the "greater love" ideal. In "Miners" the poet associates himself with the pathos of a sacrifice forgotten by future generations; the centuries "will not dream of us poor lads/ Lost in the ground." In "Greater Love," however, he has abandoned his earlier self-concern and assumed the responsibility of "pleader" for those too dedicated or too inarticulate to plead for themselves. At first an observer, Owen becomes a deeply involved participant, then advances to the more demanding and more disciplined role of intermediary. Thus the emotional force of an experienced truth submits to the control of a maturely conceived poetic purpose in "Greater Love."

The structure of the poem involves a point-by-point contrast between sensuous love and the "greater love"; the poet evokes the familiar imagery of the one in order to bring fresh meaning to the other. The contrast, therefore, is more than a revelation of pathetic discrepancies; it is the re-definition of a spiritual concept in terms of its lesser physical counterpart. Sensuous love is aroused by the beauty of lips, eyes, and limbs, and it is expressed through the voice, the heart (the emotions), and the hands. Owen uses each of these images to draw out the contrasting implications of sacrificial love. In the first stanza, for instance, the pleasurable qualities of a lover's lips (redness and warmth) are contrasted with the color of blood and the insensate coldness of stones; the lure of eyes is contrasted with the terrible vacancy of blindness:

> Red lips are not so red
>   As the stained stones kissed by the English dead.
> Kindness of wooed and wooer
> Seems shame to their love pure.
> O Love, your eyes lose lure
>   When I behold eyes blinded in my stead!

The consuming intensity of the "greater love" is described in terms of an explicit sexual analogy. Just as the sexual act represents the fruition of sensuous love, so the agonies of the dying represent the fulfillment of the "greater love." The analogy, of course, evokes a whole range of opposed associations that are too profound for irony:

> Your slender attitude
>   Trembles not exquisite like limbs knife-skewed,
> Rolling and rolling there
> Where God seems not to care;
> Till the fierce Love they bear
>   Cramps them in death's extreme decrepitude.

The fourth line touches another, less obvious contrast that embodies the spiritual doubts which had troubled Owen since his first exposure to the sufferings of war. Since God—in whom man finds the perfection of love—is apparently indifferent to the fate of the dying, man himself becomes the real exemplar of the "greater love." Thus the deeper levels of the poem reveal an irony that turns upon man's capacity for a love greater than sensuous love and greater, apparently, than the love that God bears for man. The final stanza, with its altered echo of Christ's injunction to the women of Jerusalem (Luke 23:28-29), ends with an identification of the modern soldier's sacrificial role with that of Christ:

Heart, you were never hot,
    Nor large, nor full like hearts made great with
        shot;
And though your hand be pale,
Paler are all which trail
Your cross through flame and hail:
    Weep, you may weep, for you may touch them not.

Life, of course, is the corollary of sensuous love; death is the corollary of the "greater love," the purity and intensity of which shame the ordinary expressions of love between man and woman. If, as the poet believes, "God seems not to care," Christ himself—the original exemplar of the "greater love"—voiced the same sense of dereliction that is implicit in Owen's attitude: "My God, my God, why hast thou forsaken me?" Thus the poem advances on two closely related levels of meaning. The first level involves a complex pattern of contrasts between sensuous and spiritual love; the second level suggests an analogy between two manifestations of the "greater love": Christ and the modern infantryman. Owen's basic purpose, of course, is definition. Only when we comprehend the nature of the "greater love" can we begin to understand the terrible demands that are made upon those whom that love destroys.

"Greater Love" is a key utterance because it marks a stage in the development of Owen's ability to give his inner conflicts an explicit and compelling poetic form. Another key utterance is "Strange Meeting," which was probably composed in the summer of 1918, since it is included in Owen's Table of Contents. Here the major concept is not the "greater love" but the truth upon which the "true Poets" must base their appeal to posterity. In the absence or inadequacy of other standards, the "greater love" may be the only positive guide for man in modern warfare; the self-sacrifice implicit in the "greater love" may never be necessary, however, if future generations heed the warnings of the "true Poets."

Although it takes the form of a possibly unfinished colloquy, "Strange Meeting" opens with a dramatic incident which was almost certainly inspired by Sassoon's "The Rear-Guard." Sassoon's brief narrative, it may be recalled, deals with the experience of a solitary soldier lost in the darkness of a tunnel below the Hindenburg Line; when he attempts to arouse a recumbent figure, he is confronted with the agonized face of a dead German soldier. Owen utilizes part of this experience for his own purposes:

> It seemed that out of battle I escaped
> Down some profound dull tunnel, long since scooped
> Through granites which titanic wars had groined.
> Yet also there encumbered sleepers groaned,
> Too fast in thought or death to be bestirred.
> Then, as I probed them, one sprang up, and stared
> With piteous recognition in fixed eyes,
> Lifting distressful hands as if to bless.
> And by his smile, I knew that sullen hall,
> By his dead smile I knew we stood in Hell.

Sassoon emphasizes only the physical and psychological shock of his experience in the Hindenburg tunnel; he retreats with the "sweat of horror in his hair," "unloading hell behind him step by step." Owen, however, goes far beyond the experiential effects developed by Sassoon; he remains in hell and confronts the truth behind the horror. In "Mental Cases" (written in May 1918), Owen had employed Dante's rhetorical and dramatic technique. In "Strange Meeting" he utilizes Sassoon's experience as a background for a colloquy that is again appropriately Dantesque in method and effect. In the profound silence of the tunnel ("no guns thumped, or down the flues made moan") he isolates himself from the tumult and distractions of battle ("no blood reached there from the upper ground") in order to assess the personal, artistic, and historical implications of the conflict.

The colloquy begins on a note of tenderness and reconciliation oddly at variance with the atmosphere of the "sullen hall." " 'Strange friend,' " says the narrator, " 'here is no cause to conflict.

> "None," said the other, "save the undone years,
> The hopelessness. Whatever hope is yours,
> Was my life also; I went hunting wild
> After the wildest beauty in the world,
> Which lies not calm in eyes, or braided hair,
> But mocks the steady running of the hour,
> And if it grieves, grieves richlier than here.
> For by my glee might many men have laughed,
> And of my weeping something had been left,
> Which must die now. I mean the truth untold,
> The pity of war, the pity war distilled."

Thus the pursuit of beauty is no longer possible in a world that has undergone the profound transformations suggested by the allusions in the first part of the poem. The evil of modern warfare demands a new dedication of the poet: he must speak of the violence, the suffering, the pity—the "truth untold." This enlargement of the poet's function is then viewed in terms of the future—the course of history which the apparition prophetically envisions but upon which his courage and wisdom (the fruits of his role as seer) can have no effect:

> "Now men will go content with what we spoiled.
> Or, discontent, boil bloody, and be spilled.
> They will be swift with swiftness of the tigress,
> None will break ranks, though nations trek from
>   progress.
> Courage was mine, and I had mystery,

Wisdom was mine, and I had mastery;
To miss the march of this retreating world
Into vain citadels that are not walled."

Here Owen forecasts the social and economic crises of the post-war years as well as the rise of the totalitarian state. More remarkable than the prophecy, however, is his conception of the role of the poet amid the evils of chaos and regimentation. Had he lived, the apparition would have had the insight and the skill to voice his protest, to tell the "truth untold" about war, to assert his faith in the values that men relinquish for the "vain citadels" of political absolutism and militarism. It is in this re-definition of the poet's role that "Strange Meeting" reveals a dramatic transition between the general attitudes of nineteenth-century poetry and those of the poetry written in the twenties and thirties. When men "boil bloody," the poet may no longer hunt "the wildest beauty in the world"; his function is broadly social rather than personal or aesthetic:

"Then, when much blood had clogged their chariot-wheels
I would go up and wash them from sweet wells,
Even with truths that lie too deep for taint.
I would have poured my spirit without stint
But not through wounds; not on the cess of war.
Foreheads of men have bled where no wounds were."

When "none will break ranks" from the march that leads inevitably to war, the poet emerges as seer and spokesman; he has access to a truth that immunizes him against the passions of nationalism. Thus he may no longer endorse imperialism, as did Kipling; it is not his duty to fight as a soldier or, as a poet, to deal with the external phenomena of war. This completely independent attitude is a measure of the poet's sensitivity rather than of his objectivity: "Foreheads of men have bled where no wounds were." Yet it is only through the exercise of his objectifying power (his courage and wisdom) that the poet has been able to renounce traditional claims upon his art as well as the more recent claims advanced by the stunning physical realities of modern warfare. Those physical realities must be "distilled" rather than crudely transmitted as experiential effects; the metaphor carries over to the "sweet wells" of truth, which represent a distillation of the poetic experience.

"Strange Meeting" concludes with a poignant revelation that makes pity and the "greater love" a part of the "truth untold" which must perish with the poet:

> "I am the enemy you killed, my friend.
> I knew you in this dark; for so you frowned
> Yesterday through me as you jabbed and killed.
> I parried; but my hands were loath and cold.
> Let us sleep now. . . ."

Although we assume that the two soldiers are British and German, they are not identified as such; it is the bond of humanity that must now be stressed and not the opposition of rival nationalities. Sorley described the tragic blindness of such an opposition in his 1914 sonnet "To Germany"; that blindness is now lifted, ironically, in the darkness of the "profound dull tunnel" where the truth of war lies buried with those who yearn to tell it. The lack of national identification also permits an alternative or additional interpretation of the poem; the "enemy" is the poet himself, seen as the slayer and the slain and sharing the guilt of murder as well as the innocence of the "greater love." ". . . am I not myself a conscientious objector with a very seared conscience?" asked Owen in June 1917. This interpretation, however, alters neither the basic meaning of the poem nor its external literary significance. With "Strange Meeting" Owen joins the small company of English poets who have been privileged to speak for their art in a time of crisis and change. He was the only war poet who seemed to be conscious of the implications of "war poetry" for poetry in general. The change in his own conceptions anticipates a radically altered conception of poetic purpose and method, itself a product of inadequacies which the war—and the poetry of the war—clearly revealed. The summary of nineteenth-century traditions which the Georgians represented could not cope with the moral and physical complexities of the twentieth century; poetry, if it would live, must change. Owen had time only to mark the transition, to lament the "undone years," to prophesy—as did Matthew Arnold in "Dover Beach"—the effects of absolutism and anarchy.

Although he felt that any direct participation in war would deprive the poet of his independence, Owen knew that his obligation as a "pleader" would entail his return to France. In "The Calls" and "And I Must Go"[19] he records both his resistance to that obligation and his eventual capitulation to it:

> I heard the sighs of men, that have no skill
> To speak of their distress, no, nor the will!
> A voice I know. And I must go.

Sassoon had expressed his consciousness of a similar "call" in "Sick Leave" and "Banishment." His return, however, was prompted by an emotional desire to share the sufferings of his fellows, whereas Owen felt a moral compulsion to return as a spokesman for the inarticulate—a purpose in accord with the function of the true poet as defined in the Preface and more explicitly though somewhat differently elaborated in "Strange Meeting."

Owen's arrival in France in September 1918 coincided with preparations for the last great offensive of the war, the effort

[19] Welland has proposed (in "Wilfred Owen's Manuscripts") that "And I Must Go" is actually the second part of "The Calls." The two poems possess a temporal continuity as well as an obvious thematic progression.

that was to result in the breaking of the Hindenburg Line. Just prior to or during his participation in the September attacks, the poet produced "Spring Offensive," "The Sentry" (part of the first and all of the second were sent to Sassoon on September 22), and "Smile, Smile, Smile," which is dated September 23. Two undated lyrics—"At a Calvary near the Ancre" and "Le Christianisme"—probably belong to this period because they, like the poems definitely written in September, were omitted from the Table of Contents, which in all likelihood Owen attempted to formulate before he departed for France.

"Smile, Smile, Smile" records, after the colloquial manner of Sassoon, the secret derision of the wounded as they read distorted newspaper accounts of the war, which is still being managed as if a "victory" were possible. Sassoon's *Counter-Attack* had appeared only two months before this poem was completed, so possibly Owen felt justified in renewing his own "counter-attack" on the misconceptions encouraged by the daily press. In "Spring Offensive" and "The Sentry," however, Owen seems to be experimenting with the possibilities of the brief narrative form. "The Sentry" is related in the first person by a participating observer; the fluent colloquial style is Sassoon's, as well as the range of blunt physical notation:

> We'd found an old Boche dug-out, and he knew,
> And gave us hell, for shell on frantic shell
> Hammered on top, but never quite burst through.
> Rain, guttering down in waterfalls of slime
> Kept slush waist-high that, rising hour by hour,
> Choked up the steps too thick with clay to climb.
> What murk of air remained stank old, and sour
> With fumes of whizz-bangs, and the smell of men
> Who'd lived there years, and left their curse
>   in the den,
> If not their corpses. . . .

In "Spring Offensive," on the other hand, the story is told in the third person with the poet as an omniscient but remote narrator. The style is formal, elevated, and controlled. Apparently Owen had some misgivings about the contrasting effects of "The Sentry" and "Spring Offensive," for he feared that the latter poem, because of its deliberately "poetic" technique, would evoke a *"No Compris!"* from the ordinary soldier. Although it has a clear narrative pattern, "Spring Offensive" is developed on a level that permits the introduction of richly lyrical elements:

> Halted against the shade of a last hill,
> They fed, and, lying easy, were at ease
> And, finding comfortable chests and knees,
> Carelessly slept. But many there stood still
> To face the stark, blank sky beyond the ridge,
> Knowing their feet had come to the end of the
>   world.
>
> Marvelling they stood, and watched the long grass
>   swirled
> By the May breeze, murmurous with wasp and midge,
> For though the summer oozed into their veins
> Like an injected drug for their bodies' pains,
> Sharp on their souls hung the imminent line of
>   grass,
> Fearfully flashed the sky's mysterious glass.

Here Owen succeeds in combining the virtues of objective visualization with the virtues of subjective perception; in other words, he blends a controlled, impersonal narrative development with the sensuous and imaginative immediacy proper to the lyric form. The subjective elements do not threaten the narrative continuity because the poet has deliberately withdrawn from the scene of action:

So, soon they topped the hill, and raced together
Over an open stretch of herb and heather
Exposed. And instantly the whole sky burned
With fury against them; earth set sudden cups
In thousands for their blood; and the green slope
Chasmed and steepened sheer to infinite space.

Thus Owen utilizes a narrative progression to organize and extend the insights encouraged by lyric perception. As we have seen, other poets had experimented with the brief narrative form, but they had been able to maintain neither the formal control nor the objective relationships demanded by a narrative progression. In "Spring Offensive" Owen attempts to encompass the objective as well as the subjective reality of war. In so doing he seems to have been developing a technique that would represent the significant aspects of both external and internal realities. "I do not doubt that, had he lived longer," writes Sassoon, "he would have produced poems of sustained grandeur and ample design."[20] Certainly the narrative technique employed in "Spring Offensive" would have been equal to the conceptions involved in any such poems.

Both "At a Calvary near the Ancre" and "Le Christianisme" are explicit in their indictments of formal Christianity. In poems such as "Anthem for Doomed Youth" and "Greater Love,"

---

[20] *Siegfried's Journey*, p. 92. Though Owen did not live to write the kind of verse to which Sassoon refers, nine of his poems (including "Anthem for Doomed Youth," "Futility," and "Strange Meeting") were used as songs by Benjamin Britten in his *War Requiem*, a work of extraordinary beauty and complexity first performed at the consecration of St. Michael's Cathedral, Coventry, on May 30, 1962. (The old cathedral was destroyed by German bombers in 1940.) With powerful effect, Britten employs the timeless prayers and supplications of *Missa pro Defunctis* as a background for the voice of the individual soldier caught up and destroyed in the sacrificial violence of modern warfare. Of special interest here is the composer's use of Owen's lyrics as personal, testimonial parts contributing to an artistic whole of "sustained grandeur and ample design"—a whole which the poet himself did not achieve with respect to the vision developed through the medium of lyric poetry.

Owen had explored the implications of his disillusionment with
Christianity as an external symbol, but in these two late lyrics
he writes with the casual bitterness of a man whose doubts have
settled into convictions. In early September 1918, Owen rejoined his battalion at Corbie on the Ancre River; somewhere
near Corbie he may have seen the damaged crucifix which
brought to mind a host of ironic associations:

> One ever hangs where shelled roads part.
>> In this war He too lost a limb,
> But His disciples hide apart;
>> And now the Soldiers bear with Him.
>
> Near Golgotha strolls many a priest,
>> And in their faces there is pride
> That they were flesh-marked by the Beast
>> By whom the gentle Christ's denied.
>
> The scribes on all the people shove
>> And bawl allegiance to the state,
> But they who love the greater love
>> Lay down their life; they do not hate.

The pride of churchmen and the hatred encouraged by journal-
ists and politicians oppose the spirit of the martyred Christ as
well as the spirit of the British soldier. "Le Christianisme" is
aimed more specifically at the ineffectuality of the Church as a
symbol and a medium:

> So the church Christ was hit and buried
>> Under its rubbish and its rubble.
> In cellars, packed-up saints lie serried,
>> Well out of hearing of our trouble.

One "Virgin still immaculate" has survived, but this is no
miracle; eventually "a piece of hell will batter her." Thus Owen
depicts the powerlessness of a Christianity that had failed to
act in the name of one of its basic tenets.

"The End" may also be read as a rejection of orthodox Christianity. Although it is undated, it is listed in the Table of Contents under "Doubtful" motive and this apparently is not to be interpreted as a direct and final contradiction of the spiritual values that animate so many of Owen's other poems. The mood of "The End" is clearly pessimistic, but its personifications and rhetorical tenor represent an abstract treatment of the subject rather than a spontaneous confession of disbelief:

> After the blast of lightning from the East,
> The flourish of loud clouds, the Chariot Throne;
> After the drums of Time have rolled and ceased,
> And by the bronze west long retreat is blown,
>
> Shall life renew these bodies? Of a truth
> All death will He annul, all tears assuage?—
> Fill the void veins of Life again with youth,
> And wash, with an immortal water, Age?
>
> When I do ask white Age he saith not so:
> "My head hangs weighed with snow."
> And when I hearken to the Earth, she saith:
> "My fiery heart shrinks, aching. It is death.
> Mine ancient scars shall not be glorified,
> Nor my titanic tears, the sea, be dried."

Aside from its formal excellence as a sonnet, "The End" is interesting because the poet's mother chose lines 5-6 for his tombstone at Ors. In the epitaph, however, the second question mark is omitted, thus reversing the pessimism of the sestet:

> Shall life renew these bodies? Of a truth
> All death will He annul, all tears assuage.

Thus a final ambiguity rounds off what has proved to be (aside from textual problems) the most perplexing aspect of Owen's poetry. Disputes about his orthodoxy are likely to continue until a full biography and an edition of his letters are available. It is obvious, however, that his finest work was inspired not by cynicism or despair but by a doctrine close to the heart of Christianity. This fact itself is responsible for the complexities and ambiguities that trouble so many of his readers. Owen's grasp of the implications of "pure Christianity" inevitably led to his rejection of an "impure" Christianity buried under "its rubbish and its rubble"; he held to the concept of the "greater love" as the only spiritual and poetic truth which could illuminate and possibly redeem the sufferings of the modern soldier. We may sometimes feel, however, that in doing this Owen has drawn the virtue of the "greater love" so far out of its Christian context of faith and hope that it stands in his poetry only as a source of ironic reproach or anguished appeal.

Despite Owen's extraordinary sensitivity and his efforts to reconcile that sensitivity to the demands of formal poetic art, his achievement does not measure up to the vast tragic potentialities of his material. His sense of personal involvement in the war resembled Rupert Brooke's in that it was a motive for as well as a source of poetry. Although he moves far beyond the Georgian attitude with his vision of pity, that vision was not enough. His compassion and his concept of the "greater love" grew out of his perhaps too exclusive concern with the aspects of suffering and sacrifice; these aspects do not assume their place or proportion in the total reality. Unlike Blunden, whose poetic interests range less intensely but more widely over the field of war, Owen cannot shift his eyes from particulars that represent merely a part of an enormous complex of opposed human energies comprehensible only on the historic or tragic scale. Although he attempts to give these particulars a universal significance, his vision of pity frequently obscures rather than illuminates the whole; we are likely to lose sight of the historical reality as well as the underlying tragic values that inspire the pity. In Owen's case the pity produces the poetry; only in a partial and sporadic fashion does the poetry produce pity as an effect of tragic events. Furthermore, if it is true that an enlightened compassion was apparently the only poetically fruitful point of view permitted by the nature of modern warfare, is it not also true, as Stephen Spender suggests in his essay on Owen, that "poetry inspired by pity is dependent on that repeated stimulus for its inspiration"?[21] The best of Owen's lyrics are necessarily developed in terms of a single emotion—an emotion that cannot be maintained or repeated without psychological strain or aesthetic loss. How many successful poems can be written in the tenor of "Disabled"? The very intensity of the author's compassion tends to exhaust both the emotion and the force of its stimulus. Unless pity is generated and objectified within a large tragic context, it cannot of itself support a tragic vision; as a motive for lyric poetry, it tends to become sentimental or obsessive regardless of the eloquence with which it is developed. When the compassionate attitude is apparently the only attitude with which war can be truthfully described, the possibilities of poetry are severely restricted: only passive suffering and death can provide its materials.

William Butler Yeats excluded Owen's poetry from his *Oxford Book of Modern Verse* on the basis of his judgment that "passive suffering is not a theme for poetry." A "pleader" for the sufferings of others necessarily makes those sufferings his own; "withdrawn into the quicksilver at the back of the mirror," he loses his objectivity and his sense of proportion: "no great event becomes luminous in his mind." The function of the epic narrative, of course, was to communicate that luminous effect; the epic poet, dealing with and illuminating great events, interpreted his tale in the light of heroic values. These values affected the form as well as the materials of the narrative; the epic vision deter-

[21] *The Destructive Element* (London, 1935), p. 219.

mined the attitude and technique of the poet as well as the motivations and actions of his characters. In Owen's poetry we have the physical background of war, the sense of hazard and duress, the pathos of suffering, and even a perception of tragic extremity. But these, at best, are but fragmentary aspects of the whole. They appear not as products of a unified and comprehensive poetic vision but as effects of a lyric sensibility vainly attempting to find order and significance on a level of experience where these values could not exist—where, in fact, they had been destroyed. Owen and his contemporaries inherited a sensibility deprived of vision and value; their experiences—so alien to anything dealt with by the romantic tradition—required an intellectual and imaginative discipline far beyond that provided by the vision of pity, which was itself a product of tortured sensibility. Unlike Sassoon, Owen recovered from an early experiential bias; this bias, he discovered, was as poetically unproductive as the Georgian "retrenchment" from which it was an abrupt and sensational reaction. His ironic use of romantic terms and concepts indicates the conflict between a sensibility long devoted to "Poetry" and experiences that demanded the truth. Lacking a positive and comprehensive lyric vision, Owen drew his poetry from this inner conflict while attempting to find his bearings in a period of rapid historical and artistic transition. "Strange Meeting" is his final word on the social responsibilities of the "true Poet"; but even in this statement, where the "truth untold" is seen as the pity—"the pity war distilled," Owen can present no further justification of the poet's new role than his sensitivity to suffering.

The omission of Owen's poems from *The Oxford Book of Modern Verse* provoked much censure from critics and reviewers. In a letter to Lady Dorothy Wellesley (December 21, 1936), Yeats somewhat irascibly defended his action: "When I excluded Wilfred Owen, whom I consider unworthy of the poets' corner of a country newspaper, I did not know I was excluding a revered sandwich-board Man of the revolution & that some body has put his worst & most famous poem in a glass-case in the British Museum—however if I had known it I would have excluded him just the same. He is all blood, dirt & sucked sugar stick (look at the selection in Faber's Anthology—he calls poets 'bards,' a girl a 'maid' & talks about 'Titanic wars'). There is every excuse for him but none for those who like him."[22]

The private nature of these remarks undoubtedly encouraged a measure of willful or careless exaggeration. Yeats's main and more justifiable thrust is against those who for doctrinaire political reasons had exalted the "prophetic" elements of Owen's work. Yet his case against Owen's verse strikes shrewdly—if unkindly—into the critical problem. Owen's sensibilities had indeed developed along the line Yeats indicates; "Poetry"—the "sucked sugar stick" element—was prominent in his work, although he was gradually eliminating it or making it the source of ironic reference. The "blood and dirt" or experiential element, Yeats implies, could hardly be combined in a poetically palatable manner with the sucked sugar stick of "Poetry." Yet if we drop the metaphor and its distracting associations, we may see that Owen's combination of the two is a significant aspect of his achievement and one which illustrates both his keen awareness of transition and his ability to incorporate its meaning into the substance of his poetry. For those who are also conscious of that transition, one of the most poignant effects in the poetry of World War I is created by his use of the romantic idiom to suggest, by contrast or default, what it could no longer express.

Owen's influence on the postwar poets has been summarized by C. Day Lewis, who nominates Hopkins, Owen, and Eliot as the "immediate ancestors" of the Auden group.[23] Owen's contribution, however, was less technical than inspirational.

[22] *Letters on Poetry to Dorothy Wellesley* (New York, 1940), p. 124.
[23] *A Hope for Poetry* (Oxford, 1934), pp. 2-3.

Auden, Day Lewis, and Louis MacNeice employed Owen's most notable innovation—half-rhyme—for a variety of effects, but with the exception of Day Lewis they did not seriously explore the musical possibilities of this device, which does not lend itself to every poetic purpose. It is rather as a prophet that Owen earns Day Lewis' designation as "a true revolutionary poet." Owen's protest against the evils of war has been rather unwarrantably extended to the social and economic evils of modern life; he "commends himself to post-war poets largely because they feel themselves to be in the same predicament; they feel the same lack of a stable background against which the dance of words may stand out plainly, the same distrust and horror of the unnatural forms into which life for the majority of people is being forced."[24] Owen is actually a symbol rather than a prophet; his youth, his small but eloquent body of verse, his intense dedication to the truth, his untimely and unnecessary death—all of these factors combined to make him an irresistible figure to the succeeding generation, whose "stable background" of traditional forms and values had, like Owen's, been destroyed by the war. He is a "revolutionary poet" not in the sense that he deliberately undertook any radical reformation of his art but in the sense that his work embodies, more dramatically than that of any other poet, the changing values of the time.

[24] *Ibid.*, p. 15.

As a writer Isaac Rosenberg is unusually difficult to classify; like Owen, he stands at a transitional phase of English poetry and his work represents the effort of a highly individualized talent to find itself amid rapidly shifting literary values. Although he was opposed to many of the tendencies visible in Georgian verse, his poetry is basically romantic in mode and inspiration. Up to a point in his career we can recognize certain influences and speculate about others, but beyond that point Rosenberg speaks with a voice that is undeniably his own. He pursued his visions with a single-mindedness that exasperated his Georgian friends and fellow-poets; he trusted his unsettled and sometimes wayward imaginative powers so deeply that he alienated a generation of postwar critics who could find in his "Trench Poems" neither the aggressive social purpose of Sassoon nor the explicit spiritual appeal of Owen. Yet among the soldier-poets his gift of lyrical expression was certainly unique, and his imaginative powers, when properly organized, could deal with the theme of war in a manner that invites comparison only with the more fully realized achievement of Owen.

Owen's fame, of course, has far exceeded Rosenberg's, and it may seem imprudent to suggest that their work is closely related. As soldier-poets, the two had a great deal in common; in some ways Owen is closer to Rosenberg (whom he did not know) than he is to Sassoon, who did not fully grasp the implications of his friend's poetry until after the war. Both Rosenberg and Owen served in the latter half of the conflict, when the struggle had assumed the terrible sacrificial proportions envisioned by Sorley in 1914. Both poets possessed especially sensitive artistic temperaments; both hated the physical violence and ugliness of war, though Rosenberg seemed to be more conscious of its inhibiting effects on his personal poetic development. Both poets, moreover, remained virtually unpublished and unknown until after the war; they were thus deprived of whatever stimulus or satisfaction they would have received through public recognition. Finally, they both sought to redeem their experiences by a poetic dedication to the task of interpreting the very misery and horror from which they recoiled and which in the end claimed their lives. Just as Brooke and Nichols had defined the early idealistic attitude, so Rosenberg and Owen defined the compassionate attitude which seemed to summarize all that could be thought or felt during the latter half of the war. Though they both write out of the profound personal disillusion inspired by modern technological violence and its effects on the human spirit, their poetry transcends the moods and issues of wartime disillusionment. It is in this sense that Rosenberg and Owen raise the lyric poetry of World War I to its highest and most nearly tragic level.

Of the two, Rosenberg certainly wrote under the more difficult odds. Physically and psychologically unfit for soldiering, he was miserable throughout his army life. He served as a private and was therefore cut off from any contact, social or otherwise, with minds and temperaments akin to his own. He spent nearly twenty months in the trenches or in areas near the trenches, with only two brief periods of respite. The sheer monotony and the almost constant danger to which he was exposed profoundly affected his imaginative and creative abilities. No other war poet contended against such demoralizing circumstances; it is something of a miracle that he managed to produce any work at all. Only his determination to protect his inner life as a poet and his tenuous epistolary contacts with men like Marsh, Lascelles Abercrombie, R. C. Trevelyan, Laurence Binyon, and Gordon Bottomley kept his inspiration alive. On the other hand, Owen—as did the other poets whom we have previously examined—enjoyed the privileges and the occasional amenities of rank, which, considering the hard life of the common soldier, were not inconsiderable. After a three months' period in the trenches in early 1917, Owen was invalided to England for over a year, during which time he had ample opportunity to meditate on his experiences, meet other poets, and perfect himself as a craftsman. He returned to the fighting in September 1918, but his total time in the trenches amounted to only five months. Of the major war poets—with the exception of Brooke and Nichols—Owen saw the least actual service and enjoyed the longest interlude between periods of service. These facts are mentioned here merely to emphasize the hardships under which Rosenberg struggled and to ensure a more equitable estimation of his work.

Rosenberg's early life was darkened by a poverty from which he was never free, even during his adult years. He was born on November 25, 1890, in Bristol, the son of Barnett Rosenberg, a Lithuanian, and Chasa Davidoff, a Latvian. In 1897 the family moved to London and settled in the East End, near Whitechapel. Although the Rosenbergs were poor, they led a particularly close family life—there were eight children—and did not permit their poverty to become demoralizing or degrading. Rosenberg was educated at the elementary schools of Stepney until he was fourteen, when he was apprenticed to a firm of engravers in Fleet Street. Artistic by temperament and craving for the self-expression of painting and poetry, he grew to hate the mechanical nature of his work. He attended evening classes at the Art School of Birkbeck College; his artistic promise eventually attracted the attention of three wealthy Jewish ladies, who financed his training at the Slade School. Rosenberg attended the Slade School from October 1911 until March 1914, winning several prizes for his paintings and exhibiting some of them at the Whitechapel Gallery. During this time, with the encouragement of his eldest sister, he began to write poetry; in 1912 he issued *Night and Day*, the first of three small, privately printed collections. Though his talent was recognized by a number of writers and critics, including Edward Marsh and Laurence Binyon, neither his painting nor his poetry seemed designed to invite any great public acknowledgment. His artistic independence was such that he instinctively resisted what he called the "contemporary influence" in both media. He could not lend himself to the conventionalism which would have guaranteed his painting a commercial success nor was he willing to write verse in the fashionable Georgian manner.[1]

In June 1914, having been told that tuberculosis was threatening his lungs, Rosenberg voyaged to South Africa, where he lived at Cape Town with a married sister. In May 1915 he returned to England and a few weeks later enlisted with the Suffolk Bantam Regiment. His motives reflect resignation rather than patriotic enthusiasm: "I never joined the army from patriotic reasons," he wrote Edward Marsh in late 1915. "Nothing can justify war. I suppose we must all fight to get the trouble over."[2] He quickly came to resent both the low quality of the men he was thrown among and the "brutal militaristic bullying meanness" of army ways. Of frail physique and dreamy disposition, he did not thrive as a soldier: he suffered physically from the rigorous training and the fatigue of menial labor; he was punished for absent-minded lapses in military conduct; and he was apparently the victim of racial discrimination. Transferred in early 1916 to the King's Own Royal Lancasters, he was sent to France the following June. His almost desperate letters to Edward Marsh reflect the mental deterioration of a sensitive man caught up in the stupefying and brutalizing life of the common soldier. He held on grimly to his poetry, however; as he

[1] See Horace Gregory, "The Isolation of Isaac Rosenberg," *Poetry*, LXVIII, 1 (April 1946), 30-39.

[2] Gordon Bottomley and Denys Harding, eds., *The Complete Works of Isaac Rosenberg* (London, 1937), p. 305. In a number of cases the punctuation and spelling of further quotations from Rosenberg's letters have been corrected, but without any alteration of the poet's meaning.

writes to Laurence Binyon in 1916, "I am determined that this war, with all its powers for devastation, shall not master my poeting; that is, if I am lucky enough to come through all right. I will not leave a corner of my consciousness covered up, but saturate myself with the strange and extraordinary new conditions of this life, and it will all refine itself into poetry later on."[3]

Rosenberg was occasionally fortunate enough to be assigned to rear-area duties, but aside from a brief leave in the late summer of 1917 and a two months' period of illness in a hospital later that year, he saw no relief from the "strange and extraordinary new conditions" from which he was resolved to extract whatever poetry he could. During the latter half of 1917, as he reports to a correspondent in one of his last letters, he was working on a play called "The Unicorn": "If I am lucky, and come off undamaged, I mean to put all my innermost experiences into the 'Unicorn.' I want it to symbolize the war and all the devastating forces let loose by an ambitious and unscrupulous will. Last summer I wrote pieces for it and had the whole of it planned out, but since then I've had no chance of working on it and it may have gone quite out of my mind."[4]

The play—certainly the most artistically demanding work projected by a soldier-poet—was never finished; Rosenberg was killed during the Somme retreat, on April 1, 1918. In what is probably his last letter, dated March 28, the poet addresses Edward Marsh in terms that may be extended to his struggle against the darkness of war itself:

"I think I wrote you I was about to go up the line again after our little rest. We are now in the trenches again and though I feel very sleepy, I just have a chance to answer your letter so I will while I may. It's really my being lucky enough to bag an inch of candle that incites me to this pitch of punctual epistolary. I must measure my letter by the light. . . ."[5] Time

[3] *Works*, p. 373.　　[4] *Ibid.*, p. 379.　　[5] *Ibid.*, p. 322.

was indeed short, and the end brutally abrupt: when this letter was postmarked, on April 2, Rosenberg had already been killed and hastily buried in an unmarked grave.

In the "Trench Poems" section of Rosenberg's *Complete Works* there are only twenty poems; these, with "The Dead Heroes" (from his second private collection, *Youth*, 1915) and "Marching" (from *Moses*, 1916, his third private collection) make up the total of his war verse.[6] Some of these poems, however, are negligible, being overwrought, over-ingenious, obscure, or remote from the circumstances of the conflict. Most of the others, though remarkable enough, do not reveal any conscious attitude toward the changing nature of the war; but between the spirit of Rosenberg's early elegy, "The Dead Heroes," and his later "Dead Man's Dump" lies a significant opposition, visible even in the probably unconscious irony of the contrasting titles.

Though he later expressed a dislike of Rupert Brooke's "begloried sonnets," Rosenberg's own early attitude reveals a patriotism which, if less personal, is hardly less ardent. "The Dead Heroes" memorializes, in a somewhat ingenuous and over-exuberant mood, the sacrifices of the English dead. Rosenberg's visual and verbal luxuriance contrasts sharply, of course, with Sorley's austere technique; it also differs in its imaginative intensity from Brooke's smoothly manipulated verbal and emotional effects.

> Flame out, you glorious skies,
> Welcome our brave,
> Kiss their exultant eyes;
> Give what they gave.

[6] Of these poems, only "The Dead Heroes," "Break of Day in the Trenches," and "Marching" were actually published by Rosenberg. The first appeared in *South African Women in Council*, December 1914; the other two appeared, through the offices of Ezra Pound, in *Poetry* (Chicago), December 1916.

Flash, mailèd seraphim,
Your burning spears;
New days to outflame their dim
Heroic years.

Thrills their baptismal tread
The bright proud air;
The embattled plumes outspread
Burn upwards there.

Flame out, flame out, O Song!
Star ring to star,
Strong as our hurt is strong
Our children are.

Their blood is England's heart;
By their dead hands
It is their noble part
That England stands.

England—Time gave them thee;
They gave back this
To win Eternity
And claim God's kiss.

In his Foreword to Rosenberg's *Complete Works*, Siegfried
Sassoon remarks that in the verse of his fellow war poet there
is "a fruitful fusion between English and Hebrew culture. Behind all his poetry there is a racial quality—biblical and prophetic." In certain themes and materials developed by Rosenberg
there are clear indications of his cultural and racial background,
but his imagery—perhaps more pervasively "biblical and prophetic" than his themes—is often charged with that elevated,
exotic, visionary quality that is characteristic of the great English mystic poets: Crashaw, Blake, and Francis Thompson. The
patriotic sentiments of "The Dead Heroes" are commonplace,

of course; but the quality of the imagery employed to voice these sentiments reveals an imagination that is, so to speak, outracing the conventionalities of its subject and its theme.

Rosenberg's artistic preferences, as expressed in his essays and letters, provide clues to his unusual poetic style and his recourse to an involved and frequently obscure symbolism. More than once he declares his admiration for Rossetti; he was in sympathy with the ideals of the Pre-Raphaelites, and he was attracted by the qualities of early Italian art. Blake's artistic vision he also admired profoundly. In his early verse Rosenberg experimented with a number of late nineteenth-century styles and modes: Browning's influence is visible in "Raphael," a dramatic mono-logue; the hectic eroticism of Swinburne and the minor decadents pervades such poems as "Night," "Like Some Fair Subtle Poison," and "Bacchanal"; and an incident from Francis Thompson's *Sister Songs* ("A Child's Kiss") probably inspired "A Ballad of Whitechapel." Significantly, it is Thompson who draws Rosenberg's highest praise; at their best, both poets express themselves with an intensity that is spiritual as well as sensuous. The imagery of Rosenberg's prewar verse reflects this curiously ambivalent quality; the poet explores the visionary world of William Blake (gold, fire, swords, seraphs, stars, and spears) as well as the voluptuous underworld of Swinburne (wine, roses, pearls, tresses, satin, and silver). In both worlds, perhaps, Rosenberg was seeking to express what he called, with reference to the work of another poet, "that strange longing for an indefinite ideal; the haunting desire for that which is beyond the reach of hands."[7] It is this quality of spiritual and sensuous intensity that distinguishes Rosenberg's verse from that of his tamer Georgian contemporaries. Always pressing forward to some invisible frontier, his restless imagination could never have tolerated the pleasant pedestrian meanderings of those who

[7] *Works*, p. 326.

had discovered that their poetic interests coincided agreeably with popular taste.

Rosenberg's preference for the painter-poets Blake and Rossetti is probably related both to his elaborate and frequently unsuccessful symbolism[8] and his ability—developed in his war verse when he no longer had the time or the materials for painting— to transfix the most essential elements of form and color in motion. "Louse Hunting" (February 1917) illustrates the poet's skill in arresting, after the fashion of the painter, the mobile elements of a grotesque conglomeration of bodies and limbs:

> Nudes—stark and glistening,
> Yelling in lurid glee. Grinning faces
> And raging limbs
> Whirl over the floor one fire.
> For a shirt verminously busy
> Yon soldier tore from his throat, with oaths
> Godhead might shrink at, but not the lice.
> And soon the shirt was aflare
> Over the candle he'd lit while we lay.
>
> Then we all sprang up and stript
> To hunt the verminous brood.
> Soon like a demons' pantomime
> The place was raging.
> See the silhouettes agape,
> See the gibbering shadows
> Mixed with the battled arms on the wall.
> See gargantuan hooked fingers
> Pluck in supreme flesh
> To smutch supreme littleness.

[8] In his Introductory Memoir to the first edition of Rosenberg's poems (Gordon Bottomley, ed., London, 1922), Laurence Binyon remarks that Rosenberg's early paintings were "saturated with symbolism." Binyon found one painting "impossibly complex" with obscure symbolic convolutions.

See the merry limbs in hot Highland fling
Because some wizard vermin
Charmed from the quiet this revel
When our ears were half lulled
By the dark music
Blown from Sleep's trumpet.

Here the painter's visualization is heightened by the poet's perception of ironic contrasts: the fantastic contortions of man's "supreme flesh" and the "supreme littleness" which has provoked it to such a fierce display of animal energy; the weird, nightmarish reality and the "dark music" of sleep which it has so grossly interrupted.

Another poem, "Marching" (late 1915), illustrates both the painter's eye for symmetry and color and the poet's predilection for oblique rather than direct statement:

My eyes catch ruddy necks
Sturdily pressed back—
All a red brick moving glint.
Like flaming pendulums, hands
Swing across the khaki—
Mustard-coloured khaki—
To the automatic feet.

We husband the ancient glory
In these bared necks and hands.
Not broke is the forge of Mars;
But a subtler brain beats iron
To shoe the hoofs of death
(Who paws dynamic air now).
Blind fingers loose an iron cloud
To rain immortal darkness
On strong eyes.

219

Necks, hands, feet, fingers, brain, eyes—all human faculties have been mobilized to slay or aligned to be destroyed by the "iron cloud" of death. The painter's glimpse of marching men is thus enlarged by the poet's insight into the inherited glory of the soldier's calling and the change which the techniques of modern warfare have introduced to make that calling less glorious and less heroic. Both "Louse Hunting" and "Marching" demonstrate that Rosenberg, despite the visionary and erotic tendencies of his prewar verse, was capable of dealing with materials of an altogether different order. In "The Dead Heroes" he envisions the "embattled plumes" of the slain; in "Marching," however, he sees the "mustard-coloured khaki" of the living. Rosenberg never curtailed his propensity for visionary and symbolic interpretations, but the startling contrast in imagery suggests that he had opened his eyes to a whole new range of experience.

The influences, techniques, and tendencies just enumerated do not exhaust the elements that are present in Rosenberg's rich and suggestive poetic style, but they do account for some of his most conspicuous effects; they are also responsible, in varying degrees, for what is most essential in his best and most characteristic work. Sassoon remarks that Rosenberg "was not consciously a 'war poet' "—that is, in the sense that Sassoon himself was a war poet, deliberately utilizing the materials and themes of warfare. Rosenberg's experiences in the army forced the somewhat irregular growth of an unusual lyric gift which the poet had neither the time nor the opportunity to refine; the theme of war was thrust upon him before his slowly maturing faculties were prepared to cope with it. The extreme desperation of his personal experiences, however, fostered a determination to deal—tentatively, at least—with material that he felt should be refined and enlarged to more significant proportions; hence the experimental nature and the uneven quality of much of his war verse.

"The Dead Heroes," as we have noted, is rather common-place in its elegiac and patriotic sentiment. However, two other poems that deal with the opening of hostilities are more effective in their evocation of the war's initial impact on men who were sensitive to the evil and suffering implicit in any human conflict. The first of these, "On Receiving News of the War," was written at Cape Town in August 1914. The sudden realization of universal as well as personal involvement is characteristically worked out in terms of a sensory image which captures the first chilling physical and psychological reaction and its extension to the objective world:

> Snow is a strange white word.
> No ice or frost
> Has asked of bud or bird
> For Winter's cost.
>
> Yet ice and frost and snow
> From earth to sky
> This Summer land doth know.
> No man knows why.
>
> In all men's hearts it is.
> Some spirit old
> Hath turned with malign kiss
> Our lives to mould.
>
> Red fangs have torn His face.
> God's blood is shed.
> He mourns from His lone place
> His children dead.
>
> O! ancient crimson curse!
> Corrode, consume.
> Give back this universe
> Its pristine bloom.

Thus Rosenberg, having developed a range of foreboding sensory implications, shifts to the deeper sacrificial, penitential, and regenerative motifs of the last two stanzas. Sassoon and Owen, among others, applied the themes of Christian suffering and sacrifice to the ordeals of the infantry soldier; Rosenberg's use of scriptural imagery, however, reflects an integral mode of visualization rather than a deliberate application of motif. His conception of the evil of war is primordial, universal, almost apocalyptic; it is the "ancient crimson curse" that so pervasively haunts the annals of Hebraism. Most of the other war poets were products of a conventional middle-class background and education which afforded no source of spiritual reference commensurate with their experience of war; hence they felt cut off from the past, whose sanctions were being devaluated or destroyed before their eyes. Rosenberg, on the other hand, possessed a racial and cultural heritage that had always remained protectively independent of its social context. For him that heritage constituted a natural source of reference, both with respect to imagery and the materials which supplied his myth-transforming and myth-making imagination.

The other poem dealing with the beginning of the war, "August 1914," was actually written in the spring of 1916, after Rosenberg had entered the army. It reveals a personal sense of wasted youth, of hopes and joys blasted by the war:

> What in our lives is burnt
> In the fire of this?
> The heart's dear granary?
> The much we shall miss?
>
> Three lives hath one life—
> Iron, honey, gold.
> The gold, the honey gone—
> Left is the hard and cold.

Iron are our lives
Molten right through our youth.
A burnt space through ripe fields
A fair mouth's broken tooth.

The theme of personal sacrifice is the same as that developed
by Rupert Brooke in Sonnets III and IV of 1914, but Rosenberg was not susceptible to the appeals of romantic idealism;
like Sorley, he insists that the waste is real, that there can be
no compensation for the sacrifice and suffering of war. The
clarity and economy of "August 1914," with its movement
geared so closely to three precise images—"Iron, honey, gold"—
might suggest that Rosenberg was experimenting with the technique of the Imagists, whose poetic theory opposed, among
other things, the kind of verbal luxuriance characteristic of
Brooke's better-known poems. Certainly the effectiveness of
"August 1914" depends a great deal on the striking images of
the last two lines, which evoke, in unrelated but vivid pictorial
summaries, the sense of destruction and waste. The poised, economical technique is an unusual one for Rosenberg, whose
sense of poetic form was not strong; his talent lay in expansion
and elaboration rather than in disciplined compression. If
Imagism did influence his verse (as it may well have, considering
his friendship with Ezra Pound),[9] the most relevant conclusion
that can be drawn here is that his lyrical talents, as late as 1916,
were still in the process of development. Having rejected Georgian neo-romanticism and having experimented with so many
late nineteenth-century modes, he was perhaps testing a new
poetic technique which seemed to promise some measure of
form and discipline.

[9] In a 1912 letter to Winifreda Seaton, Rosenberg expresses his admiration for the work of F. S. Flint, one of the English Imagist poets. See
Works, p. 326. For the possible effects of T. E. Hulme's ideas on Rosenberg,
see Joseph Cohen, "Isaac Rosenberg: From Romantic to Classic," Tulane
Studies in English, x (1960), 129-42.

The sense of sinister oppression voiced in "On Receiving News of the War" is again apparent in "Spring 1916," written, presumably, just before the poet's departure for France. The change depicted in the season reflects Rosenberg's renewed sensitivity to the dark moods aroused by the conflict toward which he was inevitably being impelled:

> Slow, rigid, is this masquerade
> That passes as through granite air;
> Heavily—heavily passes.
> What has she fed on? Who her table laid
> Through the three seasons? What forbidden fare
> Ruined her as a mortal lass is?
>
> .   .   .   .   .   .
>
> Who lured her vivid beauty so
> To be that strained chilled thing that moves
> So ghastly midst her young brood
> Of pregnant shoots that she for men did grow?
> Where are the strong men who made these their
>   loves?
> Spring! God pity your mood!

The season of renewal and growth has returned, but the unseen presence of war transforms spring into an empty mockery for men who are preoccupied with death. War threatens not only the individual life but also the very principle of vitality; the source of life is chilled, poisoned, ruined, and the figure of spring—so full of tender associations for the poet—has become a fearful symbol of death. Thus Rosenberg again considers the general emotional and spiritual implications of the conflict in terms that bear out his earlier remark that "nothing can justify war."

In France, as we have remarked, Rosenberg's opportunities for writing poetry were considerably reduced. Only during his infrequent periods of rest could he bring his faculties to bear on what he had experienced; still, he was determined, as he wrote to Binyon, to "saturate" himself with materials that he could use after the war. Some of the longer poems written in France are apparently the products of Rosenberg's desire to record significant moods and episodes; although these poems are among the most perceptive he wrote, they seem to be methods of poetic notation rather than finished works of art. In a few of his shorter lyrics, however, certain themes are more fully and satisfactorily developed. "Returning, We Hear the Larks," for instance, describes the effects of an incongruous beauty on men whose senses have been starved by the ugliness and danger that have encompassed their lives:

> Sombre the night is.
> And though we have our lives, we know
> What sinister threat lurks there.
>
> Dragging these anguished limbs, we only know
> This poison-blasted track opens on our camp—
> On a little safe sleep.
>
> But hark! joy—joy—strange joy.
> Lo! heights of night ringing with unseen larks.
> Music showering on our upturned list'ning faces.
>
> Death could drop from the dark
> As easily as song—
> But song only dropped,
> Like a blind man's dreams on the sand
> By dangerous tides,
> Like a girl's dark hair for she dreams no ruin
>   lies there,
> Or her kisses where a serpent hides.

Edmund Blunden deals with the same contrast in "Illusions," but he emphasizes, according to his own practice, the immediate visual and emotional aspects of that contrast. Rosenberg, on the other hand, characteristically suggests the idea of lurking danger by a recourse to images that are related to the experience through the medium of a far-ranging imagination. He is obviously thinking of Shelley's "To a Skylark"; we have the same ecstatic perception of beauty, the same mystical experience of "unbodied joy," the same imagery of showering music, and the same use of varied similes that reflect the poet's search for the precise quality of his inner experience. Shelley's resplendent similes revolve around his conception of ideal beauty; Rosenberg, however, seeks to evoke—through images that embody a sinister menace to unconscious human life—the precarious and paradoxically dangerous quality of beauty in war, where death is the reality and beauty a treacherous and destructive dream totally different from anything Shelley might have imagined. In "Spring 1916" beauty has become a masquerade for death; in "Returning, We Hear the Larks" joy has become a trap for the unwary. Thus Rosenberg continued to explore the strange effects of war on man's sensibility and on his capacity to respond to elements of natural beauty.

"Home-Thoughts from France" is a brief lyric that develops a minor, conventional theme with some degree of poignancy, but it is not otherwise a remarkable poem. Similarly, the ironic contrasts presented in "From France" are not inspired by any strong feeling or developed with any great originality; Rosenberg did not have Sassoon's facility with this kind of material, which made no great demands upon his imaginative resources:

> The spirit drank the café lights;
> All the hot life that glittered there,
> And heard men say to women gay,
> "Life is just so in France."
>
> The spirit dreams of café lights,
> And golden faces and soft tones,

And hears men groan to broken men,
"This is not Life in France."

Heaped stones and a charred signboard show
With grass between and dead folk under,
And some birds sing, while the spirit takes wing.
And this is Life in France.

Only when Rosenberg was grappling with larger, more difficult conceptions were his full poetic energies brought into play. Ironically, it is in his generally unsuccessful struggles with these larger conceptions that his verbal and imaginative powers are most clearly revealed.

"In War" is a short narrative that is marred, unfortunately, by a rather melodramatic conclusion. The poem is notable, however, for its creation of a haunting impression of timelessness; life, death, burial, pain, and weariness are depicted with the same simplicity, the same dignity, and the same concern with essentials that attend the epic narrative:

In the old days when death
Stalked the world
For the flower of men,
And the rose of beauty faded
And pined in the great gloom,

One day we dug a grave:
We were vexed
With the sun's heat.
We scanned the hooded dead:
At noon we sat and talked.

How death had kissed their eyes
Three dread noons since,
How human art won
The dark soul to flicker
Till it was lost again:

And we whom chance kept whole—
But haggard,
Spent—were charged
To make a place for them who knew
No pain in any place.

At this point the priest arrives to read the burial service and the speaker suddenly discovers that his brother is among the dead:

The good priest read: "I heard . . ."
Dimly my brain
Held words and lost. . . .
Sudden my blood ran cold. . . .
God! God! it could not be.

He read my brother's name;
I sank—
I clutched the priest.
They did not tell me it was he
Was killed three days ago.

Here Rosenberg may have been attempting to suggest the larger symbolic aspects of brotherhood and its tragically delayed recognition. His rather awkward handling of the climax, however, breaks sharply into the grave dignity of the stanzas quoted previously; the speaker's reactions are commonplace and over-emotionalized. In the final stanza these effects are almost redeemed by a return to the elevated mood of the original visualization:

What are the great sceptred dooms
To us, caught
In the wild wave?
We break ourselves on them,
My brother, our hearts and years.

If "In War" is marred by its unnecessary climax, the poem illustrates Rosenberg's fine lyrical skill, especially with regard to imagery and phrasing. Certain images—"the rose of beauty" and "death kissed their eyes"—are reminiscent of the sensuous strain in his prewar verse; here, however, they are made to serve altogether different conceptions. One phrase—"the great sceptred dooms"—has a splendor that is almost Shakespearian. Although Rosenberg is aware of the ugliness and suffering of death in war, he prefers to dwell on its less obvious aspects: the mystery of the passing of sensory life, the tragedy of the "wild wave" of death, which bears down inexorably upon the lowly and obscure—those whose lives are the chief toll of any great war. The fine restraint of the poem—the absence of external realism and the emphasis upon what is timeless and universal in human conflict—is a quality rather rare in World War I verse. That restraint, however, is imperfectly maintained; Rosenberg is still uncertain in the employment of his lyrical talents and in the realization of his larger poetic conceptions. When we think of Owen's fourteen months in England and his stimulating relationship with Sassoon, we wonder how similar experiences would have affected Rosenberg's ability to detect the weaknesses which mar even his most impressive poems. Perhaps if he had been, consciously, a "war poet," with friendships, advice, and a sense of shared poetic interests, he would have been able to view his work more objectively and bring his rather autonomous imaginative energies into line with a clearly conceived moral or social purpose.

In a letter to Edward Marsh postmarked July 30, 1917, Rosenberg gives an account of "The Daughters of War," an interesting work upon which he had apparently been engaged since his arrival in France in June 1916. Although he speaks of his long struggle to make the poem clear, he is still convinced of its intrinsic merit: "I believe my Amazon poem to be my best poem. If there is any difficulty it must be in words here and there the changing or elimination of which may make the poem clear. It has taken me about a year to write; for I have changed and rechanged it and thought hard over that poem and striven to get that sense of inexorableness the human (or unhuman) side of this war has. It even penetrates behind human life, for the 'Amazon' who speaks in the second part of the poem is imagined to be without her lover yet, while all her sisters have theirs, the released spirits of the slain earth men; her lover yet remains to be released."[10]

Neither Rosenberg's liking for the poem nor his anxiety about its lack of clarity is difficult to understand, considering its tangential symbolism and its visionary, prophetic temper. The poems we have already considered indicate that his conceptions (except in minor instances) were not limited by the external realities of everyday experience; "The Daughters of War," in fact, is a deliberate effort to escape or transcend the limitations of that experience. The attempt to capture the "sense of inexorableness" in war is as typical of Rosenberg as his effort to capture it through the medium of an elaborate, far-ranging symbolism. "In War" deals with the theme of death and its implications for the living, who helplessly await their own doom; this theme is realized through perceptions grounded in the experience of war. "The Daughters of War," although it develops the same theme, depends on the qualities of the poet's symbolic projection rather than on a "sense of inexorableness" realized in terms of the war itself. A few lines will illustrate just how far removed the poem is from the circumstances of its origin:

> I saw in prophetic gleams
> These mighty daughters in their dances
> Beckon each soul aghast from its crimson corpse
> To mix in their glittering dances.

[10] *Works*, p. 319.

230

I heard the mighty daughters' giant sighs
In sleepless passion for the sons of valour,
And envy of the days of flesh
Barring their love with mortal boughs across—
The mortal boughs, the mortal tree of life.
The old bark burnt with iron wars
They blow to a live flame
To char the young green days
And reach the occult soul; they have no
    softer lure—
No softer lure than the savage ways of death.

The undeniable grandeur of these conceptions remains isolated
and remote; although he develops the qualities of might and
inexorableness in his mythological figures, the poet does not
relate these figures in any immediate way to the particular
quality of inexorableness he discerned in modern warfare. He
has avoided the tyranny of external realism only to plunge into a
visionary world that is devoid of credibility and emotional
force:

These maidens came—these strong everliving
    Amazons,
And in an easy might their wrists
Of night's sway and noon's sway the sceptres
    brake,
Clouding the wild—the soft lustres of our eyes.

Clouding the wild lustres, the clinging tender
    lights;
Driving the darkness into the flame of day
With the Amazonian wind of them
Over our corroding faces
That must be broken—broken for evermore
So the soul can leap out
Into their huge embraces.

The "wild wave" of death, in the final stanza of "In War," suggests inexorableness much more vividly and compellingly than the "huge embraces" of the Amazons. Hardy was perhaps the only other living poet whose imagination could work successfully on this large, visionary scale; *The Dynasts*, however, maintains an effective balance between its supra-human personifications and the particularized reality of the Napoleonic Wars. In "The Daughters of War" the fault lies in the tenuous relationship between the conception and the reality and not, as Rosenberg believed, in any verbal obscurity. His struggles with the poem indicate that he felt it was not successful, but for some reason he was unwilling to abandon the mode of visionary symbolism or the somewhat remote and improbable figures of the Amazons, who are no doubt cousins of the female mythological figures of which the late nineteenth-century poets —notably Swinburne—were so fond.

Although Rosenberg's formal education was limited, he was from childhood an avid reader. His letters show an acquaintance with a surprising variety of English and American authors, and his critical judgments (expressed in his letters and in several brief essays) are sometimes as penetrating as Charles Sorley's. He would have applauded Sorley's contemptuous dismissal of the "finely trained" Georgian voice; he would also have agreed that the early idealistic response to the war followed the conventional Georgian pattern. A brief comment on some aspects of the early response indicates something of his attitude toward war poetry in general. The following passage is from a letter to Mrs. Herbert Cohen (one of the ladies who had paid for his training at the Slade School) written in early June. 1916: "The Poetry Review you sent is good—the articles are too breathless, and want more packing, I think. The poems by the soldier are vigorous but, I feel, a bit commonplace. I did not like Rupert Brooke's begloried sonnets for the same reason. What I mean is, second-hand phrases—'lambent fires,' etc.,—take from its [poetry's?] reality and strength. It [war] should be approached in a colder way, more abstract, with less of the million feelings everybody feels; or all these should be concentrated in one distinguished emotion. Walt Whitman in 'Beat, Drums, Beat' [*sic*] has said the noblest thing on war."[11]

Rosenberg's remark about "second-hand phrases" recalls Yeats's criticism of what he called the "sucked sugar stick" element in Owen's verse. Committed in different ways to the demands of the living imagination, neither Rosenberg nor Yeats could tolerate poetry that had lost its vital inner vision—its "reality and strength"—while subsisting on diminishing reserves of romantic imagery and sentiment. Brooke's popularity, as Rosenberg implies, was due to the fact that his rather emotional response was too closely related to "the million feelings everybody feels." To this "commonplace" poetry of familiar themes and threadbare phrases, Rosenberg would oppose a "more abstract" approach, one dictated by the poet's sense of the timeless within the finite historical reality. It is a tribute to Rosenberg's intellectual maturity that at this early date he anticipates Sassoon's resolution, in July 1918, to view the war in a more detached and impersonal fashion, to be, as an "independent contemplator," as much "above the battle" as he could. It is interesting, also, to note that both poets mention Whitman as a source of inspiration for the new attitude they conceived as necessary in the writing of modern war poetry.[12] Sassoon remarks that he imagined his future poetry imbued "with Whitmanesque humanity and amplitude"; Rosenberg admires Whitman as an inspired spokesman for the mood of a nation at war—the "million feelings" nobly concentrated in

[11] *Ibid.*, p. 348.

[12] Whitman's direct poetic influence, however, is not strong enough or visible enough to trace in the poets we are considering here. For an interpretation of Whitman's role as the originator of the "modern attitude" of compassionate realism in war literature, see V. S. Pritchett, "Two Writers and Modern War," *The Living Novel* (New York, 1947), pp. 167-78.

"one distinguished emotion." Both poets realized that neither patriotism nor idealism nor realism was enough; they knew that conventional patriotic sentiments could not encompass the awesome reality of a nation in arms, that idealism could not hide the new horrors of death in battle, that simple verisimilitude was empty and meaningless without the compassion that must accompany a truly tragic conception of war. The war ended, of course, before Sassoon could embody these realizations in his verse. Rosenberg, on the other hand, was deprived of the leisure necessary for the production of the kind of poetry he felt impelled to write; the visionary nature of his conceptions, furthermore, hindered their easy transmission into verse. "The Daughters of War" indicates how far he was willing to go in order to suggest the abstract or timeless implications of war; certain other poems, however, show that he was aware that the timeless must have its roots in reality—the reality in which he had earlier resolved to "saturate" himself.

"Break of Day in the Trenches," perhaps Rosenberg's best short lyric, was composed in the late summer of 1916. Despite its brevity, the poem is replete with varied meanings and suggestions, all growing naturally out of a central incident. Against a background of violence, the poet meditates on the pathetic ephemerality of beauty and human life; he considers the essential fraternity of all men as well as man's tragic self-victimization. The manner in which these themes are presented produces an effect of mystery and questioning wonder; the tone is quiet and unpretentious, reflecting the awakening consciousness rather than the reaction of an experienced and disillusioned observer. Having placed "the parapet's poppy" behind his ear, the poet musingly addresses a rat that has just jumped over his hand:

> Now you have touched this English hand
> You will do the same to a German—
> Soon, no doubt, if it be your pleasure

To cross the sleeping green between.
It seems you inwardly grin as you pass
Strong eyes, fine limbs, haughty athletes
Less chanced than you for life,
Bonds to the whims of murder,
Sprawled in the bowels of the earth,
The torn fields of France.
What do you see in our eyes
At the shrieking iron and flame
Hurled through still heavens?
What quaver—what heart aghast?
Poppies whose roots are in man's veins
Drop, and are ever dropping;
But mine in my ear is safe,
Just a little white with the dust.

Of this poem Sassoon remarks, "Sensuous front-line experience is there, hateful and repellent, unforgettable and inescapable." But there is more present, of course, than mere "sensuous front-line experience"; few other poems written during the war manage to suggest, in terms so compelling, the deeper emotional significance of the conflict and the mingled mysteries of violence, brotherhood, beauty, and death. Ironically, it is the rat—the scavenger of the trenches—that reminds us that war is above all a human activity; it is the fragile poppy that for a moment symbolizes beauty—safe, perhaps only for a moment, behind the poet's ear. Rosenberg's almost casual tone is in direct contrast to the elevated style of his symbolic poems; his imagery is simple and based directly upon the circumstances of the incident. On his own testimony, however, he did not regard such productions as "Break of Day in the Trenches" as ends in themselves; he spoke constantly of grander projects in which the experiences captured in the lyrics would be incorporated. Like Sorley, Rosenberg seemed to disdain poetry of the "small-holdings type"; no doubt his desire to write on the grand imaginative scale is responsible for the curious division in his work between the timeless, visionary mode ("The Daughters of War") and the mode which is based on the immediately realized sensuous experience ("Break of Day in the Trenches"). When these modes are brought together in the same poem—as they are in "Dead Man's Dump"—the result is an uncertain but powerful blend of lyric immediacy and tragic vision.

"I've written some lines suggested by going out wiring, or rather carrying wire up the line on limbers and running over dead bodies lying about," Rosenberg wrote to Marsh in a letter postmarked May 8, 1917. "I don't think what I've written is very good but I think the substance is, and when I work on it I'll make it fine."[13] Marsh must have replied promptly because at the end of the month Rosenberg acknowledged his reaction to the poem and added a few further comments of his own:

"I liked your criticism of 'Dead Man's Dump.' Mr. Binyon has often sermonized lengthily over my working on two different principles in the same thing and I know how it spoils the unity of a poem. But if I couldn't before, I can now, I am sure, plead the absolute necessity of fixing an idea before it is lost, because of the situation it's conceived in."[14]

It is not clear whether Rosenberg had the opportunity to revise the poem; as it now stands, "Dead Man's Dump" remains a fragmentary but impressive achievement. His difficulties, however, were not altogether due to the circumstances of composition; they are connected with the basic problem that afflicted World War I poets when they attempted to escape from the limitations of the brief personal lyric.

We have noted before, in the cases of Robert Nichols and Edmund Blunden, the consequences of intensifying and prolonging the lyric response, which is often unequal, in modern

13 Works, p. 316.
14 Ibid., pp. 316-17.

warfare, to the magnitude of the situations which produce it. When the poet attempts to depict more than an isolated impression, when he attempts to unite a series of impressions in a narrative or descriptive whole, his purpose often fails him, and he wavers between moments of lyrical intensity and a struggling narrative or descriptive advancement. If the original stimulus is strong, the poet may produce lines that superbly suggest the chaos and horror of war, but his poetry, for all that, remains fragmentary and divided in purpose and only a partial reflection of the literally overwhelming whole. On the one hand, the lyric response, intense though it may be, is limited to subjective and therefore partial and scattered impressions; on the other hand, the narrative or descriptive progression cannot embrace any really meaningful action or impart any sense of reference to the physical and spiritual totality of the war. Any attempt at rendering a meaningful action or even a simple progression of events, as we saw in Blunden's "Third Ypres," was likely to remain, for the most part, a disorganized record of sensations and subjective impressions. Under the circumstances, a detached and comprehensive account of combat experience could hardly be expected, although Arthur Graeme West's "The Night Patrol" indicates that a controlled verse narrative could be produced without recourse to isolated lyric impressions. Almost every poet who was aware of the larger implications of the conflict evinced some dissatisfaction with the limitations of the lyric mode or with the responses encouraged by that mode. Their efforts to transcend these limitations, as we have seen, were hampered by a commitment to the premises of contemporary neo-romantic poetry, which employed the lyric chiefly as a medium of personal sensibility. Neither changes in technique (an extension or intensification of the lyric mode) nor changes in attitude (the development of the compassionate response) could offer a satisfactory solution to the problem; the two poets who dealt with their experiences after the war was over—

Herbert Read and David Jones—turned not to the lyric but to entirely different modes of poetic expression.

These generalizations may again be invoked with respect to Rosenberg's "Dead Man's Dump," which is composed of descriptive, reflective, and narrative elements. The poet obviously intended to record a powerful personal experience, the effects and implications of which were too profound for a simple lyrical presentation. The experience, therefore, is prolonged by means of a slight narrative progression; it is intensified by descriptive enlargements and by reflective passages suggested by the mystery of life and death in war. Although the poem realizes a scene of frightful carnage with overwhelming visual and imaginative intensity, the elements that compose it do not merge into a satisfactory artistic whole, and we have what amounts to a succession of brilliant lyric fragments. Of course, Rosenberg admitted that the poem was a means of "fixing an idea" rather than a finished production, but he would not have sent the poem to Marsh if it represented no more than a disconnected series of private notations. He was, moreover, concerned about the unity of the work—a fact which indicates that he conceived of it as a single, independent production capable of being read and judged on its own merits.

The title, of course, suggests the callousness of modern warfare, the brutal indifference to death as well as to life; the contrast to idealized versions of death in warfare (including Rosenberg's own "The Dead Heroes") is obvious. The opening stanzas, however, present a consciousness sensitive to the tragic effects of the war, vividly depicted in the pathetic passivity of the dead. The tone approximates the contemplative restraint of the stanzas previously quoted from "In War"; we have the same impression of timelessness, an impression that is maintained throughout the poem. Also recognizable is the sacrificial motif which Rosenberg had employed earlier in "On Receiving

News of the War"; this motif suggests the mood of sympathy and compassion which is amplified to thematic proportions in the concluding section of the poem.

> The plunging limbers over the shattered track
> Racketed with their rusty freight,
> Stuck out like many crowns of thorns,
> And the rusty stakes like sceptres old
> To stay the flood of brutish men
> Upon our brothers dear.

> The wheels lurched over sprawled dead
> But pained them not, though their bones crunched,
> Their shut mouths made no moan.
> They lie there huddled, friend and foeman,
> Man born of man, and born of woman,
> And shells go crying over them
> From night till night and now.

"Dead Man's Dump" runs to eighty-six lines and consists of thirteen irregular stanzas of from two to nine lines each. The next six stanzas—forty-one lines, or about half the poem—turn to speculations on the mystery of mortality and violent death. This section of the poem, which ends with an impassioned address to "Maniac Earth," contains passages of great lyric beauty; the visionary mode, however, together with its somewhat overwrought tone, must have prompted Binyon's criticism about "working on two principles in the same thing." In the third stanza the narrative progression is halted (to be suddenly resumed, in the tenth stanza, from another point of view) and the poet begins to reflect upon death and upon the living who are so close to death:

> Earth has waited for them,
> All the time of their growth
> Fretting for their decay:

Now she has them at last!
In the strength of their strength
Suspended—stopped and held.

What fierce imaginings their dark souls lit?
Earth! have they gone into you!
Somewhere they must have gone,
And flung on your hard back
Is their soul's sack
Emptied of God-ancestralled essences.
Who hurled them out? Who hurled?

None saw their spirits' shadow shake the grass,
Or stood aside for the half used life to pass
Out of those doomed nostrils and the doomed
　　　mouth,
When the swift iron burning bee
Drained the wild honey of their youth.

In a larger narrative context these reflections could be developed without the somewhat digressive character they here assume; in a short poem, however, the shift from narrative to a heightened level of metaphysical speculation diminishes the effectiveness of both modes, especially when the latter involves material that is tangential to the situation upon which the narrative progression is based. Robert Nichols, in "Night Bombardment," attempted a similar mixture of narrative, descriptive, and reflective material; the resulting impression of disunity is similar to that we receive from "Dead Man's Dump."

In the next two stanzas the poet goes on to consider the fate of the living who move so precariously amid the dead and dying bodies of their "brothers dear":

What of us who, flung on the shrieking pyre,
Walk, our usual thoughts untouched,

Our lucky limbs as on ichor fed,
Immortal seeming ever?
Perhaps when the flames beat loud on us,
A fear may choke in our veins
And the startled blood may stop.

The air is loud with death,
The dark air spurts with fire,
The explosions ceaseless are.
Timelessly now, some minutes past,
These dead strode time with vigorous life,
Till the shrapnel called "An end!"
But not to all. In bleeding pangs
Some borne on stretchers dreamed of home,
Dear things, war-blotted from their hearts.

The speculations thus continue in a loose and unco-ordinated
fashion, turning from the apparent immortality of the living
to the mysterious abyss that separates them from those who
have been stricken. Finally, in the last stanza of the section,
the poet feverishly addresses the Earth, which had previously
been personified as a force opposed to the vitality in man and
impatient for his dissolution:

Maniac Earth! howling and flying, your bowl
Seared by the jagged fire, the iron love,
The impetuous storm of savage love.
Dark Earth! dark Heavens! swinging in chemic
smoke,
What dead are born when you kiss each soundless
soul
With lightning and thunder from your mined heart,
Which man's self dug, and his blind fingers
loosed?

The emotional intensity of these lines does not conceal the fact
that they constitute the least satisfactory portion of the poem
and one at odds with the compound of pathos and irony suggested by the title. We have departed from the narrative reality;
we have been drawn into a series of tangential conceptions and
visualizations that emerge from a specialized poetic imagination
rather than from the reality itself; the hectic tone and the
rhetorical outbursts threaten to disrupt the calm restraint of
the previous stanzas. The general theme of this section—the
power and inexorableness of the forces that bring death to
men—resembles that of "The Daughters of War," wherein
the Amazons represented those forces. Here, however, that
theme is obscured by the elaborate and distracting visualizations
that merge in an emotional climax only remotely related to the
scene confronting the poet.

In the stanzas that follow, Rosenberg suddenly reverts to
the "dead man's dump," but the narrative progression begins
at a new point. The action thus initiated is brought within the
observation of the narrator in the first part of the poem:

> A man's brains splattered on
> A stretcher-bearer's face;
> His shook shoulders slipped their load,
> But when they bent to look again
> The drowning soul was sunk too deep
> For human tenderness.

Just as there is a point between life and death where tenderness
is of no avail, so there is a range of tragedy beyond which compassion cannot penetrate. Rosenberg's experience bears out the
stoic wisdom of Sorley, who recognized that pity is irrelevant
when its object is the victim of forces beyond human control
or understanding.

The grievously wounded man is left at the crossroads with

the "older dead," whose terrible faces the poet sees under the
wheels of the limber:

> Burnt black by strange decay
> Their sinister faces lie,
> The lid over each eye,
> The grass and coloured clay
> More motion have than they,
> Joined to the great sunk silences.

Among these horribly inanimate shapes, already half-absorbed
into the earth, the dying man lies; his "drowning soul" is suspended above the "great sunk silences" which open to receive
him. As the limber approaches he struggles with death as a
swimmer struggles with the tide:

> His dark hearing caught our far wheels,
> And the choked soul stretched weak hands
> To reach the living word the far wheels said,
> The blood-dazed intelligence beating for light,
> Crying through the suspense of the far torturing
>   wheels
> Swift for the end to break
> Or the wheels to break,
> Cried as the tide of the world broke over his
>   sight.

In the doomed man—who is not an individual but a universalized symbol of death in war—is aroused a final, desperate hope;
he is beyond human tenderness or aid, but his voice sounds from
the edge of the "great sunk silences" in an ultimate plea for
human contact and recognition:

> Will they come? Will they ever come?
> Even as the mixed hoofs of the mules,
> The quivering-bellied mules,

And the rushing wheels all mixed
With his tortured upturned sight.
So we crashed round the bend,
We heard his weak scream,
We heard his very last sound,
And our wheels grazed his dead face.

Thus the poem comes to a climax that summarizes all the brutality and pathos of death in war: the helplessness of man to control the vast forces he has unleashed; the mystery of the violent passage from life to death; and the impossibility of responding to the moment of that passage, so grossly obscured by the issues and exigencies of battle. We see the dying man's last glimpse of life: the "mixed hoofs" and the bellies of the mules, and the "rushing wheels"; we also hear, with the poet, his last weak scream. Death in modern warfare is not admirable or heroic; it is passive, obscure, ignominious, and pitiable. The wheels of the limber are the wheels of war—the bloody wheels that Owen hoped to cleanse with water from the "sweet wells" of truth—and the poet, upon whose sensibility the impact falls, emerges as a powerless and horrified participant as well as a compassionate observer. Thus the meaning of the poem is drawn out to the tragic proportions of Owen's "Strange Meeting," wherein the reactions of the poet as a participant become more significant, morally, than the sum of his emotional reactions as an observer.

Although the earlier poets—Brooke, Grenfell, Nichols—were participants rather than observers, they regarded their involvement in the war either as a romantic adventure or as an opportunity for personal moral regeneration. Sassoon and Blunden, for the most part, were observers whose reactions were strongly influenced by the disappearance of that earlier sense of participation. Toward the end of the war, Owen and Rosenberg began to think of themselves as participants who shared the guilt as well as the knowledge of death and suffering; this is the point of view which draws "Strange Meeting" and "Dead Man's Dump" so closely together. Both poems are based on Frederic Manning's premise that war is a "peculiarly human activity." As such, it cannot be condemned on mere idealistic or humanitarian terms: "To call it a crime against mankind is to miss at least half its significance; it is also the punishment of a crime." Owen contemplated the "dead smile" of his enemy in hell; Rosenberg heard the last "weak scream" of his dying comrade; both poets confronted the ultimate implications of organized human violence and were conscious not only of the crime but of the guilt and the punishment.

In "Dead Man's Dump," therefore, Rosenberg does not depend upon the effects of mere realism nor is his presentation actuated by the moods and motives of disillusion. As in "Strange Meeting," we know neither the combatants nor the issues of the struggle; we see its effects only in terms of human suffering and sacrifice. Although the poem was inspired by the same compassion that distinguishes most of Owen's work, Rosenberg's attitude of calm detachment magnifies and ennobles that emotion; we have a pity that is too vast for its identification with one object and too profound to seek its expression in the outward emotional reaction of the observer. If the true poetry of the war, as Owen claimed, was in the pity, Rosenberg's pity is an effect produced in the reader by the revelation of a larger poetic truth and not an attitude consciously applied or developed by the poet. In "Dead Man's Dump" the poetry produces the pity; pity does not produce the poetry. Thus the compassionate attitude becomes a means of interpreting the tragedy of war rather than an emotional response to the "crime against mankind."

The irregularity and disunity of "Dead Man's Dump" are partly due to the circumstances of composition, partly to a mixture of different modes and intentions, and partly to Rosenberg's uneven poetic technique and his rather vague sense of form. Although there is some evidence that he was influenced by the disciplines of Imagism in some of his shorter lyrics, his style, his methods of development, and the quality of his imagination were in direct opposition to the ideals of that movement. His style is often rhetorical and diffuse; his development is loose and erratic; and his imagination, though brilliant with respect to details, frequently lacks coherence in form and conception. Unlike Owen, whose meticulous sense of form sought expression in the sonnet or in the perfectly balanced lyric, Rosenberg seemed more intent on capturing his inspiration through spontaneous imagery rather than on the process of shaping that inspiration in a harmony of words, rhythms, rhymes, and stanzas. Even when they achieve a successful lyric expression, his insights are apparently meant to serve large symbolic projections rather than limited lyric revelations: images integral to "Returning, We Hear the Larks" (one of his best lyrics) are later incorporated as incidental effects in the final draft of a portion of "The Unicorn." In his less successful lyrics he is sometimes obscure, sometimes conventional, and sometimes without genuine inspiration; in his most ambitious poems his inspiration outruns his capacity to give it a unified and coherent expression. In these longer poems he deals with elevated abstractions in the grand style, but that style, like the abstractions, has little relationship to the underlying reality of the war. Except for a few of his shorter lyrics, Rosenberg was unable to unite thought and expression in a single, harmoniously complete poetic entity. "Dead Man's Dump"—brilliant in parts, perceptive, compelling, but fragmentary and inchoate—is an epitome of his defects as well as of his qualities as a poet. Although these qualities are considerable, they hardly warrant the claim that Rosenberg is a "greater poet" than Owen;[15] his tragic vision, it is true, approximated that of Owen, but his

[15] See Marius Bewley, "The Poetry of Isaac Rosenberg," *Commentary*, VII, 1 (January 1949), 34-44.

expression of that vision does not measure up to the range, the variety, and the craftsmanship inherent in Owen's work.

If Rosenberg failed to achieve his promise, there is, as Yeats said of Owen, "every excuse for him." His art and personality were both highly vulnerable to the disruptive tendencies of the war. He seized desperately, however, at the sensations and revelations which confronted him; as he remarked in one of his letters to Marsh, "these rare parts must not be lost." The parts that the poet preserved are rare enough, since they project, with extraordinary lyric skill, a personal vision of the war that remained free, for the most part, from extraneous moods and attitudes. He was apparently conscious of some of the deficiencies of his work, since his poems were sent on to his friends rather apologetically, and he always welcomed their critical comments and advice. As he stated in one of his last letters, he planned to put all his "innermost experiences" in a grand poetic drama—"The Unicorn"—which was to transcend the crude particularities of war by means of an elaborate symbolism. He struggled to preserve and extend the truth of the inner vision at a time when every force seemed bent on destroying it. Although he momentarily entertained the idea of publishing his war lyrics in an inexpensive pamphlet form, he had no delusions about the temporary fame of the "soldier-poet"; publication, however humble, was simply a means of ensuring the preservation of his verse. Unlike most of his contemporaries, who were caught up in their interpretation of the war as a present actuality, he constantly looked to the future for a complete realization of his talents and his inner vision. Considering his obscure and precarious existence in the trenches, that hope in itself constituted an extraordinary profession of poetic faith.

Rosenberg's effort to escape from the limitations of the brief personal lyric follows a pattern we have observed in the practice and the theory of other World War I poets, most of whom, in one way or another, sought to enlarge the range of their responses. His remarks that war should be approached in "a colder way, more abstract"; his efforts to follow that dictum in poems like "Dead Man's Dump"; and his incomplete experiments with a more objective form, that of the poetic drama, demonstrate his own independent effort to free his work from the limitations of the lyric as a medium of war poetry. However, through his poetic insight, his tragic perceptions, his "compassionate realism," and his effort to envision the war in terms of larger artistic conceptions, Rosenberg at times made the lyric a means of momentary revelation as eloquent and as moving as these limitations would permit. It is in the exercise of this superior lyric power that he joins the company of the most perceptive and sensitive poets of the war.

In what is probably his last poem, " 'Through These Pale Cold Days,' " Rosenberg speaks not for himself but for his generation and the extremity to which it had been brought. The mood of the final year of the war is characteristically evoked in terms of the ancient sorrows and hopes of Hebraism:

> Through these pale cold days
> What dark faces burn
> Out of three thousand years,
> And their wild eyes yearn,
>
> While underneath their brows
> Like waifs their spirits grope
> For the pools of Hebron again—
> For Lebanon's summer slope.
>
> They leave these blond still days
> In dust behind their tread
> They see with living eyes
> How long they have been dead.

It is this same profound concern—purified of lesser attitudes and emotions—that Sorley felt for the shattered destiny of the war generation. In his early prophetic sonnet, "A Hundred Thousand Million Mites We Go," he too speaks in terms of a restless, visionary quest:

> A hundred thousand million mites we go
> Wheeling and tacking o'er the eternal plain,
> Some black with death—and some are white with woe.
> Who sent us forth? Who takes us home again?

Blunden is also thinking of the collective fate of his generation when he admits, in "Zero," the appalling inevitability of the conflict: "It's plain we were born for this, naught else." But it is only in the "profound dull tunnel" of Owen's "Strange Meeting" that the quest is in some sense ended; it is here that the poet confronts and acknowledges the old issues of inevitability and hope, of responsibility and reconciliation, of man's bondage to warfare and his hunger for the peace of "Lebanon's summer slope." In different ways these three poets were aware that war has no real significance unless it is viewed in terms that are larger and more universally valid than those of patriotism, humanitarianism, or simple personal involvement. The lyric only partially sufficed for the expression of this awareness, which lay within the bounds of inner experience and discovery but which seemed to demand, in virtue of its profundity, a fuller and more objective expression in narrative or dramatic form.

CHAPTER VII · THE "HIGHER REALITY": HERBERT READ

AMONG the soldier-poets who survived the war—Nichols, Graves, Sassoon, and Blunden—not one returned to his battle experiences as the source of further poetic inspiration. Their wartime verse grew so directly out of their personal sufferings that, when the guns at last were silent, they had little desire to re-create what Blunden in a moment of saddened retrospect called "the lost intensities of hope and fear." Moreover, their themes and techniques had been so closely adapted to those "lost intensities" that they were no longer relevant in a world confronted with the diffused issues of an uncertain peace. Of the poets we have examined, only Rosenberg looked beyond the stress of battle for the opportunity to refine his "innermost experiences" into a drama comprehensive enough "to symbolize the war and all the devastating forces let loose by an ambitious and unscrupulous will." If Rosenberg had lived to complete these intentions in "The Unicorn," he would have found himself in the company of two other poets whose imaginative powers would also be devoted—though in directly opposite ways—to refining the crude materials of a war that had passed into history. Significantly, these two poets—Herbert (now Sir Herbert) Read and David Jones—had not committed themselves to the limited terms of the wartime lyric response; their imaginations, free from experiential or emotional bias, were therefore capable of relating the struggle to moral and historical values that for a number of reasons had been beyond the scope of wartime verse.

Although he had written and published war poetry during and after the conflict, Read did not begin his most impressive work—*The End of a War*—until 1931. Published separately in 1933, *The End of a War* is comparatively brief (about 400 lines) and seems to have little in common with Jones's novel-length *In Parenthesis*. Jones began *In Parenthesis* in 1928, but this rather long narrative poem was not completed until 1937, when the nations of Europe, in Owen's phrase, were again about to "boil bloody." Though dissimilar in almost every respect, these two productions represent the final stages of a rapidly evolving poetic impulse that had originated in 1914. In this and the following chapter we shall attempt to follow the critical and creative adjustments through which any "new" poetry seeks to correct its excesses, modify its techniques, and extend its control over unfamiliar materials.

Both Read and Jones enjoyed a number of literary advantages over the poets who wrote during the fighting. By 1930 the appearance of several major war novels and autobiographical accounts had signalized the fact that the interpretation of personal experience had entered a broader and more consciously evaluative phase; it was possible, after the lapse of a dozen years, to see the war in its historical context and to discern the tragic patterns behind the particulars rendered so memorably by the wartime poets. Both Read and Jones, moreover, were able to profit artistically by the efforts of their predecessors to break away from prewar conventions as well as the limitations of the personal lyric response. They could not avoid being strongly influenced by what the soldier-poets had accomplished, or—more importantly—by what they had failed to accomplish. Finally, Read and Jones both benefited by the experimental turn that English poetry in general took after 1912. The revolt of the Imagists, the popularity of Hopkins' posthumously published verse, the emergence of an entirely new type of poetic statement in the work of T. S. Eliot—all were symptomatic of the dissatisfaction that poets felt with a tradition that had outlived its usefulness with respect to the complex issues of modern life. The influence of Eliot is especially strong in Jones's *In Parenthesis*, while Read's work is marked by the style and technique of the Imagists. Thus both poets were enabled to treat aspects and levels of the war for which their contemporaries had no serviceable medium save the attitudes and techniques encouraged by the employment of the brief personal lyric.

Certainly the most significant feature of postwar verse is the change from the brief lyric mode to the long philosophic poem (Read's *The End of a War*) and to the heroic narrative (Jones's *In Parenthesis*). Accompanying this change is a shift from a generally subjective to a generally objective visualization; the response to the reality of war no longer required a presentation in terms of urgent personal reactions. Read, in fact, dissociates his poetry from the act of moral judgment as well as from the emotions aroused by the physical phenomena of war. On the other hand, Jones incorporates the lyrical sense of immediate physical involvement (developed so compellingly by the poets of 1914-1918) into a context of narrative development based on the objective visualizations of the heroic poem. Indeed, Jones's *In Parenthesis* might be seen as the culmination of those tendencies—noted either in the verse or in the comments of Nichols, Sassoon, Blunden, and Rosenberg—toward an objectively visualized, unified, and comprehensive narrative poem that would encompass the general human significance of war as well as its complex, fragmented physical reality.

The soldier-poets of 1914-1918 dealt chiefly with the particulars of technological warfare and the effects of scientifically manipulated violence on human beings. With Read and Jones, however, the emphasis falls upon the more universal aspects of violence and evil. Both poets, of course, utilize their personal experiences of the war; but their work is an artistically ordered interpretation of human nature as it reveals itself amid circumstances of extraordinary physical and moral stress. Although their productions differ radically, they share the same formal artistic intention, that of relating the experience of modern warfare to the values implicit in the general range of human experience.

Herbert Read was born in a remote rural area of Yorkshire, near Kirbymoorside, in 1893. He was the son of a farmer and spent his most impressionable years absorbing the sights, sounds, and rhythms of the Yorkshire countryside. This happy period—sensitively recorded in The Innocent Eye[1]—was terminated in 1903 by the death of his father; the farm was sold and the family dispersed. After five years in a Halifax boarding school, Read was forced to earn his living as a bank clerk in Leeds. Although his ambitions at this time were rather vague, he was determined to continue his education. He therefore enrolled at the University of Leeds when he was eighteen, ostensibly to study law but actually looking forward to a literary career of some kind. The war intervened, however, and as a consequence of his membership in the Officers' Training Corps at Leeds, he received his commission in January 1915. In the course of his three years' service in France with the Yorkshire Regiment he was promoted to captain and won both the Military Cross and the badge of the Distinguished Service Order. Read returned to England in May 1918, after the Somme retreat, and was demobilized in January 1919. Although his subsequent activities as teacher, editor, critic, and aesthetician have earned him an eminence in modern art and letters, our concern here is naturally limited to his early poetic theory and practice.

It was not until he was about to enter the University of Leeds that Read discovered the realm of poetry. As he states in The Innocent Eye, his early admirations centered successively around Tennyson, Blake, Ralph Hodgson, Donne, Browning, and—most importantly—the Imagists. His first compositions, written between 1910 and 1915, show the influence of Blake, Hodgson, and Yeats; they appeared in June 1915 as Songs of Chaos. Read's

[1] London, 1933.

first war poems were written in 1915, within a few weeks of his arrival in France. During 1915-1916 a number of these, together with some prose pieces, were printed in the *Gryphon*, the students' magazine at Leeds. By this time he had thoroughly absorbed the doctrines of the Imagists, who were opposed to the neo-romantic manner and the "vague generalities" of the Georgians. Read's impression of the winter landscape at Ypres is objective, concentrated, "hard and clear":

> With a chill and hazy light
> the sun of a winter noon
> swills
> thy ruins.
>
> Thy ruins etched
> in silver silhouettes
> against a turquoise sky.
>
> Lank poles leap to the infinite,
> their broken wires
> tossed like the rat-locks of Maenades.
>
> And Desolation broods over all,
> gathering to her lap
> her leprous children.
>
> The sparrows whimper
> amid the broken arches.

Emotionalism and sentiment are rigidly excluded here; the pictorial effect of desolation strikes the reader as it originally struck the observer, who has selected and organized his details—his images—with that single effect in mind. We have a reduction of the scene to its essential pictorial elements rather than the expansion of a personal reaction. The impression, however, is obviously limited by its visual simplicity and verbal brevity. Although a certain clarity of outline is achieved by the elimination of subjective elements, the poet is still working within the physical and psychological confines of the lyric mode and does not seek to present his subject in terms more comprehensive than those of the visualization itself.

Read's participation in the Imagist protest against outworn nineteenth-century poetic attitudes and techniques is nevertheless quite important. With precocious critical intelligence Sorley had discerned the hollowness of contemporary verse; Rosenberg had also demonstrated his independence of the fashionable Georgian manner. As a young poet Read, too, had found that manner completely out of touch with the realities of the twentieth century. In 1939 he thus summarized the conditions which led to the emergence of Imagism: "We were in revolt, just before the War, against certain tame conventions which Hopkins (though we did not then know it) had described as Parnassian—a poeticism, or poetry derived from poetry, which Bridges represented at its best, Alfred Noyes at its worst. Masefield had tried to break through this literary stuffiness with a violence which was merely of words, not of essence or attitude; and the Georgians, with Rupert Brooke and Lascelles Abercrombie at their head, had only given a fresh coat of paint to the creaking Pegasus."[2]

The new movement proposed "the eternal aesthetic ideal—an ideal of form, indifferent to the nature of the subject-matter." This ideal was to be achieved through the practice of a well-defined doctrine: "What was aimed at, by means of precision of expression and vitality of image, was above all an aesthetic entity—a poem, that is to say, which had a clear crystalline objectivity, due to sincerity of feeling, exactness of expression, and the consequent virtues of precision, economy and vividness."[3] Since the "aesthetic entity" was "indifferent to the nature

[2] "The Present State of Poetry," *Kenyon Review*, I, 4 (Autumn 1939), 359.
[3] *Ibid.*, p. 360.

of the subject-matter," any kind of experience, theoretically, could be accommodated by it:

"The War came, but that did not make any essential difference to our poetry. I myself wrote imagist poems in the trenches, and did not see or feel any inconsistency in the act. War was one thing, and poetry was another; and if war was to be expressed in poetry, the imagist technique was as adequate as any other."[4]

Six of the Imagist poems that Read composed in the trenches are printed under the title of "The Scene of War" in his *Collected Poems*.[5] "Villages Démolis," "The Crucifix," and "The Refugees" depict, without superfluous comment, the destruction and disruption of war; like the previously quoted impression of Ypres, they depend upon an economical selection of vivid pictorial elements which evoke their own response in the reader. The objectivity of "Villages Démolis" illustrates how far the Imagist doctrine was removed from the attitudes and techniques of Brooke's introspective sonnets:

> The villages are strewn
> In red and yellow heaps of rubble:
>
> Here and there
> Interior walls
> Lie upturned and interrogate the skies amazedly.
>
> Walls that once held
> Within their cubic confines
> A soul that now lies strewn
> In red and yellow
> Heaps of rubble.

[4] *Ibid.*
[5] Norfolk, Conn., 1951. Previous collections were published in 1926 and 1935.

The three remaining poems of "The Scene of War" are not, however, so successful, perhaps because they deal with material that is not amenable to the Imagist treatment. Despite Read's claim regarding the indifference of the Imagist ideal to subject-matter, there were clearly areas of inner experience that the Imagist technique could not easily penetrate. Both "Fear" and "The Happy Warrior" attempt to portray the psychological effects of warfare, but both amount to little more than abbreviated notations. In "The Happy Warrior" the realistic and satiric impulse is not much different from Sassoon's; it has merely been compressed to conform to the Imagist principle of verbal economy:

> His wild heart beats with painful sobs,
> His strain'd hands clench an ice-cold rifle,
> His aching jaws grip a hot parch'd tongue,
> His wide eyes search unconsciously.
>
> He cannot shriek.
>
> Bloody saliva
> Dribbles down his shapeless jacket.
>
> I saw him stab
> And stab again
> A well-killed Boche.
>
> This is the happy warrior,
> This is he. . . .

The principle of economy has likewise arbitrarily reduced the narrative of "Liedholz" to little more than a series of laconic observations:

> We met in the night at half-past one,
> Between the lines.

257

Liedholz shot at me
And I at him;
And in the ensuing tumult he surrendered
    to me.

. . . .

In broken French we discussed
Beethoven, Nietzsche and the International.

He was a professor
Living at Spandau;
And not too intelligible.

The dimensions of this incident are much more fully evoked in *Ambush*, a brief prose narrative reprinted under the title of "The Raid" in the enlarged edition of *The Innocent Eye*.[6] However, the Imagist principle of detachment in "Liedholz" entailed no shift from subjective to objective emphasis such as we have discerned in Sassoon's prose account of his Hindenburg tunnel experience or in Blunden's prose version of the pillbox episode described in "Third Ypres."

Although he was applying a theory that seemed to eliminate some of the more objectionable characteristics of "poeticism," Read began to find himself at variance with the Imagist creed as early as 1916. Toward the end of that year the *Gryphon* printed two poems that show how much he had been disillusioned by the failure of the Somme Offensive. Both poems were titled "Truth for a Change"; one of them (reproduced in *The Innocent Eye*) advances a concept of "truth" that is obviously contrary to the Imagist ideal:

Such a lad as Harry was
Isn't met with every day.
He walked the land like a god,

[6] New York, 1947.

Exulting in energy,
Care-free,
His eyes a blue smile
Beneath his yellow curling locks;
And you'd wonder where a common
    laborer got
Those deep Rossetti lips
And finely carven nose. . . .
I saw him stretch his arms
Languid as a dozing panther,
His face full to the clean sky—
When a blasted sniper laid him low:
He fell limp on the muddy boards
And left us all blaspheming.

The peculiar awkwardness of this poem is due to the fact that Read was attempting to combine the Imagist principles of detachment and economy with the motives of curative realism. Unlike Owen, whose poetry embodies an organic relationship between theme and the elements of form, Read could not resolve the opposition between an emotionally experienced truth and the theoretically established demands of formal expression. An "aesthetic entity" that emphasized purely formal relationships could not effectively present the cruder aspects of the war, especially when the revelation of those aspects was motivated by anger and disillusionment.

By early 1918, conscious of the shortcomings of Imagist theory and practice, Read had formulated his own somewhat more generalized ideal of poetic art. In an essay entitled "Definitions towards a Modern Theory of Poetry,"[7] he set forth his axioms with respect to the primacy of emotion over external formal elements. He also attacked the Imagists for their "decorative"

[7] Published in *Art and Letters*, I, 3 (January 1918). This quarterly, founded by Read and Frank Rutter, was issued somewhat irregularly between July 1917 and the spring of 1920.

tendencies and their carelessness in the matter of "aesthetic selection."

Commenting upon this early essay in *The Innocent Eye*, Read remarks: "I can look back with amusement on its earnest solemnity now, but I think it reflects something of the contradiction that was being forced on us by our daily experience. We were trying to maintain an abstract aesthetic ideal in the midst of terrorful and inhuman events. In my own case I am certain that this devotion to abstract notions and intellectual reveries saved me from a raw reaction to these events. But as the war went on, year after year, and there seemed no escape from its indignity except death, some compromise between dream and reality became necessary. The only worthy compromise, I even then dimly realized, was a synthesis—some higher reality in which the freedom of the mind and the necessity of experience became reconciled. If I had been older that solution might have been a philosophy; but I was not contemplative enough for that, nor wise enough. I therefore sought the solution in art: in a poetry which would represent my aesthetic ideals and yet at the same time deal with the experience that threatened to overwhelm me. The result was a series of war poems, some of which I afterwards destroyed, but most of which I published in a small volume to which I gave the title *Naked Warriors*."[8]

Thus it was Read's general preoccupation with aesthetic theory as well as the practice of the Imagist technique itself that kept his verse free from the characteristics that marked the personal response. Although it was at first adequate for a detached representation of pictorial elements, the Imagist technique—as Read's own efforts demonstrate—proved that it could not cope satisfactorily with the elements of inner experience. Some kind of compromise had to be effected between the opposed requirements of the purely intellectual and the purely

[8] *The Innocent Eye*, pp. 102-103. (This and the following references are to the 1947 edition.)

experiential; the demands of the one had to be reconciled with the demands of the other. Both Sassoon and Rosenberg, it will be recalled, indicated their growing consciousness that some degree of intellectual remoteness, some principle of formal control, was necessary for the poetic representation of experience; but Read was the only poet to work out some practical solution to the problem on critical and theoretical grounds. The longer poems of *Naked Warriors* are, therefore, the result of Read's dissatisfaction with the ordinary lyric form as well as with the more disciplined Imagist technique; they embody a deliberate effort to organize and expand the inner experience of warfare.

On the title-page of *Naked Warriors* is an epigraph that suggests Read's sense of man's physical and spiritual vulnerability to the violence of modern warfare: "And there were some that went into the battle naked and unarmed, fighting only with the fervor of their spirit, dying and getting many wounds." It was a general sense of vulnerability that developed the fraternal bond among soldiers who became keenly aware of their common destiny of suffering and death; like Owen, they found the "greater love" a source of strength, the only positive to prevail over the law of violence. In "My Company" Read deals with this familiar theme as a leader who has been gradually drawn into the corporate life of his unit:

> In many acts and quiet observances
> You absorbed me:
> Until one day I stood eminent
> And I saw you gather'd round me,
> Uplooking,
> And about you a radiance that seemed to beat
> With variant glow and to give
> Grace to our unity.

Later, amid the scenes of battle, there is a curious but quite natural rejection of this identification with his men and his involvement in their fate:

> I can assume
> A giant attitude and godlike mood,
> And then detachedly regard
> All riots, conflicts and collisions.
>
> The men I've lived with
> Lurch suddenly into a far perspective;
> They distantly gather like a dark cloud of birds
> In the autumn sky.

His original feeling reasserts itself, however, and he submits to the bond of love and the self-sacrifice that it entails:

> Then again I assume
> My human docility,
> Bow my head
> And share their doom.

Many other soldier poets wrote of the fraternal bond, but Read probed more deeply into the nature of that bond by exploring the conflict between the sense of individuality and the demands of a corporate existence which would inevitably consume that individuality. "My Company" is thus an attempt to define a subtle and significant relationship which most poets were content to depict in terms of its external emotional manifestations. Unlike Owen, who characteristically deals with the bond of love as a spiritual principle that summons up a host of ironic parallels and contrasts, Read just as characteristically analyzes love as a psychological principle and the source of an acute inner division.

Both "The Execution of Cornelius Vane" and "Kneeshaw Goes to War" are narratives that deal with the effect of war on the lives of individual soldiers. The emphasis, however, is not on the dramatic representation of external events but on the

revelation of character and attitude. The individual consciousness, instead of being utilized as a means for the communication
of an external reality, is itself the subject of careful analysis.
Cornelius Vane is a shirker who cannot understand why he is
being shot for cowardice; in his flight from the battle line he
instinctively rejoices in the mild warmth and beauty of spring,
but he is unable to comprehend the imperatives of a conflict
from which he just as instinctively recoils:

> The sentence duly confirmed,
> One morning at dawn they led him forth.
> He saw a party of his own regiment,
> With rifles, looking very sad.
> The morning was bright, and as they tied
> The cloth over his eyes, he said to the assembly:
> "What wrong have I done that I should leave these:
> The bright sun rising
> And the birds that sing?"

Cornelius Vane is of course no hero, but his cowardice is not
presented as totally despicable. In a war of unprecedented violence, representing the conflict of abstract ideological and economic interests, the absence of positive heroic virtues cannot be
categorically condemned. Like "Liedholz," the poem is sometimes so devoid of imaginative depth that its lines have a decidedly pedestrian effect: "For nearly a year Cornelius peeled
potatoes/ And his life was full of serenity." If "The Execution
of Cornelius Vane" is a plea for tolerance in the matter of
cowardice, the subject did not, or could not, evoke a fully
realized and compelling poetic form. Like Sassoon's and Owen's
soldier-suicides, Vane is a pitiable figure, but his death does not
arouse pity because Read appeals to the reader's understanding
rather than to his emotions.

"Kneeshaw Goes to War" is more successful in its depiction of
a character whose passivity forever bars him from a participation

in any meaningful human action.[9] Like his more sophisticated contemporary, J. Alfred Prufrock, Ernest Kneeshaw confronts the world without joy and without any real hope; even the urgings of sex cannot force him out of his dream-constricted self:

> Ernest Kneeshaw grew
> In the forest of his dreams
> Like a woodland flower whose anaemic petals
> Need the sun.
>
> Life was a far perspective
> Of high black columns
> Flanking, arching and encircling him.
> He never, even vaguely, tried to pierce
> The gloom about him,
> But was content to contemplate
> His finger-nails and wrinkled boots.

As a soldier en route to the scene of war Kneeshaw has some intimation of the potentialities of life and action when he views the forest of masts in the harbor of Boulogne:

> This forest was congregated
> From various climates and strange seas:
> Hadn't each ship some separate memory
> Of sunlit scenes or arduous waters?
> Didn't each bring in the high glamour
> Of conquering force?
> Wasn't the forest-gloom of their assembly
> A body built of living cells,
> Of personalities and experiences
> —A witness of heroism
> Co-existent with man?

[9] In his philosophical romance, *The Green Child* (London, 1935), Read introduces another Kneeshaw as the brutal antagonist of Olivero and the Green Child.

This image of coherent forces and purposeful destinies unified to one great end becomes a symbol of spiritual freedom, of release from passivity and despair:

> And that dark forest of his youth—
> Couldn't he liberate the black columns
> Flanking, arching, encircling him with dread?
> Couldn't he let them spread from his vision
>   like a fleet
> Taking the open sea,
> Disintegrating into light and colour and the
>   fragrance of winds?

These, however, are only romantic musings which emphasize the pathetic limitations of Kneeshaw's character. Later, after a series of demoralizing battle experiences, Kneeshaw is struck by a shell; he loses a leg and is sent back to England. There, haunted by loneliness and fear, he meditates on his failure to accept the challenge of life. Even Judas was animated by a rational purpose in his betrayal of Christ; but Kneeshaw succumbed to an ignoble passivity, the moral implications of which have now been revealed by the war:

> The forest gloom breaks:
> The wild black masts
> Seaward sweep on adventurous ways:
> I grip my crutches and keep
> A lonely view.
>
> I stand on this hill and accept
> The pleasure my flesh dictates
> I count not kisses nor take
> Too serious a view of tobacco.
>
> Judas no doubt was right
> In a mental sort of way:

> For he betrayed another and so
> With purpose was self-justified.
> But I delivered my body to fear—
> I was a bloodier fool than he.

Like Cornelius Vane, he is content to live on a purely instinctive level; but at the end he at least understands that, although human actions cannot be judged dogmatically, a man must shape his life around an irreducible moral law:

> I stand on this hill and accept
> The flowers at my feet and the deep
> Beauty of the still tarn;
> Chance that gave me a crutch and a view
> Gave me these.

> The soul is not a dogmatic affair
> Like manliness, colour, and light;
> But these essentials there be:
> To speak truth and so rule oneself
> That other folk may rede.

In the narrative sections of the poem Read provides an account of Kneeshaw's experiences in the front lines; the violence of war is, of course, a crucial element in his process of self-discovery. Although these experiences are detailed enough to afford a convincing background for that process, they do not assume a disproportionate value nor do they reflect any separate and narrowly corrective intent. The war is not envisioned as a self-contained totality (as it is, for instance, in Owen's "Apologia pro Poemate Meo") but as a climactic phase in the revelation of character; Kneeshaw's "exposure" to suffering evokes understanding on the moral and psychological level rather than compassion on the experiential level. Other poets often used their characters merely as media for the communication of limited states of consciousness—shock, anger, grief, misery, despair; Read, however, deals with these effects as they operate on previously existing traits and attitudes. By employing a longer narrative form and a detached, impersonal technique, he succeeded in avoiding the experiential bias inherent in the limited personal response and established a fuller, more flexible pattern for utilizing the more significant experiences of war.

Both "The Execution of Cornelius Vane" and "Kneeshaw Goes to War" were written while the conflict was still in progress. How these productions stand in the evolution of Read's poetic practice is indicated in *The Innocent Eye*: ". . . I think I may say that by the end of the war I had discovered myself and my style—that is to say, I had made an equation between emotion and image, between feeling and expression. So long as I was true to this equation, I need not be afraid of influences or acquired mannerisms. Poetry was reduced to an instrument of precision."[10]

Such an equation, of course, is in danger of remaining only an equation; and one feels that the aesthetic theorizing that saved Read from a "raw reaction" to the war also inhibited an adequate realization of the sensuous levels of experience. If other war poets weighted the equation too heavily in favor of feeling and emotion, Read stressed the formal, intellectual element to such a degree that the simple sensuous content is virtually excluded. Nevertheless, the fact that he felt it necessary to work out such an equation again demonstrates the existence of a problem that troubled nearly every war poet: how could the profound and bitter truths of a new range of human experience be objectified in a form that would encompass the universal as well as the particular aspects of those truths? Read clarifies the problem, but he does not really solve it because his equation is a principle of division and exclusion rather than one of organic wholeness.

[10] *The Innocent Eye*, p. 105.

When the surviving wartime poets sought to re-create their experiences, they turned to the prose narrative as if to fill in the temporal and physical context of the limited personal response. It is perhaps significant, in view of the detached and impersonal nature of his wartime poetry, that Read has left no detailed record of his life as a soldier; his verse needed no expansive prose supplement because it was motivated by an impersonal ideal of form rather than by the pressures and extremities of battle experience. Although he narrates two brief battle episodes in *In Retreat* (1925) and *Ambush* (1930), these are carefully controlled prose distillations with little autobiographical significance. Like the earlier poems of character analysis, *The End of a War* does not grow out of personal experience, nor does it deal directly with battle. Taking an isolated factual incident as the basis for his poem, Read sought to reveal the deeper spiritual attitudes that operated as motives and forces beneath the familiar external events of the conflict. In so doing he follows even more rigorously the "equation" responsible for the effects of order and control in his earlier poems. *The End of a War*, consequently, is an abstract rather than a mere transcript of experience; economy, precision, and control are exercised in an effort that is primarily intellectual and definitive.

Although it is predicated upon a series of violent actions, *The End of a War* is not a narrative poem; the central incident is summarized in an Argument. On November 10, 1918, an officer of a British battalion, a Lieutenant S—, is informed by a wounded German officer that the village the British infantrymen are approaching is undefended. When the battalion halts in the *place*, however, several machine guns open fire from the church tower and other points; a hundred men are killed or wounded. The survivors quickly bayonet the hidden gunners, and a corporal runs back to deal with the German officer who had tricked them. The officer meets his fate impassively. Later, the British find the dismembered body of a young girl who had been violated and tortured by the Germans. Lieutenant S—, sick and weary of the day's events, seeks relief in slumber. He awakens in the morning to the sound of bells announcing the Armistice.

The three characters who are most importantly involved in these events—the German officer, the murdered French girl, and the English officer—provide the poem with its three parts: "Meditation of the Dying German Officer," "Dialogue between the Body and the Soul," and "Meditation of the Waking English Officer." Each character voices a distinct attitude toward the war, and each attitude in turn reveals contrasting spiritual beliefs. Thus Read deliberately avoids any contact with the external incident; as he announces in a postscript to the poem, his interest lies in an objective presentation of the reality behind the violence: "It was necessary for my poetic purpose to take an incident from the War of 1914-1918 which would serve as a focus for feelings and sentiments otherwise diffuse. The incident is true, and can be vouched for by several witnesses still living. But its horrors do not accuse any particular nation; they are representative of war and of human nature in War. It is not my business as a poet to condemn war (or, to be more exact, modern warfare). I only wish to present the universal aspects of a particular event. Judgment may follow, but should never precede or become embroiled with the act of poetry. . . ."

Thus by implication Read speaks out against the main tendencies of World War I poetry, which found its most powerful motive in the condemnation of modern warfare and its most common technique in the emphasis upon particular rather than upon universal aspects. In a sense, *The End of a War* was designed to say all that had been left unsaid by other poets. Certainly no other war poet ventured so far into what Read called the "higher reality" that lay beyond the confused phenomena that assaulted the mind and the senses.

The first part of the poem, "Meditation of the Dying German Officer," reveals the philosophy of a man who has placed all his faith in action. In betraying the British battalion at the cost of his own life, he has followed the only imperative he knows: fanatic loyalty to Emperor, Flag, and Empire. His life as a soldier has been animated by the political ideal of calling all Europe to "one life, one order and one living." For him the war has been no catastrophe but a daring enterprise justified by a mystic concept of German supremacy:

> For that dream I've given my life and to the last
> fought its listless enemies. Now Chaos intervenes
> and I leave not gladly but with harsh disdain
> a world too strong in folly for the bliss of dreams.
>
> I fought with gladness. When others cursed the day
> this stress was loosed
> and men were driven into camps, to follow
> with wonder, woe, or base delirium
> the voiceless yet incessant surge
> then I exulted . . .
>
>   The first week
> I crossed the Fatherland, to take my place
> in the swift-wing'd swoop that all but ended
> the assay in one wild and agile venture.
> I was blooded then, but the wound
> seared in the burning circlet of my spirit
> served only to temper courage
> with scorn of action's outcome.
> Blooded but not beaten I left the ranks
> to be a leader. Four years
> I have lived in the ecstasy of battle.
> The throbbing of guns, growing yearly,

has been drum music to my ears
the crash of shells the thrill of cymbals
bayonet fiddlers' bows and the crack of rifles
plucked harp strings. Now the silence
is unholy.

Woven through these thoughts are deeper speculations about
faith and belief, about the meaning of life and death. Unlike
his Christian friend Heinrich, the German officer is a non-
believer; for him, death is simply an absorption into the Unknown. He dismisses the Christian God as a cold abstraction,
an inert essence that fades with the dying mind. His faith grows
out of a nationalist *mystique*, an idealistic materialism that
draws its strength from an affirmation and not a denial of self:

Faith in self comes first, from self we build
the web of friendship, from friends to confederates
and so to the State. This web has a weft
in the land we live in, a town, a hill
all that the living eyes traverse. There are lights
given by the tongue we speak, the songs we sing,
the music and the magic of our Fatherland.
This is a tangible trust. To make it secure
against the tempests of inferior minds
to build it in our blood, to make our lives
a tribute to its beauty—there is no higher aim.
This good achieved, then to God we turn
for a crown on our perfection: God we create
in the end of action, not in dreams.

As a fatalist, the officer calmly submits to his extinction. The
body is to become a clod, but the "rare ethereal glimmer of
mind's own intensity" will momentarily survive before it too
is extinguished "in the darkest void of Nothing." That "last
light" breaks

with a sigh
against the ultimate
shores of this world
so finite
so small
Nichts

Thus the final impression of finiteness and nothingness accords
with the officer's spiritually negative philosophy. His purposeful-
ness and strength are derived from materialistic values; when
he is deprived of life and the opportunity for action, there is,
literally, nothingness.

The second part of the poem, "Dialogue between the Body
and the Soul of the Murdered Girl," discloses the story behind
the atrocity discovered in the village. We learn that the French
girl was slain for spying on the Germans; like the German
officer, she sacrificed her life for her country. The officer was
motivated by grandiose political ideals and his duty as a soldier,
but the French girl acted out of a simple love of her native
land. Her death, in fact, has the aspect of martyrdom, since
the Body proclaims Christ as the source of its strength and
assures the Soul of its eventual salvation. The Soul, however,
cautions against pride and presumption in this respect; the
consciousness of a positive patriotic or religious faith is not
a prerequisite for the crown of martyrdom:

A bright mantle fell across your bleeding limbs.
Your face averted shone with sacred fire.
So be content. In this war
many men have perished not bless'd
with faith in a cause, a country or a God
not less martyrs than Herod's Victims, Ursula's Virgins
or any mass'd innocents massacred.

The Body, secure in its blessing of faith and in its consciousness
of justified sacrifice, refuses to admit that men who die without

belief in a cause deserve to be called martyrs; their deaths are darkened with bitterness and resignation: "Such men give themselves not to their God but to their fate/ die thinking the face of God not love but hate." The Soul, however, reveals the danger of such a narrow judgment by implying that faith itself may be subject to the delusions of pride: "Those who die for a cause die comforted and coy;/ believing their cause God's cause they die with joy." Thus the dialogue, which has developed harmoniously up to these final exchanges, ends on an ambivalent note that suggests the depth and complexity of the whole problem of belief as it is brought to a test amid the extraordinary conditions of war.

In the third and final section of the poem, "Meditation of the Waking English Officer," Lieutenant S— is roused from sleep by church bells and the voices of peasants chanting a litany of thanksgiving. It is the morning of November 11; the war is over. Hardly able to believe the fact of his survival, the officer begins to reflect upon the events of the previous day and upon the conflict in general:

> First there are the dead to bury
> O God, the dead. How can God's bell
> ring out from that unholy ambush?
> That tower of death! In excess of horror
> war died. The nerve was broken
> fray'd men fought obscenely then: there was no fair
>   joy
> no glory in the strife, no blessed wrath.
> Man's mind cannot excel
> mechanic might except in savage sin.
> Our broken bodies oiled the engines: mind was grit.

His meditation thereupon turns to the implications of his own motives, or lack of motives, as a soldier. He at once dissociates himself from the attitude of the pacifist:

273

Shall I regret my pact? Envy that friend
who risked ignominy, insult, gaol
rather than stain his hands with human blood?
And left his fellow men. Such lonely pride
was never mine. I answered no call
there was no call to answer. I felt no hate
only the anguish of an unknown fate . . .

.   .   .   .

Listless
I felt the storm about me; its force
too strong to beat against; in its swirl
I spread my sapling arms, toss'd on its swell
I rose, I ran, I down the dark world sped
till death fell round me like a rain of steel
and hope and faith and love coiled in my inmost
    cell.

Thus, unlike his German counterpart, the English officer has
participated in the war without any positive convictions. At
first, it is true, he "vowed devotion to the rights of man" and
determined to "fight for peace once it came again," but in the
stress of war this vague idealism had turned to bitterness. Indeed,
his "life's inconstant drift" has forced him to question such
basic spiritual doctrines as the uniqueness and immateriality
of the individual soul:

God not real, hate not real, the hearts of men
insentient engines pumping blood
into a spongy mass that cannot move
above the indignity of inflicted death:
the only answer this: the infinite is all
and I, a finite speck, no essence even
of the life that falls like dew
from the spirit breathed on the fine edge
of matter, perhaps only that edge

274

a ridge between eternal death and life eternal,
a moment of time, temporal.

If the individual human life is viewed merely as a finite moment
in a sea of infinity, there can be no God, no self, and no soul;
men are subject to the vast physical forces that govern the
universe. Any appeal to a paternal God is therefore useless.
Fact, fate, and chance determine all:

> Where all must be, there is no God
> for God can only be the God of prayer
> an infinitely kind Father whose will
> can mould the world, who can
> in answer to my prayer, mould me.
> But whilst I cannot pray, I can't believe
> but in this frame of machine necessity
> must renounce not only God, but self.
> For what is the self without God?
> A moment not reckoned in the infinite.

Thus the Englishman has been brought to a position that resembles the spiritual negativism of the German. But if there
is no self, no God, and no meaning to the life of man, how
is it that the German, who was full of "power and pride,"
lies defeated? Though possessing no "visionary purpose" of
their own, the meek have triumphed. This paradox leads to the
crux of the spiritual problem:

> Now I see, either the world is mechanic force
> and this the last tragic act, portending
> endless hate and blind reversion
> back to the tents and healthy lusts
> of animal men: or we act
> God's purpose in an obscure way.

Although he does not have the simple faith of the French girl,
the Englishman cannot accept the negativism implicit in the

philosophy of the German. Now that he has survived the war, he must seek a tentative premise upon which to order his life. He must believe that the war served some higher purpose, that it was "a fire to burn our dross." He must believe that man's destiny does not lead backward to savagery but forward to some "inconceived span":

> To that end worship God, join the voices
> heard by these waking ears. God is love:
> in his will the meek heart rejoices
> doubting till the final grace a dove
> from Heaven descends and wakes the mind
> in light above the light of human kind
> in light celestial
> infinite and still
> eternal
> bright

The German officer's reverie ended in death and in the anticipation of nothingness after death; the English officer, however, "wakes" to the possibilities of faith and is willing to live in the hope that a "final grace" may justify his choice between the alternatives of "mechanic force" and divine love. With that hope he joins the litany of the peasants.

In form and technique *The End of a War* is suited admirably to its analytical purpose. The three-part division corresponds to the paradoxically intimate relationship among the three characters (slayer, slain, and avenger) as well as to the contrasting spiritual attitudes they represent. The soliloquies of the slayer and the avenger—one greeting death, the other life—are balanced by the dialogue between the body and soul of the slain, which reveals, through its dialectical form, a new dimension to the problem of faith and motive. Read emphasizes in his postscript that the act of judgment "should never precede or become embroiled with the act of poetry." Hence the three-part structure is meant to effect a significant juxtaposition rather than a dramatic unity. Out of the partitioned complexities of motive, attitude, and feeling, the reader must create his own unity and formulate his own judgment. He is poised between the reality from which the poet has abstracted his material and the expanding implications of the "higher reality."

Read's purpose is reflected in his use of language and imagery as well as in the dialectical mode of his development. Though the metrical and stanzaic pattern is irregular and the verse occasionally has the fluency of natural speech rhythms ("Life ebbs with an easy flow/ and I've no anguish now"), the general poetic effect is one of heightened exposition. Read does not eschew the sensuous image ("When the last jump comes/ and the axe-head blackness slips through flesh"), but for the most part his figures condense rather than expand his meaning. In Wilfred Owen's "Strange Meeting" the texture of imagery is one with the texture of meaning; Read, however, employs the image to summarize an idea that is part of a larger expository texture:

> The universe swaying between Nothing and Being
> and life faltering like a clock's tick
> between a pendulum's coming and going.

A degree of prosaic formality is almost inevitable in verse devoted to the unfolding of ideas and attitudes, and Read has not entirely escaped this effect.[11] Yet the language of his poem has a meditative quality which, in the first part, sounds somberly in "the empty silence of retreating life." Similarly, in the third part, the spontaneous joy of the English officer is aroused and accompanied by the "litany/ of simple voices and the jubilant

[11] Nor has he escaped the penalty of trying to avoid it. The worst lines in the poem—"The bells of hell ring ting-a-ling/for you but not for me. . . ." (Part III)—are derived from the opening of an old Salvation Army song. The echo is stylistically incongruous and devoid of poetic resonance.

bell"; this joy is gradually modulated into the calm hope expressed in the final lines. The interchange between the body and soul of the murdered girl—presented not as a progressive meditation but as a rapid sequence of claims and counter-claims —reflects a fundamental opposition that is significantly suspended in the two final couplets. Read combines lyric, narrative, dramatic, and expository elements in a verbal medium that is flexible and resonant enough to accommodate itself to each mode of development.

The End of a War deals with a level of reality that the poets who wrote between 1914-1918 could not easily explore. They were much too deeply involved in the particular aspects of the conflict to contemplate abstract problems of value and belief; their whole inspiration was necessarily bound up with more urgent issues. Read, of course, benefits by his distance from the event, by the aesthetic "equation" developed in his own wartime verse, and by the essentially critical and philosophical temper of his mind. Of the verse written between 1914-1918, perhaps Owen's "Strange Meeting" comes closest to the high meditative quality of *The End of a War*. Both poems rise above the flux of experience to unfold a particular wisdom; both poems invoke positive values that are opposed to the regressive tendencies of war. Unlike the contrasting characters of *The End of a War*, however, the Englishman and the German of "Strange Meeting" are reconciled by the bond of love. Since they are grounded in individualized attitudes, the subtle tensions of *The End of a War* permit no such reconciliation. Owen attempts an emotional and intuitive synthesis, Read a rational analysis of motive. The complexities of human nature, he implies, do not favor any easy resolution of the fundamental spiritual oppositions that war so dramatically reveals.

It has been pointed out before that Read, in treating the "higher reality" of war, seems to neglect the lower but indispensable reality of sensuous experience. The extent to which he has separated these two complementary realities is indicated by the fact that the narrative elements of *The End of a War* are presented in a prefatory note. The poem cannot be comprehended without a knowledge of the external incidents upon which it is based; the prose summary, though complete in itself, is slight in substance and development. This separation of narrative elements from the analysis of character and motive simplifies the poet's task, of course; he is free of the manifold artistic problems which any sequence of violent events must present. These problems, however, are avoided rather than solved. The emphasis is simply transferred from the level of sensuous experience to the higher level of motive and belief. *The End of a War* is no doubt a remarkable poem, but an arbitrary separation of the realities involved produces only a limited realization of their combined artistic potentialities. If Shakespeare had prefixed a brief prose summary of *Hamlet* to the most important soliloquies, the result would have been poetry of a high order, but the dramatic dimensions of the play would have been lost. This analogy may suggest how far *The End of a War* fails to measure up to its external dramatic potentialities. Read's poetic "equation" between formal and emotional elements eventually produced an "instrument of precision" that severed rather than joined the two realities of inner and outer experience.

It is interesting to contrast the level of Read's short prose narrative, *In Retreat*, to the level of *The End of a War*. The prose narrative is a sensitive yet factual first-person account, "A Journal of the Retreat of the Fifth Army from St. Quentin, March, 1918." Although *In Retreat* is externally concerned with the sequence of emergency measures necessitated by a rapid military withdrawal, Read's participation unifies the story and heightens it with the drama of personal experience. We thus have a narrative dimension of carefully blended objective and subjective elements. Sometimes the story is told through a series of tense military dispatches; sometimes the sense of crisis is more intimately communicated through images that vividly suggest the quality of inner experience:

"The gradual accumulation of our anxiety should be realized. Every minute seemed to add to its intensity. By ten o'clock or so, our hearts were like taut drum skins beaten reverberantly by every little incident.

"Then the skin smashed. Bodily action flickered like flame, the sense of duration was consumed away."[12]

The combination of objective and subjective elements is clearly revealed in the final paragraph, wherein the author touches upon the personal and heroic aspects of the whole episode:

"When evening came and the hills of Moreuil were faint in the twilight, we were still traveling along the western road. No guns nor any clamor of war could be heard: a great silence filled the cup of misty hills. My weary horse drooped her head as she ambled along, and I, too, was sorrowful. To our northeast lay the squat towers of Amiens, a city in whose defense we had endured hardships until flesh had been defeated, and the brave heart broken. My mind held a vague wonder for her fate—a wonder devoid of hope. I could not believe in the avail of any effort. Then I listened to the rumbling cart, and the quiet voices of the men about me. The first stars were out when we reached Guignemicourt, and there we billeted for the night. In this manner we marched by easy stages down the valley of the Somme, halting finally at Salenelle, a village near Valery, and there we rested four days."[13]

The rhythm and tones of this passage come close to poetry, but it is a poetry different from that of *The End of a War*. The passage is compounded of the same materials that Read excludes from his poem: the sense of action, effort, and physical involve-

[12] *The Innocent Eye*, p. 180.
[13] *Ibid.*, p. 212.

ment—seen here in a compelling summary that embodies a variety of emotional effects. Read has observed that "poetry is creative expression: prose is constructive expression."[14] As a factual, "constructive" prose narrative, *In Retreat* does not go beyond the bounds of action and the inner experience directly related to that action. *The End of a War*, however, isolates what Read regards as a more significant level of wartime experience—a level that can be explored and interpreted only through the medium of the creative imagination. Thus the prose narrative preserves the dramatic continuity of the actual experience, whereas *The End of a War* abstracts, divides, and precipitates the morally significant elements of a complex actuality. The materials of wartime poetry are taken over by prose, and poetry itself moves upward to the level of the "higher reality."

If Yeats excluded Owen's poetry from his *Oxford Book of Modern Verse*, he made a point of mentioning, in his Introduction, that he had included Read's *The End of a War*. Yeats's principles of selection (in this matter, at least) were consistent, for the best work of these two poets represents a culmination of opposed tendencies. Owen was by nature a romantic, although some of his most important poems are developed in terms of the discrepancy between the reality of war and the neo-romantic traditions of his time. For Read, however, the break with these conventions was abrupt and complete; he felt that the attenuated romantic tradition no longer had any vital relationship to what the modern poet—especially the war poet—had to say. The Imagist creed provided a formula and a discipline, but the "higher reality" of war could no more be encompassed by an Imagist poem than it could by a conventional lyric. Hence Read's experiments with the verse narrative, the brief prose narrative, and the philosophical poem. Owen was a practicing

[14] *English Prose Style* (New York, 1952), p. x.

poet rather than an aesthetician; he did not theorize, as far as we know, about the problems that Read attempted to solve. Nevertheless, the contrast between his earlier verse and the best of his later poems indicates a shift in attitude that generally corresponds to the change that is externally visible in Read's poetry. Owen, however, took advantage of this shift in attitude and embodied its tensions and conflicts in his verse; he did not seek a poetic reformation in terms of a doctrine that rejected the techniques to which he had become habituated. Except for his assertion that the "true Poets" should be concerned with the "truth" of war rather than with traditional poetic pursuits, he did not seek to impose arbitrary limitations on the substance of his poetry. Although his careful manuscript revisions indicate that he was increasingly aware of the opposition between this "truth" and the distortions encouraged by the personal response, he did not dissociate himself from the reality of sensuous experience. His last poems—especially "Spring Offensive"—point to the probability that he, like Read, had developed something of an equation between the claims of the intellect and those of sensuous experience. Owen's equation, however, did not emphasize one element at the expense of the other. His soldiers do not represent opposed beliefs or ideologies, nor are they abstracted types; they live and die in a world that is as vividly realized, in its ugliness and pain, as any world of beauty and delight. The calm impersonality of his last poems suggests that Owen was beginning to work out his own conception of the "higher reality" and his own technique for exploring it. Had he survived, he would no doubt have produced, as Sassoon puts it, "poems of sustained grandeur and ample design"— or perhaps a single poem that, within an "ample design," would have particularized the level of sensuous experience that Read somewhat arbitrarily avoids.

With *The End of a War* we have obviously come a long way from the substance of action and achievement that characterizes the heroic narrative. The problems of motive and belief with which Read deals could hardly exist for the epic poet, whose values were simple, clear, and unquestioned. Nor could there be any problems about internal or external realities; heroic motives involved heroic action, and a treatment of the one could not be isolated from a treatment of the other. For the epic poet there could be no compromise with the broad dimensions of physical actuality, no equation imposed on the relations between matter and form. Read approximates the epic technique only in his objective attitude, which is achieved not by a mastery of the physical dimension but by an exclusion of that dimension from his poem. The necessities which prompted this exclusion are visible in the development of World War I verse. The soldier-poets had extended the traditional lyric forms and techniques to their limit; they had also extended the range of lyric perception to new areas of experience—areas which seemed to demand a broader and more objective poetic form. Although Read attempts to provide such a form in *The End of a War*, he goes too far in his reaction against the limitations implicit in the personal response. He excludes not only that response but also the very materials which forced the soldier-poets to revise their conceptions, to readjust their attitudes, to alter their techniques—the materials which were, in fact, demanding a radical expansion rather than a contraction of sensibility.

These considerations provide a background for understanding David Jones's *In Parenthesis*, which unites internal and external realities in a new poetic dimension—a dimension in which the expanded sensibility achieves order and significance within the form of the heroic poem.

CHAPTER VIII · THE HEROIC VISION:
DAVID JONES

AMONG the critics who reviewed *In Parenthesis* when it first appeared in 1937,[1] Herbert Read perhaps came closest to the meaning and the external literary significance of the poem when he remarked that it was "as near a great epic of the war as ever the war generation will reach."[2] We have seen what the war generation produced; and as we look back upon a literary account that is now apparently closed, Read's statement still holds true—even if the term "epic" is extended to certain substantial prose narratives also inspired by the war. In designating *In Parenthesis* as a modern epic, however, Read was not being merely polite or appreciative; he had in mind both the unique qualities of the poem and the special difficulties that afflicted nearly every World War I poet who felt that the struggle afforded themes and materials beyond the range of simple lyric presentation.

Although David Jones is somewhat better known as an artist than he is as a poet, he has lived, even as a water-colorist of some distinction, quietly and in comparative obscurity. His own modesty and reticence have combined with critical neglect to make him certainly the least known of World War I poets. *In Parenthesis* itself, though it is by far the longest single poem about the war, is in no sense a personal record; and we cannot think of using it, as we frequently use the verse of Sassoon and Owen, as an accurate index to the poet's range of experiences and emotions. Although the poem is, among other things, an intimate revelation of inner experience, that inner experience is not offered as a personal account in the guise of fiction

[1] Originally published by Faber and Faber, *In Parenthesis* was republished in the United States by the Chilmark Press in 1962.
[2] "A Malory of the Trenches," *London Mercury*, xxxvi (July 1937), 304-305.

but as a self-subsisting product of the creative imagination. Thus Jones's independence and impersonality contrast markedly with the earlier poets' conception of their work as necessarily expressive of personal emotions and attitudes.

The son of a Flintshire Welshman and an English mother, Jones was born in Brockley, Kent, on November 1, 1895. When he was fourteen his love of drawing and painting had so far outrun his academic interests that he entered the Camberwell School of Art, where he studied until the outbreak of the war. Although he volunteered for service in August 1914, he was rejected because he did not measure up to the required physical standards. He nevertheless became a soldier in January 1915 and spent the next ten months in infantry training. From late 1915 to 1918 he served in France with the Royal Welch Fusiliers (the regiment of Robert Graves and Siegfried Sassoon). Jones's experiences during the early months of the war—from December 1915 to July 1916—have been translated into the materials of *In Parenthesis*. After the war he attended the Westminster Art School from 1919-1921. He also became a pupil of Eric Gill's and was converted to Roman Catholicism—facts important to the outward emphasis on ritual and liturgy in *In Parenthesis*, as well as to the underlying spiritual orientation of the poem.

In the twenties Jones was quite active as a painter and an engraver. He completed a series of wood engravings for such works as *Gulliver's Travels*, the Book of Jonah, and *The Chester Play of The Deluge*; he also produced copper engravings of scenes from *The Ancient Mariner*. This predilection for literary subject-matter is the only indication we have that his tastes and talents were eventually to be turned toward the writing of poetry. Since 1927 he has confined himself largely to water-coloring, and it is in this field that he is best known today. His first publication was *In Parenthesis*, which won the Hawthornden Prize for 1938. In 1952 he published *The Anathemata*, a difficult but richly poetic work which received an award from the National Institute of Arts and Letters. In both his paintings and his verse we have evidence of an extraordinary imagination, delicate, profound, and remarkably allusive in its conceptions. The two stark but symbolic illustrations in *In Parenthesis* (they are parts of larger drawings executed as designs for engravings) demonstrate these qualities in a graphic medium; they also complement the intricate and elliptical verbal medium which the poet has developed as an essential element of his style.

Critics less acute than Herbert Read have been perplexed by the form of *In Parenthesis*, and, indeed, the poem seems to fall among that class of literary productions which elude conventional definitions. Hence some preliminary description of its characteristics may be helpful. *In Parenthesis* is a 40,000-word narrative (about 8,000 words shorter than Stephen Crane's *The Red Badge of Courage*) which is divided into seven parts of varied lengths. Each part follows the stages of a British infantry unit's movement from its depot in England to the great summer battle (obviously the Somme Offensive) which is destined to consume it. The story is told sometimes in prose, sometimes in verse; the fundamental conception—considering the level of sensibility, the texture of the language, and the compressed or elliptical verbal technique—belongs, however, to the realm of poetry rather than to that of prose. The author looks to the ancient Welsh epic poem as well as to the French *chanson de geste* as his models; numerous literary allusions (in the form of titles, epigraphs, and echoes in the text), in addition to other characteristics, make it clear that the author has consciously attempted to write a modern heroic poem. The employment of heroic elements, however, does not exclude a lyric intensity of presentation; indeed, the particular and unique quality of *In Parenthesis* is its blend of intellectualized, impersonal consciousness and immediate, sensuous perception.

The story of *In Parenthesis* is quite simple. There is no formal plot; the narrative progresses, of course, but the substance of the work depends upon a carefully maintained level of poetic awareness rather than upon any complication and resolution of the action. This poetic awareness extends from the simple to the complex, from particulars as evanescent as a gun-flash to the profounder meanings inherent in an act of heroism or the fact of death. Although there are a half-dozen characters whom the author depicts with greater care than the other soldiers in the story, these characters do not act or interact in any extraordinary way. They are, in fact, modes of a shifting consciousness which the author manipulates at will. The narrative moves forward with events: it slows when they slow; it accelerates when they accelerate. External events, rather than the story or the characters, dictate the climax in the final part of the poem. Thus the author employs character and action as media of poetic revelation, as textures upon which a generalized experience of war is projected and interpreted.

The opening scene is an infantry camp in England; the occasion is the battalion parade prior to embarkation for France; the time is early December 1915. In a brief serio-comic prelude that reveals the human element behind the solemn formalities of military ritual, we are introduced to the central characters: Mr. Jenkins, Sergeant Snell, Corporal Quilter, Lance-Corporal Lewis, and Private John Ball, who, more than any other person, is the focus of perception in the poem. Having presented a group of varied personalities, the narrative proceeds. We follow the battalion to France; we move with it from place to place, always closer to the front lines; we finally advance to the trenches under cover of darkness. This series of events concludes on Christmas Day, 1915. The narrative picks up again in early June 1916. We feel the mounting tension as the preparation for the Somme Offensive begins. The final action of the poem deals with the July attack that destroys John Ball's platoon. Ball is wounded but survives; he is, as we learn at the end, "the man who was on the field . . . and who wrote the book."

Thus the story is not extraordinary in any way; dozens of war novels, good and bad, have been put together out of the same material. Yet the whole pattern—preparation, initiation, experience, and a final, purposeful consummation in a time of terrible crisis—is profoundly typical of the common infantryman's experience in the war. Jones tells the story not, however, for itself but for the objective framework of action which he has designed to encompass another, deeper level of sensibility. This objective framework of simple yet significant action was, as we have seen, beyond the powers of the earlier poets; they were too much preoccupied with the sensuous re-creation of the isolated personal experience to be able to unite separate experiences into a meaningful, coherent whole. Having projected an action which follows the pattern of external events, Jones is free to observe and interpret the isolated personal experience; he is also able to integrate it into the action he has initiated.

Of the main characters we really know very little. We are acquainted with one or two facts about John Ball's life as a civilian, but these are introduced by way of contrast to his status as a soldier. With surprisingly few details, however, Jones is able to suggest a whole personality—or rather a whole sensibility. His characters are individuals, but they are distinguished from one another not so much by traits as by degrees of sensibility and insensibility. They live less by what they are and do than by what they see and feel. This may be illustrated by an incident from Part I of the poem. Private Ball, late for parade, unsuccessfully tries to slip into the rear rank:

> . . . Captain Gwynn does not turn or move or give any
> sign.
> Have that man's name taken if you please, Mr. Jenkins.
> Take that man's name, Sergeant Snell.
> Take his name, corporal.

Take his name take his number—charge him—late on parade—the Battalion being paraded for overseas—warn him for Company Office.

Have you got his name Corporal Quilter.

Temporary unpaid Lance-Corporal Aneirin Merddyn Lewis had somewhere in his Welsh depths a remembrance of the nature of man, of how a lance-corporal's stripe is but held vicariously and from on high, is of one texture with an eternal economy. He brings in a manner, baptism, and metaphysical order to the bankruptcy of the occasion.

'o1 Ball is it—there was a man in Bethesda late for the last bloody judgment.

Corporal Quilter on the other hand knew nothing of these things.

(pp. 1-2)

Thus Lewis' crude but sympathetic jibe breaks the impersonal litany of condemnation. The plodding insensibility of Quilter is then contrasted to the humane awareness exhibited by Lewis. Two touches illuminate the characters and attitudes of both men. This method, once established, gradually develops the sensitivity of the reader to the significance of such subtle distinctions.

Jones has occasion to introduce a number of minor characters who are actually little more than names—or, in some cases, not even names. Yet when these characters are made to serve as a focus for some poetic revelation, they are momentarily invested with qualities that make them, despite their anonymity, quite human. For instance, a soldier in a village *estaminet* is depicted dreaming of his Thames-side home:

The man from Rotherhithe sipped very gravely, his abominable beer; sometimes he held his slowly emptying glass to the light; when he replaced it on the marble, he

did so without the faintest audibility. He looked straight-
eyed and levelly; through bunched heads, through the
Sacred Heart, done in wools, through the wall, through the
Traffic Control notice, on the board, outside, opposite;
through all barriers, making as though they are not, all
things foreign and unloved; through all things other and
separate; through all other things to where the mahogany
cornices of *The Paradise*—to the sawdust thinly spread
. . . the turned spirals that support the frosted panes they
call through, half-open, from the other bar, is a good job
o' work. . . . Nat West put that in when they enlarged
the house; he got the wood cheap when they broke up *The
Golden Vanity*—at the Royal Albert, in the cholera year.
. . . Surrey Commercial stevedores call drinks for the
Reykjavik mate . . . she's lying across the water and goes
out tonight . . . she's bound for the Skagerrak with plant
from Ravenhills.

(pp. 112-113)

Thus Jones does something quite different with the common
wartime theme of nostalgia. He enhances his poetry by his
fidelity to human nature; he does not attempt to draw on the
conventionally "poetic" images and emotions of nostalgia. The
man from Rotherhithe is mentioned only two or three times
in the poem; we are strongly conscious, however, of the mood
he momentarily represents. Most of the minor characters of
In Parenthesis are employed, at one time or another, as a
means of revealing a particular mood, attitude, or perception
that enriches the psychological verisimilitude of the poem and
prevents the accumulation of nearly indistinguishable super-
numeraries.

If the story and the characters of *In Parenthesis* are basically
simple, other aspects of the poem are decidedly complex. The

narrative method, for example, is fragmentary and impressionistic, alternating between dramatic and lyrical elements that
represent both objective and subjective realities. A rapid succession of scenes, dialogues, and descriptions carries the story
forward. Through compression, ellipsis, unorthodox punctuation,
and typographical variety the author creates a verbal medium
that corresponds with his flexible narrative technique. Though
Jones's literary allusiveness sometimes impedes the flow of the
story, his narrative progression is seldom obscure, since it is
linked with the progress of objective, external events. Within
this progression are interspersed impressionistic and lyrical elements. Thus the following passage from Part I is a texture of
interwoven dramatic, lyrical, and descriptive visualizations that
are perfectly intelligible despite their discontinuity:

> Some like tight belts and some like loose belts—trussed-
> up pockets—cigarettes in ammunition pouches—rifle-bolts,
> webbing, buckles and rain—gotta light mate—give us a
> match chum. How cold the morning is and blue, and how
> mysterious in cupped hands glow the match-lights of a
> concourse of men, moving so early in the morning.
>
> The body of the high figure in front of the head of the
> column seemed to change his position however so slightly.
> It rains on the transparent talc of his map-case.
>
> The Major's horse rubs noses with the horse of the
> superior officer. Their docked manes brush each, as two
> friends would meet. The dark horse snorts a little for the
> pulling at her bridle rein.
>
> In 'D' Company round the bend of the road in the half-
> light is movement, like a train shunting, when the forward
> coaches buffer the rear coaches back. The halt was unex-
> pected. How heavy and how top-heavy is all this martial
> panoply and how the ground seems to press upward to
> afflict the feet.

The bastard's lost his way already.
Various messages are passed.

(p. 5)

The effect is one of complex sensibility, especially when the narrative point of view is considered. Though the omniscient narrator controls the story and focuses the generalized as well as the individualized consciousness (cf. the daydream of the man from Rotherhithe), Jones, when following the actions and impressions of John Ball, frequently employs the second person. Thus the reader himself is brought a stage closer to the immediate experience of warfare; he shares, in an intimate fashion, the sensations and emotions of the protagonist. In the following passage from Part II the point of view shifts from third-person plural to second person, then to third-person singular, then back to second person. Having reached another stage in their movement to the front lines, the soldiers are descending from a bus:

> They heavily clambered down, in their nostrils an awareness and at all their sense-centres a perceiving of strange new things.
> The full day was clear after the early rain. The great flats, under the vacant sky, spread very far. It was not that the look of the place was unfamiliar to you. It was at one to all appearances with what you knew already. The sodden hedgeless fields—the dykes so full to overflowing to bound these furrows from these, ran narrow glassy demarkations. The firm, straight-thrust, plumb-forward way, to march upon; the black bundles labouring, bent to the turnips for each wide plot; the same astonishing expanse of sky. Truly the unseen wind had little but your nice body for its teeth— and '02 Weavel's snuffle would depress anyone—but what was the matter with that quite ordinary tree. That's a very usual looking farm house. The road was as Napoleon had

left it. The day itself was what you'd expect of December.

He noticed that the other three, his marching companions, in that section of four, were unusually silent, who
normally were so boringly communicative. He supposed
them too tired to talk. Certainly they might well be—the
day had been strenuous enough from its sleepy beginnings
at four o'clock—or did they share with him his inward
restiveness, deep in the bowels, so dry for your tongue's
root.

(pp. 18-19)

This passage is in the past tense, but Jones quite often shifts
to the present, especially when the second-person point of view
is used. Such a device, of course, strengthens the impression of
immediacy; the action is simultaneous with the reader's experience of it. Nearly the whole of Part VII, which deals with
the major battle action of the story, is narrated in the second
person and in the present tense. The result, as we shall see later,
is probably the most powerfully sustained and compelling
account of modern battle action yet written.

Jones's narrative technique, for all its freedom and flexibility,
is highly disciplined. It has neither the formal control of rhyme
or meter nor the ordinary patterns that govern descriptive, narrative, or dramatic prose. Yet the poet is in complete control;
he selects and blends his materials so effectively that we are
always conscious of a formal artistic principle. In the matter
of narrative technique, that principle determines the appropriate
mode of presentation, point of view, tense, pace, proportion, and
climax. All of these elements of narrative art are uniquely
developed in *In Parenthesis*; their fine inter-adjustment, considering the technical problems connected with each, is further
evidence of a clearly conceived formal principle. In such a poem
as Nichols' "The Assault," the formal principle is almost completely absent; the poet simply duplicates, in verse, the con-

fusion experienced by his protagonist. Jones, on the other hand, has deliberately fashioned his own technique for revealing and controlling the multifarious aspects of war—so confusing, so elusive, and so apt to distort the poet's vision. Jones utilizes his unusual narrative art to develop (as he tells us in the Preface to In Parenthesis) "The complex of sights, sounds, fears, hopes, apprehensions, smells, things exterior and interior, the landscape and paraphernalia of that singular time and of those particular men." This, of course, is the very material that the earlier poets had sought to communicate through the limited techniques of the conventional lyric and the distorted visualizations of the personal response.

When we consider the poetic rather than the narrative aspects of In Parenthesis, we are more specifically concerned with Jones's sensibility and its relationship to word and image. The language of the poem, like the narrative technique, is extremely flexible and varies according to the objective circumstances and the mode of presentation. If the narrative mode is developed through the medium of prose (as it is in the last two sections of Part I), the language possesses a heightened quality similar to that employed by Herbert Read in In Retreat (one of the few pieces of contemporary war writing for which Jones has professed an admiration):

> So they went most of that day and it rained with increasing vigour until night-fall. In the middle afternoon the outer parts of the town of embarkation were reached. They halted for a brief while; adjusted puttees, straightened caps, fastened undone buttons, tightened rifle-slings and attended each one to his own bedraggled and irregular condition. The band recommenced playing; and at the attention and in excellent step they passed through the suburbs, the town's centre, and so towards the docks. The people of that town did not acclaim them, nor stop about their business—for it was late in the second year.

By some effort of a corporate will the soldierly bearing of the text books maintained itself through the town, but with a realisation of the considerable distance yet to be covered through miles of dock, their frailty reasserted itself —which slackening called for fresh effort from the Quilters and the Snells, but at this stage with a more persuasive intonation, with almost motherly concern.

(pp. 6-7)

Even here, however, the verbal texture and the selection of impressions indicates the fundamentally poetic quality of Jones's imagination.

In other passages, which may or may not fall into the typographical pattern of verse, the verbal texture is either elliptical or highly compressed; and conventional syntax yields to a rapid series of almost overlapping impressions. Thus in Part VII we witness the death of Mr. Jenkins:

Mr. Jenkins half inclined his head to them—he walked just barely in advance of his platoon and immediately to the left of Private Ball.
> He makes the conventional sign
and there is the deeply inward effort of spent
> men who would
make response for him,
and take it at the double.
He sinks on one knee
and now on the other,
his upper body tilts in rigid inclination
this way and back;
weighted lanyard runs out to full tether,
> swings like a pendulum
> and the clock run down.
Lurched over, jerked iron saucer over tilted brow,
clampt unkindly over lip and chin

nor no ventaille to this darkening
    and masked face lifts to grope the air
and so disconsolate;
enfeebled fingering at a paltry strap—
buckle holds,
holds him blind against the morning.
    Then stretch still where weeds pattern the chalk predella
—where it rises to his wire—and Sergeant T. Quilter takes
over.

(pp. 165-166)

Neither the cause nor the nature of the fatal wound is mentioned; there is no attempt to dramatize the situation in terms
of external action. The details of the swinging lanyard, the
tilted helmet, and the fingering of the helmet strap suggest
the paroxysms of death much more vividly than any extended
description. Passages like the foregoing have the truth of lyric
immediacy as well as the truth of a dramatically visualized
action. Even when the action is critical and the narrative tempo
rapid, the interwoven lyric elements reveal the poetic essence
of the situation.

Occasionally Jones will expand the impressions evoked by
an event, rather than contracting or compressing them. Certainly
the best instance of this occurs at the conclusion of Part II,
when Private Ball undergoes his first experience of shell-fire.
Here the author expands the sensations of a few seconds into
an extraordinary summary of impressions that encompasses the
physical, sensuous, emotional, and moral implications of an
exploding artillery shell. No other World War I poet has captured so accurately the sheer physical impact of such an
occurrence; no other poet has attempted to suggest, at the same
time, the fundamental inhumanity of that particular form of
violence. Sergeant Snell is reprimanding Private Ball on a
lapse in military deportment:

296

On addressing commissioned officers—it was his favourite theme. John Ball stood patiently, waiting for the eloquence to spend itself. The tedious flow continued, then broke off very suddenly. He looked straight at Sergeant Snell enquiringly—whose eyes changed queerly, who ducked in under the low entry. John Ball would have followed, but stood fixed and alone in the little yard—his senses highly alert, his body incapable of movement or response. The exact disposition of small things—the precise shapes of trees, the tilt of a bucket, the movement of a straw, the disappearing right boot of Sergeant Snell—all minute noises, separate and distinct, in a stillness charged through with some approaching violence—registered not by the ear nor any single faculty—an on-rushing pervasion, saturating all existence; with exactitude, logarithmic, dial-timed, millesimal—of calculated velocity, some mean chemist's contrivance, a stinking physicist's destroying toy.

He stood alone on the stones, his mess-tin spilled at his feet. Out of the vortex, rifling the air it came—bright, brass-shod, Pandoran; with all-filling screaming the howling crescendo's up-piling snapt. The universal world, breath held, one half second, a bludgeoned stillness. Then the pent violence released a consummation of all burstings out; all sudden up-rendings and rivings-through—all taking-out of vents—all barrier-breaking—all unmaking. Pernitric begetting—the dissolving and splitting of solid things. In which unearthing aftermath, John Ball picked up his mess-tin and hurried within; ashen, huddled, waited in the dismal straw. Behind 'E' Battery, fifty yards down the road, a great many mangolds, uprooted, pulped, congealed with chemical earth, spattered and made slippery the rigid boards leading to the emplacement. The sap of vegetables slobbered the spotless breech-block of No. 3 gun.

(p. 24)

In the first paragraph Jones employs what has been called the psychology of crisis; the trivialities of experience, during the few seconds of the shell's approach, assume a clarity and a fixity beyond the measure of their relevance. These trivialities assume a compelling poetic relevance, however, because they convey a psychological truth appropriate to the experience. One must note, too, that the point of view shifts from the physical sensations of Private Ball to the more objective perceptions of the narrator; it is the latter, remote and impersonal, who provides the perspective necessary for the accurate artistic representation of the whole experience. It is the narrator and not Private Ball (he has retired to the barn) who perceives the final, incongruous, but memorable detail: "The sap of vegetables slobbered the spotless breech-block of No. 3 gun." Thus, in order to recreate the full dimensions of an experience, Jones utilizes the device of complex sensibility. He shifts from subjective sense-data to objective notation, selecting and blending so that every sensation, every perception, every impression achieves its full poetic effect. This technique, of course, permits the poet to free himself from the limited visualizations of the personal lyric response, for that response is incorporated within an objectified narrative progression and co-ordinated with an externalized point of view.

Jones has an artist's eye for vivid and evocative detail, as is demonstrated by the particulars which so effectively round off the passage above. He is also quite alert to other aspects of physical experience and employs a variety of sensations and perceptions to create the impression of immediacy. Sometimes this impression is based on simple sensuous notations:

> Metalled eyelet hole in waterproof pall hanging glides cold across your upward tilted cheek with that carrying party's unseen passing—the smell of iodine hangs about when it's used so freely.
>
> (p. 46)

Sometimes the notation is more complex in its effect on the reader, as in this description of a cruel and haphazard violence: "Wastebottom married a wife on his Draft-leave but the whinnying splinter razored diagonal and mess-tin fragments drove inward and toxined underwear" (pp. 157-158). Sometimes a familiar set of impressions will be used to evoke impressions of another, less familiar scene, as in this unusual description of No Man's Land:

> The untidied squalor of the loveless scene spread far horizontally, imaging unnamed discomfort, sordid and deprived as ill-kept hen-runs that back on sidings on wet weekdays where waste-land meets environs and punctured bins ooze canned-meats discarded, tyres to rot, derelict slow-weathered iron-ware disintegrates between factory-end and nettle-bed. Sewage feeds the high grasses and bald clay-crop bears tins and braces, swollen rat-body turned-turtle to the clear morning.
>
> (p. 75)

Jones employs the same device to evoke the monotony and dreariness of a rainy day in the trenches:

> The morning bore all that quiet broken only by single and solitary action that consorts with wet weather. That kind of day when kitchen-helps half-open doors in areas, poke pink hands to hurrying tradesmen: How wet you are Mr. Thoroughgoods—a shocking morning for you. And with the door's slam there is nothing in the street at all but rain between the buildings and you settle down to a very wet morning indeed.
>
> (pp. 84-85)

Almost any page of *In Parenthesis* will afford similar examples of Jones's sensibility with respect to the physical experiences of warfare. His extraordinary care in creating an accurate and

authentic background is illustrated by the elaborate notes to
the poem. These occupy thirty-four pages and comprise 219
separate entries (some of which are multiple notes). Of these,
105 are source notes or explanations of literary allusions; the
remainder (114, or over half) are devoted to explanations of
military terminology and the techniques of trench warfare. The
passing of the years has, of course, made some of this material
obscure; and notes are necessary, especially when soldiers' slang
is involved. However, this necessity itself demonstrates how
closely Jones attempts to approximate the reality. Of all the war
poets, he comes closest to the actual, particularized experience
of life in the front lines—not in terms of a limited, purposeful
realism but in terms of a receptive poetic sensibility alert to the
essential significance of scenes and events and their impact on
human beings.

Another characteristic of Jones's style is his use of extended
images. These images usually involve imaginative enlargements
which are poetic visualizations in their own right; such visualizations are intended to illuminate a special quality or perception
which the poet wishes to emphasize. Here, of course, Jones is
adopting the principle of the epic simile, one of the most common conventions of the epic and heroic poem. An extended
personification, for example, is employed to suggest both the
arbitrary, obscene finality of death, and, through a continuing
metaphor, the grimly ironic parallel between violent death and
the sex act. (In "Greater Love," it will be recalled, Owen used
the same parallel, but with somewhat different implications):

But sweet sister death has gone debauched today and stalks
on this high ground with strumpet confidence, makes no
coy veiling of her appetite but leers from you to me with
all her parts discovered.
By one and one the line gaps, where her
fancy will—howsoever they may howl for their
virginity

she holds them—who impinge less on space
sink limply to a heap
nourish a lesser category of being . . .

(pp. 162-163)

An extended simile is used to define the mixed, indeterminate
mood of soldiers at daybreak, when they are roused for the
front-line ritual of "stand-to." Here the adaptation of the epic
convention is quite obvious; in this case, hardly any other device
could so effectively convey the quality of the emotions involved:

> An eastward alignment of troubled, ashen faces; delicate
> mechanisms of nerve and sinew, grapple afresh, deal for
> another day; ill-matched contesting, handicapped out of
> reason, spirits at the ebb bare up; strung taut—by what
> volition keyed—as best they may.
>
> As grievous invalids watch the returning light pale-bright
> the ruckled counterpane, see their uneased bodies only
> newly clear; fearful to know afresh their ill condition; yet
> made glad for that rising, yet strain ears to the earliest
> note—should some prevenient bird make his kindly cry.

(p. 61)

Even when he is using a conventional image to describe the
most common sound in warfare—that of a bullet passing overhead—Jones gives the simile a turn that perfectly expresses the
emotional as well as the physical effect of the experience: "Occasionally a rifle bullet raw snapt like tenuous hide whip by spiteful
ostler handled" (pp. 42-43). In the passage that recounts the
wounding of Private Ball, Jones summons an extraordinary
range of images to depict the sensations of a soldier advancing
into vicious machine-gun fire and being struck by that fire.
Each image suggests a particular quality of apprehension, fear,
or fright; all are combined in an accelerated context that preserves the dramatic and psychological urgency of the situation:

301

But you seek him alive from bushment and briar—
        perhaps he's where the hornbeam spreads:
he finds you everywhere.
Where his fiery sickle garners you:
fanged-flash and darkt-fire thrring and thrrung athwart
thdrill a Wimshurst pandemonium drill with dynamo druv
staccato bark at you like Berthe Krupp's terrier bitch and
rattlesnakes for bare legs; sweat you on the sudden like
masher Bimp's back-firing No. 3 model for Granny Bodger
at 1.30 a.m. rrattle a chatter you like a Vitus neurotic,
harrow your vertebrae, bore your brain-pan before you can
say Fanny—and comfortably over open sights. . . .
And to Private Ball it came as if a rigid beam of great weight
flailed about his calves, caught from behind by ballista-
baulk let fly or aft-beam slewed to clout gunnel-walker . . .
                        (pp. 182-183)

Thus impressions of painful or unpleasant sound (the dynamo,
the car's backfire) are interspersed among images that suggest
the indiscriminate effect of traversing machine-gun fire (the
sickle), the malignant, knee-level sweep of the bullets (the
terrier and the rattlesnake), and the sheer physical impact felt
by the wounded (the beam, the catapult, and the ship's boom).
For Jones the world of physical sensation evokes a complex of
relationships and analogies that is limited only by the memory
and the imagination. Out of that complex, rather than out
of the stock of conventional poetic ideas, images, and emotions,
he has fashioned a work which goes beyond surface "realism"
and deep into the heart of human experience.

Up to this point we have spoken of Jones's narrative art and
his lyric sensibility, both of which must assure him a high place
among World War I poets, if not among the postwar poets in
general. These two elements alone, however, could not elevate
In Parenthesis to the status of a near-epic. In fact, Jones's com-

mitment to the level of particularized sensuous experience would seem to forestall the kind of development that one would expect of an epic poem. Certainly this commitment inhibited any measure of objectivity, proportion, order, and control among the lyric poets who wrote during the war. One would also have to admit that the action of *In Parenthesis* is not essentially heroic action; the protagonist of the poem is hardly a protagonist at all, and he is certainly not made in the mold of the epic hero. No reader can deny, however, that the poem produces a special effect that cannot be attributed merely to the felicitous blending of narrative and lyrical elements.

The basic narrative pattern of *In Parenthesis*, as we have observed, involves the fortunes (it would be more accurate to say the inner experience) of men who undergo the sequence of preparation, initiation, seasoning, and consummation in a crucial battle. The primary ingredient of the work, therefore, is action and not the passive suffering depicted by the wartime lyric poets. Jones has obviously undertaken to narrate a whole action, an action that is complete and significant in itself. Thus *In Parenthesis* has much more in common with *The Battle of Maldon* than, say, Sassoon's *Counter-Attack* or Blunden's "Third Ypres." As *Maldon* stops short with the deaths of the East Saxons, so also *In Parenthesis* stops short with the deaths of John Ball's comrades and the wounding of Ball himself. In both cases the battle is over for the corporate unit whose courage, loyalty, and physical endurance have been brought to the ultimate test. From the point of view of the heroic narrative, there is nothing more to say; the story has reached its climax and its natural conclusion. Jones has therefore projected his poem not in terms of unrelated or loosely related lyric fragments but in terms of a unified, completed action that is based, as we shall see, on a particular conception of wartime experience.

One of the marks of the epic poem is the creation of a temporal or historical perspective which embraces the distant past as well as the present; the narrative reality is thus permeated with inherited racial traditions and legends which, as they accumulate by way of analogy or simple poetic enrichment, produce the effect of a vital and significant historical continuity. World War I poetry, we have seen, is notable for its bitter sense of temporal discontinuity with respect to both art and life; the past afforded no analogy or source of poetic enrichment to make the ordeals of modern warfare less intolerable. This lack of historical perspective seriously weakened the moral and artistic qualities of the poetry written during the war; any event, no matter how deeply it affects the sensibilities, ceases to be morally or even physically significant when it is isolated from all other events. In *In Parenthesis*, however, Jones deliberately creates a rich background of historical analogy and reference through which his story takes on an added dimension. The experiences of John Ball, changed though they are by the techniques of twentieth-century warfare, are viewed in relation to past conceptions and depictions of heroism in combat as transmitted in such works as Aneirin's *Y Gododdin, The Mabinogion,* Malory's *Morte d'Arthur,* and the *Chanson de Roland.* Thus Jones presents his story in a racial, national, and cultural context that establishes an implicit standard for heroic action and endurance. From this the poet derives a double effect. When an analogy is discerned between the heroic past and the heroic present, we are impressed by the fundamental unity of human experience. When, on the other hand, a striking contrast exists, we are conscious of ironic discrepancies which emphasize the unprecedented violence and suffering imposed by the conditions of modern technological warfare. The literary-historical background of *In Parenthesis* is, therefore, a major formative element of the poem, since this background gives meaning and value to the sequence of external events as well as to the sensations and attitudes of the individual soldier. The individual response does not serve merely as a focus for limited emotional reactions;

through its relationship to the heroic past it is universalized and ennobled. Despite the uniqueness of his experiences, the World War I infantryman, as Jones depicts him, confronts the same ordeals and challenges that have confronted the warriors of all ages.

Jones's re-creation of the heroic spirit is largely dependent upon certain devices—analogy, allusion, reference, imitation, adaptation, echo—which implicitly or explicitly evoke both the heroic past and the elevated style of the epic poem. We have already mentioned his use of the epic simile as a means of capturing complex sensations and perceptions. Another aspect of this device is revealed, however, when we consider its effects simply as an adapted epic convention. We become conscious, of course, of the heroic background out of which the author's conception of the present action grew; we are also conscious of the poetic objectivity necessary for the formulation of such a device, since the epic simile requires both a considerable range of visualization and a sensitivity to the poetic relationships involved. Jones's use of the Homeric time-reference also has a double aspect. In the following passage from Part VII (a portion of the narrative which relates the passing of seconds before the zero hour of attack) the poet heightens the contrast between the routine events of ordinary life and the concurrent moments —agonizing ones for the soldier—just before the signal is given for the advance:

> So in the fullness of time
>> when pallid jurors bring the doomes
>> mooring cables swipe slack-end on
> barnacled piles,
> and the world falls apart at the last to siren screech and
> screaming vertical steam in conformity with the Company's
> Sailings and up to scheduled time. . . .
>
> (p. 159)

Anyone familiar with Homer's practice of marking the time of day by reference to commonplace daily occurrences will appreciate the parallels and contrasts that this device suggests.

The long boast, which is usually uttered by the hero just prior to combat, is another epic feature which the poet has used. In Part IV of *In Parenthesis* a dispute develops among members of Ball's platoon about tactics and strategy. The argument quickly shifts to heated claims and counter-claims concerning length of military service and the experience derived from that service. At this point Dai, a Welsh soldier clad in an oversized greatcoat, begins a long account (five pages) of his own extraordinary experiences. The passage is a composite of legend, myth, and history of which Dai, as a common soldier, could hardly have been conscious. The poet simply uses Dai as a spokesman for a racial memory, obliterated by the years, which might be supposed to exist as a part of the national heritage. Although this memory is vocalized through the medium of the modern infantryman's speech, Jones models the passage on Taliesin's boast in the court of Maelgwin:

> I was with my Lord in the highest sphere,
> On the fall of Lucifer into the depth of hell
> I have borne a banner before Alexander;
> I know the names of the stars from north to
> south;
> I have been on the galaxy at the throne of the
> Distributor;
> I was in Canaan when Absalom was slain. . . .[3]

Similarly, Dai boasts at length of having been present at all the great military exploits of history and legend: the fall of Lucifer, the twelve battles of Arthur, the defeat of Artaxerxes, the Roman invasion of Britain, David's victory over Goliath.

[3] *Taliesin*, from *The Mabinogion*, trans. Lady Charlotte Guest (London, 1906), p. 273.

As a member of Caesar's Xth Fretensis, he was even present at the crucifixion of Christ. Jones draws his references from Welsh legend and romance, from Nennius, from Malory, from *Widsith*, from Caesar, from the *Chanson de Roland*, and from the Bible. The tone is both comic and serious; it shifts from the humor of soldiers' slang and outrageous exaggeration to the diminuendo of the quiet eyewitness report: "I saw Him die." The theme throughout is, of course, "I was there," and the passage closes appropriately with the old refrain, "Old soldiers never die."[4] The speaker, in contrast to the impressive heroic personages who usually make such boasts, is a common infantryman in an ill-fitting army overcoat; he dies obscurely in the great attack described in Part VII. Thus Jones evokes the epic past and gives it a modern context which emphasizes both the continuity of human experience and the incongruity of the heroic attitude amid the novel circumstances of modern war.

Another epic convention is recalled at the end of Part III, when John Ball, posted as a night sentry, listens to the scurryings of rats in No Man's Land. The birds of prey commonly depicted hovering ominously over the epic battlefield are imagined as having undergone a transformation similar to man's:

Those broad-pinioned;
blue-burnished, or brinded-back;
whose proud eyes watched
        the broken emblems
droop and drag dust,
suffer with us this metamorphosis.
These too have shed their fine feathers; these too have slimed their dark-bright coats; these too have condescended to dig in.
The white-tailed eagle at the battle ebb,
        where the sea wars against the river

---

[4] American soldiers of World War II would recognize a parallel to Dai in the omnipresent Kilroy, a wraith who left his mark—"Kilroy was here"—from Scotland to North Africa.

the speckled kite of Maldon
and the crow
have naturally selected to be un-winged;
to go on the belly, to
sap   sap   sap
with festered spines, arched under the moon;
furrit with whiskered snouts the secret parts
of us.

(p. 54)

Thus Jones interweaves past and present in a purely imaginative visualization that vividly suggests the ignoble aspects of modern warfare, in which men have been forced to dig and fight like beasts.

Certainly the most pervasive method that Jones employs to recall the heroic spirit lies in the analogy between the events of *In Parenthesis* and those of Aneirin's *Y Gododdin*. Although most of the soldiers in John Ball's regiment are Londoners, there are enough Welshmen present to make the Welsh literary and historical background an effective source of reference and analogy. The epigraphs to each part of *In Parenthesis* indicate how Jones conceived his work as a modern heroic poem with relationships to the songs and stories of the legendary past. These songs and stories themselves echo a still remoter past; the present is thus made meaningful in terms of the age-old human struggle to defend the values implicit in a racial or national identity. In his General Notes (Note 4, pp. 191-192), the poet clearly indicates his intention of relating the crisis of the present to the broad but obscure historical flux of which Y *Gododdin* is a remnant: "The whole poem has special interest for all of us of this Island because it is a monument of that time of obscurity when north Britain was still largely in Celtic possession and the memory of Rome yet potent; when the fate of the Island was as yet undecided. . . . So that the choice of fragments of this poem as 'texts' is not altogether without point in that it connects us with a very ancient unity and mingling of races; with the Island as a corporate inheritance, with the remembrance of Rome as a European unity."

Thus Jones, unlike the earlier war poets, displays a strong sense of historical continuity; he is alert for meaningful parallels and precedents, and by means of these parallels and precedents he endows the present with the combined sense of drama and destiny with which we usually view the distant past.

Tradition ascribes Y *Gododdin* to the poet Aneirin (fl. 600), who may have been the son of Caw-ab-Geraint, a chief of the Gododdin. The Gododdin were a Brythonic tribe living, in the sixth century, in the area between the Forth and the Tyne rivers. Their most important town, Caer Eiddyn, occupied the site where Edinburgh now stands. Toward the end of the sixth century a king named Mynyddawg planned an expedition against the Saxons of Deira, his traditional enemies. The Saxons held an important road junction called Catraeth, and their presence posed a serious threat to Mynyddawg's dominion. The expedition was composed of three hundred youths of noble blood— the flower of the Brythonic peoples. After a year of training at Mynyddawg's court, the small force advanced into the territory of the Saxons; at Catraeth they charged their more numerous foes, hurling themselves upon the enemy with extraordinary courage. At the end of a week's fighting every Brython had been killed except one, and Catraeth was still occupied by the Saxons. The poem, therefore, tells the story of a defeat; but the defeat, like that related in *Maldon*, is a glorious one. Aneirin was present at Catraeth as both priest and bard; as the only survivor, he was taken prisoner by the Saxons.

Y *Gododdin* is composed in an irregular stanzaic form of from six to twenty lines. Although it celebrates the heroism of a particular enterprise and the courage of individual warriors, the poem is not primarily a narrative. Each stanza develops some facet or interpretation of the battle in a way that has best been described by Thomas Parry. *Y Gododdin,* he remarks, "is not epic poetry, in the sense that it relates the exploits of heroes of the past and makes a story out of them, as the *Iliad* or the *Aeneid* does. The fact is, Aneirin was singing of men he knew. . . . His heroes are contemporaries. He gives us no story to tell us of the feasting at Caer Eiddyn, nor yet about the expedition to Catraeth; we have to gather all that. Rather he expresses the sense of loss he feels for one after another of the lads who fell, and sometimes for all of them together, lingering regretfully and falteringly over his memories of the past and the 'exultation,' and comforting himself with the recollection that the company tasted the chief virtue of a man in that dark age, namely, the power to fight and to slay. It is of the loss to the tribe, the Gododdin, that he speaks; rarely does he reveal his own sorrow. Nevertheless, in this impersonal quality and in his detached statements lies hidden the true emotion of his heart, which his reserve only deepens. That is an important function of economy and reserve in poetry (unintentional here perhaps); to hint rather than to state, to imply rather than to assert. And it is by virtue of this personal anguish, which makes its own way into sight, without the poet's revealing it himself, that this splendid poem may be called lyrical."[5]

Y *Gododdin,* one might add, may not be epic poetry in the formal sense, but it communicates the heroic spirit nearly as well as any epic narrative. Gwyn Williams classifies it as "a heroic poem made up of a series of lyrical fragments," the whole exhibiting "a high degree of poetic craftsmanship," including end rhyme, internal rhyme, alliteration, and assonance.[6] Though figures of speech are rarely employed, the poet makes use of "arresting contrasts" which gain strength from the simplicity and directness of the style.

[5] *A History of Welsh Literature,* trans. H. I. Bell (Oxford, 1955), p. 7.
[6] *An Introduction to Welsh Poetry* (Philadelphia, 1952), p. 24.

Jones's poem parallels Y *Gododdin* in two respects. First, the course of external events is roughly the same. The three hundred young Brythons who train for a year and then advance into hostile territory despite hopeless odds and certain doom surely have their modern counterparts in John Ball's battalion. In each case the poet celebrates the sufferings, the heroism, and the collective fate of the fighting unit. Through the use of epigraphs from Y *Gododdin*, Jones suggests a correspondence between the stages leading to the Battle of Catraeth and those leading to the desperate attack which destroys John Ball's battalion. In both poems, it should also be pointed out, it is the poet who survives to tell the story. Secondly, both poems stress the lyrical element rather than the narrative. *In Parenthesis* follows the course of external events more closely than does Y *Gododdin*, but neither poem depends upon mere narrative action for its primary effect. Jones's simple but eloquent dedication echoes, in its formal tone, the impersonal elegiac quality discerned by Parry in the older poem:

> THIS WRITING IS FOR MY FRIENDS
> IN MIND OF ALL COMMON & HIDDEN
> MEN AND OF THE SECRET PRINCES
> AND TO THE MEMORY OF THOSE
> WITH ME IN THE COVERT AND IN
> THE OPEN FROM THE BLACKWALL
> THE BROADWAY THE CAUSEWAY
> THE CUT THE FLATS THE LEVEL THE
> ENVIRONS AND THOSE OTHERS
> FROM TREATH FAWR AND LONG
> MOUNTAIN THE HENDREF AND YR
> HAFOD THE PENTRE PANDY AND Y
> DARREN THE MAELORS THE BOUNDARY
> WALLS AND NO. 4 WORKING
> ESPECIALLY PTE. R.A. LEWIS-GUNNER
> FROM NEWPORT MONMOUTHSHIRE

KILLED IN ACTION IN THE BOE-
SINGHE SECTOR N.W. OF YPRES
SOME TIME IN THE WINTER 1916-17
AND TO THE BEARDED INFANTRY
WHO EXCHANGED THEIR LONG
LOAVES WITH US AT A SECTOR'S
BARRIER AND TO THE ENEMY
FRONT-FIGHTERS WHO SHARED OUR
PAINS AGAINST WHOM WE FOUND
OURSELVES BY MISADVENTURE

Although Jones does not stress this elegiac element in the course of his poem, he is as aware as Aneirin of the tragic implications of the war for his generation, which entered the "parenthesis" of 1914-1918 with much the same spirit that animated the Gododdin as they marched toward Catraeth. Through recourse to almost forgotten standards of heroic endeavor, he has preserved that spirit with greater fidelity to physical fact and poetic truth than any other World War I writer.

Part VII of *In Parenthesis* has remarkable virtues of its own as a sustained battle narrative with unmistakably heroic overtones. The action begins at 4 A.M. of a day early in July; it concludes twenty-four hours later with the wounding of John Ball and the advance of fresh reserves through Ball's exhausted battalion. We follow the action through Ball's inner and outer experience; he emerges, in this final section, as the observing and recording consciousness. That consciousness is the medium for a sustained lyrical visualization that renders sensations, feelings, and emotions of an extraordinary range and intensity. The whole attack is a pattern of heroic endeavor amid novel, inhuman circumstances. Heroism asserts itself in unexpected ways and in unlikely personages, and the poet honors this heroism by singing of it in the epic manner and thus linking it to the great heroic deeds of the past.

Even before the attack begins, Wastebottom, Talacryn, and Lance-Corporal Aneirin Lewis are killed by the heavy shellfire; Lewis, cruelly dismembered, is "unwholer, limb from limb, than any of them fallen at Catraeth." One soldier loses his nerve and becomes violently hysterical; he is found "all gone to pieces and not pulling himself together nor making the best of things"— an ironic understatement, couched in the cheerfully inane phraseology of the non-combatant, which cuts through any purely emotional response to the scene. Amid this nightmare two well-tailored Old Army officers calmly discuss trivial memories of their days in India; ". . . but the comrade close next you screamed so after the last salvo that it was impossible to catch any more the burthen of this white-man talk." (Jones is adept at these minor ironies of situation, which are all the more effective because they have no purposive ironic intent.) Finally the moment comes to rise and move forward to "death's sure meeting place":

> Tunicled functionaries signify and clear-
> voiced heralds cry
> and leg it to a safe distance:
> leave fairway for the Paladins, and Roland
> throws a kiss . . .
> and Mr. Jenkins takes them over
> and don't bunch on the left
> for Christ's sake.
>
> Riders on pale horses loosed
> and vials irreparably broken
> an' Wat price bleedin' Glory
> Glory
> Glory Hallelujah
> and the Royal Welsh sing:
> Jesu
> lover of me soul . . . to *Aberystwyth*. (p. 160)

"But that was on the right with/ the genuine Taffies," adds
the poet. He then proceeds, after the fashion of the epic list,
to name the varied sections of London and Wales which have
produced the men of Ball's miscellaneous unit:

> . . . but we are rash levied
> from Islington and Hackney
> and the purlieus of Walworth
> flashers from Surbiton
> men of the stock of Abraham
> from Bromley-by-Bow
> Anglo-Welsh from Queens Ferry
> rosary-wallahs from Pembrey Dock
> lighterman with a Norway darling
> from Greenland Stairs
> and two lovers from Ebury Bridge
> Bates and Coldpepper
> that men called the Lily-white boys. . . .
>
> Of young gentlemen wearing the Flash,
> from reputable marcher houses
> with mountain-squireen first-borns
> prince-pedigreed
> from Meirionedd and Cyfeiliog.

(pp. 160-161)

Homer, of course, names only the leaders whose fortunes he
intends to trace; the common men are too numerous to mention, and the epic poet is properly concerned with the deeds of
heroes rather than with the deeds of the ordinary warrior. As
a modern war poet for whom the standards of heroic conduct
have been altered but not obliterated, Jones is interested in the
fortunes of the common infantryman. In the passage above he
actually emphasizes, by way of contrast to the ancient heroic
background, the prosaic and unheroic nature of the modern
infantryman's origins.

Despite the rain of artillery shells and the sweep of machine-gun fire, the first wave moves inexorably ahead, motivated by some power independent of normal volition:

> But red horses now—blare every trump without economy,
> burn boat and sever every tie every held thing goes west
> and tethering snapt, bolts unshot and brass doors flung
> wide and you go forward, foot goes another step further.
>
> (p. 163)

The first objective is attained, and Sergeant Quilter (Mr. Jenkins has been killed) organizes the survivors for an advance into the woods behind the German front line. The enemy is retreating, but the British have lost so heavily that their progress is disorganized and uncertain. Quilter is killed; the confusion threatens to become a panic when the "tripod's clank" indicates a possible German counter-attack. At this point, however, leadership and heroism manifest themselves in a most unlikely personage:

> But for the better discipline of the living,
> a green-gilled corporal,
> returned to company last Wednesday
> from some Corps sinecure,
> who'd lost his new tin-hat, his mousey hair and
>   pendulous
> red ears like the grocery bloke at the Dry
> said his sentences.

His words cut away smartly, with attention to the prescribed form, so that when he said do this they bloody did it, for all his back-area breeze-up high.

For Christ knows he must persuade old sweats with more than sewn-on chevrons or pocket his legatine prestige and lie doggo.

But he'd got them into line at the prone, and loosing off with economy; and he himself knelt at the further beech bole to control their fire.

(p. 172)

Certainly the "green-gilled corporal" affords a remarkable contrast to the passive or paralyzed figures that were commonly depicted by the wartime poets. Their strong sense of personal disillusion and disaffection, grounded in outraged humanitarian instincts, blinded them to the essential continuity of human experience; they saw and reported mere particulars, mere sensations, mere emotions, or, at the most, they felt a tragic sense of human waste. Their negative conception of the soldier as victim rather than hero prevented any positive, comprehensive depiction of significant military action. Jones writes of particulars, sensations, and emotions, and he is conscious of the sacrificial aspects of the war; but his understanding of the heroic spirit and its manifestation in modern warfare establishes order and significance for these bewildering phenomena. Despite his unprepossessing appearance and the rather desperate situation which confronts him, the "green-gilled corporal" conducts himself with fortitude and dispatch in restoring the "Disciplines of the Wars." If that act is accepted as a heroic positive, the particulars of battle experience assume their proper measure of relevance and value.

Soon after this episode, the forward units are ordered to consolidate their positions. John Ball and his comrades begin to dig; the engineers string barbed wire; the signallers set up telephone lines; the wounded are carried back ("you mustn't spill the precious fragments, for perhaps these raw bones live"); and Father Larkin is observed "talking to the dead." After dark, however, Ball's unit is ordered to attack the positions directly ahead, where the enemy still remains entrenched. It is during this early morning attack that John Ball is wounded by machine-gun fire. The last five pages of the narrative tell of his efforts to drag himself back toward his own lines; here Jones bases his material, as well as his elevated lyric tone, on the passages in the *Chanson de Roland* which describe the last moments of the hero.

As he crawls painfully in the dark, Ball cannot decide whether or not to abandon his rifle. His indecision becomes the theme of the passage; he is torn between the urge for self-preservation and his soldierly regard for his weapon. In the old French epic, Roland is similarly concerned about the fate of his sword Durendal; he attempts to shatter it upon a rock, when defeat and death are certain, because he does not wish the weapon to become the trophy of a Saracen. The sword, however, cannot be broken, and as a last resort Roland places it beneath his body before he dies. His actions are thus in accord with the heroic conception of honor, which extends to the warrior's weapons and armor as well as to his conduct. In his own extremity, Ball's thoughts revolve around his weapon as a power and as a symbol of soldierly pride and dedication:

> It's difficult with the weight of the rifle.
> Leave it—under the oak.
> Leave it for a salvage-bloke
> let it lie bruised for a monument
> dispense the authenticated fragments to the
>   faithful.
> It's the thunder-besom for us
> it's the bright bough borne . . .
>
>   (p. 183)

In the epic narrative the weapons and armor of the hero are often described in great detail; the poet took special delight in dwelling upon supernatural origins and virtues, and he recounted the rich battle histories of sword and shield. By way of contrast, Jones presents the virtues of the infantryman's rifle in the threadbare but somehow appropriate and significant parlance of the gunnery instructor:

> . . . it's the soldier's best friend if you care for the working parts and let us be 'aving those springs released smartly in Company billets on wet forenoons and clickerty-click and one up the spout and you men must really cultivate the habit of treating this weapon with the very greatest care and there should be a healthy rivalry among you—it should be a matter of very proper pride and
>
> Marry it man! Marry it!
> Cherish her, she's your very own.
>
> Coax it man coax it—it's delicately and ingeniously made—it's an instrument of precision—it costs us tax-payers, money—I want you men to remember that.
>
> (pp. 183-184)

Despite the fact that his rifle is a standardized factory product, the relationship between the soldier and his weapon is an intimate one, as intimate as that between Roland and his Durendal. The modern soldier may not give his rifle a noble name, but he knows its characteristics as well as he knows the features and the habits of a friend:

> You've known her hot and cold.
> You would choose her from among many.
> You know her by her bias, and by her exact error at 300, and by the deep scar at the small, by the fair flaw in the grain, above the lower sling-swivel—
> but leave it under the oak.
>
> (p. 184)

The line, "Leave it under the oak," serves as a refrain; its recurrence preserves the thematic unity of the passage and helps to maintain the elevated lyric tone, which approaches, in its total effect, the intensity of song. The Roland-Durendal parallel becomes explicit in the following lines:

It is not to be broken on the brown stone under the gracious tree.
It is not to be hidden under your failing body.
Slung so, it troubles your painful crawling like a fugitive's irons.

(p. 184)

In his slow progress toward the rear and safety Ball must make his way through the bodies of the slain. In an elegiac fantasy he sees the "Queen of the Woods" distributing flowers among the intermingled bodies, British and German. The distinction between friend and enemy is obliterated; all have died honorably as soldiers and they share equal rewards:

Some she gives white berries
                some she gives brown
Emil has a curious crown it's
                made of golden saxifrage.
Fatty wears sweet-briar,
he will reign with her for a thousand years.
For Balder she reaches high to fetch his.
Ulrich smiles for his myrtle wand.
That swine Lillywhite has daisies to his chain—you'd hardly credit it.
She plaits torques of equal splendour for Mr. Jenkins and Billy Crower.
Hansel with Gronwy share dog-violets for a palm, where they lie in serious embrace beneath the twisted tripod.
Siôn gets St. John's Wort—that's fair enough.
Dai Great-coat, she can't find him anywhere—she calls both high and low, she had a very special one for him.

(pp. 185-186)

Weak from exhaustion and loss of blood, Ball is finally forced to abandon his rifle. He must "leave it under the oak," but his final qualms are produced by the same conceptions that motivate Roland's efforts to destroy his sword:

> You're clumsy in your feebleness, you implicate your tin-hat rim with the slack sling of it.
>
> Let it lie for the dews to rust it, or ought you to decently cover the working parts.
>
> Its dark barrel, where you leave it under the oak, reflects the solemn star that rises urgently from Cliff Trench.
>
> It's a beautiful doll for us
> it's the Last Reputable Arm.
>
> But leave it—under the oak.
> leave it for a Cook's tourist to the Devastated Areas and crawl as far as you can and wait for the bearers.
>
> (p. 186)

The narrative ends with Ball's consciousness of the reserves who are moving forward to renew the advance. The strength of the old corporate unit has been expended; new strength flows in for new battles, and the great war, with its ceaseless demand for fresh heroism and suffering, moves beyond the limits of the story:

> Lie still under the oak
> next to the Jerry
> and Sergeant Jerry Coke.
>
> The feet of the reserves going up tread level with your forehead; and no word for you; they whisper one with another;
> pass on, inward;
> these latest succours:
> green Kimmerii to bear up the war.
>
> (p. 187)

The poem closes with a paraphrase of four lines from the *Chanson de Roland* (lines 2095-2098):

The geste says this and the man who was on the field . . . and who wrote the book . . . the man who does not know this has not understood anything.

(p. 187)

Thus Jones implies that the truth of the poetic narrative, based on personal experience, will be borne out by objective historical accounts[7] and that the truth of war depends on the two complementary points of view. The historical account cannot deal with the particulars of personal experience; that area must have an objective reference for the ordering and evaluation of particulars. In *In Parenthesis*, therefore, the historical-heroic elements of past and present—their points of resemblance as well as their points of contrast—serve as a unifying principle for a poetic interpretation of the phenomena of modern warfare.

Unlike most of the wartime poets, Jones had no public school or university background; as a young art student, however, he read and absorbed a great deal—especially in Chaucer, Malory, Shakespeare, Milton, Coleridge, and Browning. The richly allusive nature of *In Parenthesis* demonstrates the effect of this early reading on his imaginative processes. Other aspects of the poem—formal and technical aspects not directly accounted for in the Notes—all suggest that he was affected by the major literary developments of the twenties, or, more accurately, by the larger cultural circumstances that were responsible for those developments. Jones's account[8] of his chief literary interests after the war affords something of an index to the contemporary influences at work in *In Parenthesis*, though the poet insists

---

[7] In his edition of the *Chanson de Roland*, T. A. Jenkins interprets *"geste"* (l. 2095) as referring to "sober written history" to which the poet appeals for corroboration. See T. A. Jenkins, ed., *La Chanson de Roland* (New York, 1924), pp. 153, 127.

[8] In a personal letter to the author, May 2, 1962.

that these influences, "while no doubt positive," were not as direct or as dominant as most critics have supposed. "By 1928," Jones writes, "I had read a good many 'war novels' but *extremely little* 'war poetry.'" Before beginning his poem (rather tentatively, in 1928), he had read T. S. Eliot's *The Waste Land*, but "practically none" of Ezra Pound's verse and "very little" of James Joyce—though Joyce's influence is present in *In Parenthesis* in "an oblique kind of way." Jones attributes the form and technique of his narrative less to direct literary influences than to what he calls the "civilizational situation" of the postwar era. If a number of poets "are of a certain turn of mind their problems are inevitably likely to be the same and they are likely to solve them 'artistically' in much the same way." Hence to speak too categorically of "direct" influences is a critical presumption that fails to account for the creative process, which is really a transmutation of many diverse elements with many different degrees of relationship to the work in question. "What one is 'influenced' by," writes Jones, "is the *absolute* necessity to find a 'form' that somehow or other 'fits' the contemporary situation." The wartime poets were also conscious of this necessity, but their spontaneous revolt against Georgianism did not of itself produce new forms that would "fit" their experiences. In dealing with the conflict as a part of the contemporary actuality, Jones participates in the more deliberate postwar effort to restore poetry to a more genuinely creative function in modern life.

In Parenthesis is thus clearly a product of the decades between the two great wars; that is to say, it could not have been written in its present form before 1920, and it is doubtful whether some of the unusual characteristics we have discussed could again be brought into precisely the same poetic combination today. Unlike his surviving contemporaries, Sassoon and Blunden, Jones took full advantage of the new freedoms that postwar literature seemed to demand as it sought to accom-

modate itself to the deepening complexities of modern consciousness. This is all the more remarkable, in one sense, when
we consider the fact that he was not a published poet until 1937.
It is very likely, however, that this late start excluded any premature commitment to the conventional modes of Georgian
verse or to the styles and techniques evolved by the poets who
wrote during the war years. In general, we may discern in Jones's
work the same experimental, innovative spirit that is manifest in
the productions of T. S. Eliot, Ezra Pound, James Joyce, and
Virginia Woolf. *In Parenthesis* owes many of its specific techniques, however, to the radically new conception of poetic art
that Eliot employed in "Gerontion," *The Waste Land*, and
"The Hollow Men."

In his General Notes Jones alludes to Eliot as "the greatest
English poet of our own time"; but, if imitation is the sincerest
form of praise, *In Parenthesis* is a fuller acknowledgment of
the older poet's stature and influence. Eliot's emphasis upon the
contemporaneity of past and present, his juxtaposition of narrative, lyrical, and dramatic elements, his reliance upon a loosely
associative rather than a logical continuity, his projection of
a complex sensibility as a medium of development—all of these
practices and techniques Jones has adopted not slavishly but
with the originality and authority of an independent talent.
He has fully understood the potentialities of Eliot's methods
and has utilized those methods for his own purposes. For
example, just as Eliot employs an anthropological background
in *The Waste Land* to dramatize the continuity of man's spiritual life and to point out the disappearance of spiritual values
in modern civilization, so also Jones evokes the heroic background in order to establish the essential continuity of heroic
experience, to depict the extraordinary nature of the demands
made upon the heroism of the modern soldier, and to organize
and control the otherwise meaningless data of modern warfare.
In both cases the background is evoked by parallels, analogies,

contrasts, allusions, and explicit reference; in both cases the background of the remote past and the foreground of the present are merged in a unified poetic conception. (It may be pointed out, incidentally, that the backgrounds of both *The Waste Land* and *In Parenthesis* require an elaborate apparatus of notes for their elucidation.) Jones's frequent shifts from the narrative to the lyrical and dramatic modes correspond roughly to Eliot's technique in *The Waste Land*; the lack of conventional continuity and logical transition between different modes, different scenes, and different visualizations also characterizes both poems. Again, Jones's use of a shadowy spectator-protagonist—John Ball—as a focus of a generalized poetic consciousness corresponds to the older poet's use of Gerontion (in "Gerontion") and Tiresias (in *The Waste Land*) as a means of projecting his own themes and sensibilities. As Eliot remarks in his Notes to *The Waste Land*, "What Tiresias *sees*, in fact, is the substance of the poem." What John Ball sees is largely the substance of *In Parenthesis*, although Jones may momentarily shift the focus of consciousness to other characters. It is for this reason that we know so little about John Ball; information about his past, his traits, and his appearance would be irrelevant to his function in the poem. Since Jones employs a shifting or generalized focus of consciousness through which he objectifies his sensations and perceptions, his work is not distorted by the limitations of the personal response. He would surely agree with Eliot's dictum that "poetry is not a turning loose of emotion, but an escape from emotion; it is not an expression of personality, but an escape from personality." Ball is Jones, of course, but only in the sense that Eliot is Tiresias; both poets have objectified their consciousness for purposes of self-discipline as well as for purposes of formal presentation.

Eliot's influence on Jones in the matter of language cannot be accurately determined because Eliot's break with traditional conceptions of the "poetic" was the signal for a general reformation of poetic technique. It is obvious, however, in many of the passages quoted above that Jones depends a great deal upon the diction and rhythms of colloquial speech; like the language of "Prufrock," the language of *In Parenthesis* is natural and informal rather than formally "poetic." In Part II of *The Waste Land* ("A Game of Chess"), Eliot makes full use of contrasting inflections and rhythms to depict the characteristic preoccupations of two levels of society. Jones is equally sensitive to the effects that can be gained through the use of contemporary language and freely incorporates the accents of living speech into his poetic context. Thus the spoken word often communicates more than it signifies; under certain conditions it can evoke the central dramatic or poetic quality of a scene. An example of this occurs in Part III of *In Parenthesis*. As Ball's unit moves into the front line under cover of darkness, the men must feel their way through a maze of obstacles and entanglements; verbal warnings must be relayed down the groping file:

> The repeated passing back of aidful messages assumes a cadency.
> Mind the hole
> mind the hole
> mind the hole to left
> hole right
> step over
> keep left, left.
> One grovelling, precipitated, with his
> gear tangled, struggles to feet again:
> Left be buggered.
> Sorry mate—you all right china?—
> lift us yer rifle—an' don't take on so
> Honey—but rather, mind
> the wire here
> mind the wire

mind the wire
mind the wire.

Extricate with some care that taut strand—it may well be
you'll sweat on its unbrokenness.

(p. 36)

In "A Game of Chess" Eliot employs colloquial repetition with
the same dramatic purpose if not with the same effect:

> HURRY UP PLEASE ITS TIME
> Well, that Sunday Albert was home, they had a
>   hot gammon,
> And they asked me in to dinner, to get the beauty
>   of it hot—
> HURRY UP PLEASE ITS TIME
> HURRY UP PLEASE ITS TIME
> Goonight Bill. Goonight Lou. Goonight May.
> Goonight. Ta ta. Goonight. Goonight.
> Good night, ladies, good night, sweet ladies,
>   good night, good night.

The last sentence may be recognized as an ironic echo of
Ophelia's lines in *Hamlet*. Sometimes Jones creates a similar
(but not ironic) contrast by juxtaposing a literary echo to the
broad accents of contemporary Cockney speech:

> Anyway it was a cert they were for it to do battle with
> him to-morn in the plain field. There was some bastard
> woods as Jerry was sitting tight in and this mob had clickt
> for the job of asking him to move on—if you please—an'
> thanks very much indeed, signally obliged to yer, Jerry-boy.

(p. 138)

In his Preface Jones comments on the pervasiveness of Cockney
accents and expressions in his work; he also speculates about
the occasional poetic value of soldiers' profanity and obscenities

326

(which, unfortunately, "conventional susceptibilities" prevented him from utilizing). Considering the other techniques that Jones adapted from *The Waste Land*, it would not be improper to suggest that the selection and blending of disparate language elements is an art that he could have learned only from Eliot.

The parallels indicated above cannot, of course, be pressed too far; *The Waste Land* and *In Parenthesis* differ widely in materials, inspiration, theme, and purpose. When they are viewed, however, simply as specimens of poetry written between the two great wars, their general relationships in the matter of technique can hardly be denied. Against the collective background of pre-World War I verse their resemblances become more striking and more significant, for in that broader perspective both works may be seen as embodiments of a much more flexible and comprehensive conception of poetic art. It is not unlikely that future literary historians may bring the two poems into an even closer relationship. If *The Waste Land* is the most comprehensive attempt to deal poetically with the spiritual and cultural effects of World War I, *In Parenthesis* is the most comprehensive attempt to deal with the novel physical and psychological conditions of that conflict.

Jones's profound sensory awareness, his perception of fleeting "inscapes," and his rich poetic vocabulary all suggest (perhaps inevitably) the influence of Gerard Manley Hopkins, who is mentioned twice in Jones's Notes as the source of brief allusions. The postwar poets learned a great deal from Hopkins but found him a rather dangerous model; his verbal and metrical innovations were so extraordinary, so idiosyncratic, that any close imitation of them tended to jeopardize the individual poetic talent. Jones does not imitate Hopkins' more obvious verbal mannerisms, but he has apparently assimilated something of his ability to discern the significant form or pattern of things. In Parts II, III, and IV of *In Parenthesis* Jones describes certain natural phenomena (clouds, landscapes, moonlight, winter fog, dawn) in a way that recalls Hopkins' vivid prose notations as well as certain passages in his poetry. The following description, for instance, might have come from Hopkins' *Notebooks*:

> There spread before him on the blue warp above as though by a dexterous, rapid shuttling, unseen, from the nether-side, a patterning of intense white; each separate bright breaking through, sudden and with deliberate placing—a slow spreading out, a loss of compact form, drifting into an indeterminate mottling.

(p. 20)

The manner is again Hopkins' in this description of a scene that might have inspired one of Paul Nash's depictions of somber ruin along the Western Front: "Slime-glisten on the churnings up, fractured earth pilings, heaped on, heaped up waste; overturned far throwings; tottering perpendiculars lean and sway; more leper-trees pitted, rownsepykèd out of nature, cut off in their sap-rising" (p. 39). Jones's habits of ellipsis, his asyntactical formations, his use of particular epithets, and his unorthodox compounds are also strongly reminiscent of Hopkins.

Much of what has already been said in this and in previous chapters anticipates our concluding remarks concerning Jones's attitude toward the war and toward the relations between war and poetry. While reading *In Parenthesis*, we are aware, perhaps above all else, of what might be described as an attitude of humane objectivity. Jones's imagination was not encumbered by the limited personal, political, or humanitarian motives which inspired the poetry of the war years; the passing of time, of course, had diminished the urgency of such motives and demonstrated their ephemerality. More importantly, the heroic-historical background which Jones developed for his poem emphasized the fundamental and enduring qualities revealed by any human conflict—courage, strength, loyalty—rather than the reactions that grow out of personal emotions and attitudes.

Jones views the conflict not as a poet interested only in the drama of his own exposure to danger and possible death, not as a disillusioned idealist or humanitarian, not as a pathetic victim of circumstances, but simply as a poet who grasps, with a steady eye and a steady mind, the particularities of trench warfare as well as the universals that lie hidden in the confusing flux of danger, fear, suffering, courage, and death. Jones is not even interested in the "truth" of war—the "truth" sought by misguided realists—if this "truth" means only an exaggerated emphasis on war *as war*. As he remarks in his Preface, "I did not intend this as a 'War Book'—it happens to be concerned with war."

Jones's objectivity, then, would seem to exclude nearly all of the major attitudes, motives, moods, and emotions that produced the poetry written during the war. If this objectivity excludes so much, what does it include? What are the positives implicit in poetic objectivity as far as modern war poetry is concerned?

The epic or heroic poem embodies values that apply to the form and spirit of the narrative as well as to the characters and the action. The heroic narrative is objective, impersonal, and absolutely faithful to human nature and experience. Indeed, the objectivity of the epic poet is such that he may be said to have no attitudes; he allows his story to tell itself without commentary or interpretation. There is no anger, no grief, no condemnation, no condonation, and no pity. These the poet must evoke, if he is true to his art, in the imagination of his reader. He must also evoke a sense of particularized time and place; he must create a meaningful historical or racial perspective for the action in which his hero is engaged; his representation must be comprehensive yet accurate, with parts justly proportioned to the whole; above all, his poem must embody a scale of values against which the efforts and aims of his characters must be measured. Jones has attempted, with a considerable degree of success, to approximate these qualities in *In Parenthesis*. When the conditions of modern warfare do not permit such an approximation, he utilizes the discrepancy to emphasize—without irony and without bitterness—the discontinuities of which the earlier poets were so painfully conscious. In either case he is in full control of his material; he is able to give it order, form, proportion, and clarity because he preserves his intellectual remoteness from the flux of sensation and event. Thus his freedom from extraneous emotions and attitudes allows him to devote his attention to more significant aspects of the conflict as well as to the problems of form related to their most effective presentation.

The conditions of modern warfare encouraged Jones to depart from the epic form and spirit in one important respect. The epic poet was prohibited by the terms of his art from exploring the thoughts and sensations of his characters. Jones, on the other hand, has made the thoughts and sensations of his characters the very medium of his narrative. In doing this he follows the precedent of the wartime poets, who instinctively felt that the scope and violence of modern warfare could best be registered in terms of its impact on the individual sensibility rather than in terms of its political implications or in terms of military triumphs and defeats. Unlike his predecessors, who expressed their personal reactions to the war through the limited medium of the lyric, Jones took special pains to objectify and control the subjective element in his work: he projected his sensibility into a character who serves as the central focus of sensation and perception. Thus Jones can shift freely between the comprehensive, generalized consciousness of the narrator and the more immediate, more individualized consciousness of John Ball. In either case he has objectified his own perceptions and incorporated them into a context of narrative and dramatic action. He thereby adds another valuable dimension—that created through the medium of a vivid sensory awareness—to the modified heroic form which he has utilized so effectively.

The general poetic objectivity of *In Parenthesis* does not exclude the expression of certain attitudes which, in view of the nature of the war, would have been almost impossible to repress. It is in this sense that Jones's objectivity must be interpreted as a "humane" objectivity. Anger, pity, and sympathy are sometimes visible in his work, but it is important to remember that these attitudes do not dominate or otherwise affect the character of his poetic vision. In other words, the quality of a scene or incident may evoke an emotion, but the emotion is an effect and not a predisposing cause of the visualization. Thus Jones, in the midst of his description of the exploding artillery shell, reveals a momentary anger at the men of science who have lent their minds to a perversion of science; the shell is "some mean chemist's contrivance, a stinking physicist's destroying toy." Occasionally his anger is directed against civilian optimism and insensitivity. In Part VII he mocks civilian attitudes toward the wounded with a bitterness that is not natural to him. The bearers who are carrying a wounded soldier "mustn't spill the precious fragments, for perhaps these raw bones live":

> They can cover him again with skin—in their candid coats, in their clinical shrines and parade the miraculi.
> The blinded one with the artificial guts—his morbid neurosis retards the treatment, otherwise he's bonza—and will learn a handicraft.

Nothing is impossible nowadays my dear if only we can get the poor bleeder through the barrage and they take just as much trouble with the ordinary soldiers you know and essential-service academicians can match the natural hue and everything extraordinarily well.

Give them glass eyes to see
and synthetic spare parts to walk in the Triumphs, without
anyone feeling awkward and O, O, O, its a lovely war
with poppies on the up-platform for a perpetual memorial
of his body.

(pp. 175-176)

Here Jones seems to be deliberately echoing the angry sarcasm of
Sassoon rather than voicing his own deeply felt attitudes. At
this particular time in the action of the poem (July 1916) the
mood of disillusion and rejection had not yet been so clearly
articulated; hence the tone of the passage is somewhat anachro-
nistic and does not accurately reflect the attitudes prevailing at
that time (see Chap. III). Perhaps in writing of the Somme
Offensive Jones merely sought to suggest something of the
emerging disillusion that was to inspire Sassoon's satiric attacks
on civilian complacency. In any case these expressions of anger
and bitterness are rare in *In Parenthesis*; they are related not
to Jones's major themes but rather to the attitudes that might
seem natural to the characters in the poem.

Although he has a sense of national and racial continuity
more profound than that of any other war poet, Jones is free
from any narrow nationalistic or patriotic bias. In view of his
general objectivity this is, of course, not surprising. Neither is
it surprising to find that the great political and military issues
of the war do not concern him. These issues lay beyond the
grasp of the ordinary soldier, who did not worry about problems
he could not comprehend or situations he could not control:
"You know no more than do those hands who squirt cement
till siren screams, who are indifferent that they rear an archi-
tect's folly; read in the press perhaps the grandeur of the
scheme" (p. 87). Like the earlier poets, Jones expresses no
animosity toward the enemy; during the war hatred was a luxury
only civilians could afford. His humane objectivity, however,

entails more than an absence of hatred. In his Dedication he mentions "the enemy front-fighters who shared our pains against whom we found ourselves by misadventure." In the same broadly sympathetic spirit he can occasionally glance behind the enemy's lines to visualize the effects of the day's violence:

> But all the old women in Bavaria are busy with their novenas, you bet your life, and don't sleep lest the watch should fail, nor weave for the wire might trip his darling feet and the dead Karl might not come home. . . .

> O clemens, O pia and
> turn all out of alignment the English guns amen.

> (p. 149)

These unexpected insights are a result of Jones's comprehensive poetic vision, which is not distorted by conventional wartime emotions. For Jones, as for Sorley before him, the war was not a simple physical confrontation of nations in arms. It was, indeed, a "misadventure" which made both anger and enthusiasm pointless. The intermingled bodies of German and British, described toward the end of Part VII, testify to the superior truth of the comprehensive poetic vision. The dead mutely proclaim a fellowship that is far more profound and compelling than the abstract enmity that caused them to kill one another.

When Jones voices pity it is not for man, who must endure the sufferings of war as a logical consequence of his capacity to wage it, but for the beasts who can bear no responsibility in the matter: "And mules died: their tough clipt hides that have a homely texture flayed horridly to make you weep, sunk in their servility of chain and leather" (p. 149). Unlike Owen, Jones found little poetry in pity; pity was an emotion that might be aroused under certain circumstances, but the full reality of war was much too complex to be viewed through the eyes of pity alone. Actually Jones was as fully aware as Owen of the sacrificial aspects of the conflict. He sees the sacrifice, however, in terms of Christian ritual and symbolism; he invokes specific conceptions rather than emotions. A pattern of Catholic liturgical reference runs throughout the poem, including quotations from the Rubrics for the Good Friday Office (p. 27), from the Tenebrae for Good Friday (p. 153), and from the Dominican Office of the Dead (p. 157). There are echoes from the prayers of the Mass (p. 162) and numerous Scriptural allusions. The two illustrations in the book are rich with Christian sacrificial symbolism; opposite the second illustration are six Scriptural quotations, each of which bears directly or indirectly on well-known Judeo-Christian sacrificial themes. Jones obviously sought to interweave and eventually bring together two separate conceptions of the World War I infantry soldier: the heroic conception and the sacrificial conception. Positive, aggressive heroism of the epic character is seldom possible in modern war; a man may perform valiantly in action, but for every valiant moment there are weeks of inactivity, boredom, suffering, and fear. Thus the virtues of the modern infantryman are Christian virtues—patience, endurance, hope, love—rather than the naturalistic virtues of the epic hero.[9] The modern soldier, Jones suggests, dies as the scapegoat or as the lamb; the ancient rite of expiation is re-enacted on a vast scale. Jones's soldiers are not passive victims, however. They fight, with varying degrees of courage, until they die. They die obscurely, but their death is not pitiful because it is significant in terms of the heroic tradition and in terms which the circumstances of modern war seem to have suggested to nearly every World War I poet: those of Christian sacrifice and expiation.

In his Preface Jones stresses the fact that the action of *In Parenthesis* occurs before the Somme battles of 1916 had altered the character of the war. After July 1916, he remarks, "things

---

[9] Beowulf's transformation in the hands of the unknown Christian poet is an interesting and not altogether remote parallel.

hardened into a more relentless, mechanical affair, took on a more sinister aspect":

"The wholesale slaughter of the later years, the conscripted levies filling the gaps in every file of four, knocked the bottom out of the intimate, continuing, domestic life of small contingents of men, within whose structure Roland could find, and, for a reasonable while, enjoy, his Oliver. In the earlier months there was a certain attractive amateurishness, and elbow-room for idiosyncrasy that connected one with a less exacting past. The period of the individual rifle-man, of the 'old sweat' of the Boer campaign, the 'Bairnsfather' war, seemed to terminate with the Somme battle" (p. ix).

Considering the special values that Jones invokes in his poem, could an *In Parenthesis* have been written about a similar series of events occurring in 1917 or 1918? This, of course, was the period in which Sassoon, Blunden, Rosenberg, and Owen found their particular inspirations. Jones seems to imply that he chose the earlier part of the war because it would have been more difficult, if not impossible, to discern significant patterns and values in the later part. If this inference is accepted, the efforts of the aforementioned poets may be viewed with more tolerance; they were indeed dealing with intractable material. Even Jones admits that in writing *In Parenthesis* he has "attempted to appreciate some things, which, at the time of suffering, the flesh was too weak to appraise." Jones was, however, eventually capable of appraising them; despite the fact that he was dealing with the same levels of sensuous experience explored by the earlier writers, he produced the only poetry of the war that is not distorted by ephemeral emotions or limited by subjective attitudes.

Toward the end of his Preface Jones comments on the major problem faced by the modern war poet: the opposition between poetic sensitivity and the new phenomena which that sensitivity seeks to encompass and interpret. He proposes no solution to this problem; rather, he admits the existence of a dilemma which certainly cannot be resolved on mere critical or aesthetic grounds:

"It is not easy in considering a trench-mortar barrage to give praise for the action proper to chemicals—full though it may be of beauty. We feel a rubicon has been passed between striking with a hand weapon as men used to do and loosing poison from the sky as we do ourselves. We doubt the decency of our own inventions, and are certainly in terror of their possibilities. That our culture has accelerated every line of advance into the territory of physical science is well appreciated—but not so well understood are the unforeseen, subsidiary effects of this achievement. We stroke cats, pluck flowers, tie ribands, assist at the manual acts of religion, make some kind of love, write poems, paint pictures, are generally at one with that creaturely world inherited from our remote beginnings. Our perception of many things is heightened and clarified. Yet must we do gas-drill, be attuned to many newfangled technicalities, respond to increasingly exacting mechanical devices; some fascinating and compelling, others sinister in the extreme; all requiring a new and strange direction of the mind, a new sensitivity certainly, but at a considerable cost" (p. xiv).

Is the opposition between the spirit of poetry and the spirit of modern science forever irreconcilable? Or does the dilemma of the modern poet represent a transitional stage in literature corresponding to those stages in the past that have aroused similar doubts and dilemmas? How can the methods and paraphernalia of modern warfare be accommodated to the poetic vision? The questions implicit in Jones's remarks cannot be easily answered, but they do illuminate the problem that the poet must face:

"We who are of the same world of sense with hairy ass and furry wolf and who presume to other and more radiant affinities, are finding it difficult, as yet, to recognise these creatures of chemicals as true extensions of ourselves, that we may feel for them a native affection, which alone can make them magical for us. It would be interesting to know how we shall ennoble our new media as we have already ennobled and made significant our old—candle-light, fire-light, Cups, Wands and Swords, to choose at random" (p. xiv).

To be conscious of the present dilemma is perhaps the most that can be asked of the modern poet. Certainly Jones's consciousness of it is responsible for the unusual form of *In Parenthesis*, which embodies a "new sensitivity" and a new method of expressing and controlling that sensitivity. The poets who wrote during the war were beginning to be conscious of the dilemma, but circumstances forced them to rely on traditional methods and forms; we have seen how inadequate they proved to be. Utilizing his ingenuity and imagination, the new freedoms of postwar verse, the forgotten resources of epic poetry, and the "new sensitivity" developed by the wartime poets, Jones fashioned an original work which testifies to the perennial power of poetry to adapt itself to new circumstances and to renew its vitality through the processes of that adaptation. His achievement, therefore, has implications that bear not only on modern war poetry but on modern poetry as a whole.

When World War I came to a close, the lyric impulse suddenly lapsed, not because the best poets were dead, but because that impulse was grounded on ephemeral attitudes and limited emotional reactions; Owen's "Strange Meeting" is the only poem written during the war that approaches the enlarged vision of Eliot's *The Waste Land*. Within the next decade it became clear that Owen and Eliot represented the two major lines of rebellion against the Georgian "retrenchment"; with Hopkins (whose verse, by coincidence, was first made available in 1918), they were singled out as the "ancestors" of the Auden group and designated as the source of a new "hope for poetry."

In a sense, Jones's work is a culmination of the two most important poetic developments of the postwar years—the two developments that, taking the Georgian position as their point of departure, had represented separate but related efforts to assimilate the materials of contemporary life. The impulse that began with Brooke's decorous response from within the "deep meadows" of Georgian peace and forgetfulness ends with a poem that encompasses not only the individual soldier's experience of modern warfare but also the heroic spirit which illuminates and, in a way, vindicates that experience.

Although it is obvious that the poets who wrote during the war years did not satisfactorily resolve their artistic problems—which were reducible, essentially, to a profound conflict between matter and form—they at least recovered the initiative that the Georgians had so listlessly abandoned. In so doing they were contributing (though only Owen was conscious of it) to a renewal of the positive relationships between poetry and contemporary life. Unfortunately, the phrases "war poetry" and "the war novel" have come to connote literary efforts strenuously devoted to an exposure of the "truth" of modern war, as if this truth were different from any other kind of truth. Considering the special motives that inspired the literature of World War I, this development is natural, though it tends to divorce the concerns of war literature from the concerns of literature as a whole. For this reason, perhaps, the evolution of World War I verse has not yet been generally acknowledged as an important development in twentieth-century poetry. Although Owen's particular contributions have been evaluated with respect to his influence on later poets, the general processes of intensification and enlargement—implicit in varying degrees in the work of nearly every writer we have examined—have been viewed as if they were relevant to war poetry alone.

Most of the difficulty here stems from the fact that *In Parenthesis*, if it has been recognized at all, has not been related to the tendencies apparent in the evolution of wartime verse. Jones himself was fully aware of the fact that in modern war poetry, as in no other form of writing, the new comes into dramatic and significant contact with the old. Viewed as products of the technological process, the dynamo and the long-distance artillery piece have both transformed human life; but although we have become habituated to the beneficent uses of electricity, we are still shocked, in war, by the effects of cordite and amatol: a concentrated artillery barrage strikes more profoundly at man's consciousness—and therefore more directly at his spiritual resources—than any of the less sinister products of modern technology. But as Wordsworth had anticipated, the depiction of the world created by chemistry and physics requires a special effort from the poet, who, "carrying sensation into the midst of the objects of the science itself," must effect a "transfiguration" of these objects so that they may become imaginatively meaningful. The war poets, however, came to grips with this problem amid circumstances Wordsworth could hardly have foreseen; they lacked the forms, the techniques, and even the motives to accomplish such a transfiguration. Yet, so deeply were they affected by the moral and physical impact of scientific warfare, their verse embodies an almost instinctive effort to carry sensation, at least, into an area of violence that briefly represented the frontier of modern poetry.

However, even Jones admits that the transfiguration of the symbols and instruments of science poses a continuing dilemma for the modern artist. Contrary to Wordsworth's expectations, science cannot easily be welcomed "as a dear and genuine inmate of the household of man." Yet the effort to transfigure—even though it is tentative and only partially successful—is in itself essential to the vitality of poetry. In a world of swift and sometimes catastrophic change, we must be prepared to concede that poetry will perhaps never win a complete victory over its materials. But poets cannot retrench or regress on that account.

They must live precariously on the frontiers of an expanding consciousness; they must adapt their attitudes and techniques to the rhythms of modern life; they must discover or invent the forms necessary for the representation of contemporary experience. If the poetry of World War I has taught us this, it has justified itself not only in its own terms but also in terms of what it has illustrated for modern literature.

A SELECTED BIBLIOGRAPHY

Aldington, Richard. *Death of a Hero*. New York, 1929.

Barbusse, Henri. *Under Fire*, trans. Fitzwater Wray. London, 1917.

Bayley, John. *The Romantic Survival*. London, 1957.

Berry, Francis. *Herbert Read*. (The British Council and the National Book League: Writers and Their Work, No. 45.) London, 1953.

Bertram, Anthony. *Paul Nash*. London, 1923.

Bewley, Marius. "The Poetry of Isaac Rosenberg," *Commentary*, VII, 1 (January 1949), 34-44.

Binyon, Laurence. *The Four Years*. London, 1919.

Blunden, Edmund. *The Mind's Eye*. London, 1934.

———. *Nature in English Literature*. London, 1929.

———. *Pastorals*. London, 1916.

———. *Poems, 1914-30*. London, 1930.

———. *The Shepherd and Other Poems of Peace and War*. London, 1922.

———. *Undertones of War*. London, 1928.

———. *The Waggoner and Other Poems*. London, 1920.

———. *War Poets: 1914-1918*. (The British Council and the National Book League: Writers and Their Work, No. 100.) London, 1958.

Bowra, Sir Maurice. *Heroic Poetry*. London, 1952.

———. *Tradition and Design in the Iliad*. Oxford, 1930.

Brereton, Frederick, ed. *An Anthology of War Poems*. London, 1930.

Bridges, Robert. "On the Dialectal Words in Edmund Blunden's Poems," *Society for Pure English*, Tract V. London, 1921.

Brittain, Vera. *Testament of Youth*. New York, 1933.

Brooke, Rupert. *Complete Poems*. London, 1933.

———. *1914, and Other Poems*. London, 1915.

Brown, Hilton. *Rudyard Kipling.* New York, 1945.

Buchan, John. A *History of the Great War.* 4 vols. Boston, 1923.

Chadwick, H. M. *The Heroic Age.* Cambridge, Eng., 1912.

Chadwick, H. M., and N. K. Chadwick. *The Growth of Literature.* 3 vols. Cambridge, Eng., 1932-1940.

Chew, Samuel. *Thomas Hardy.* New York, 1928.

Clarke, George H., ed. A *Treasury of War Poetry.* Boston, 1917. Second series, 1919.

Cohen, Joseph. "Isaac Rosenberg: From Romantic to Classic," *Tulane Studies in English,* x (1960), 129-142.

———. "The Three Roles of Siegfried Sassoon," *Tulane Studies in English,* vii (1957), 169-185.

———. "Wilfred Owen's Greater Love," *Tulane Studies in English,* vi (1956), 105-117.

Coulson, Leslie. *From an Outpost and Other Poems.* London, 1917.

Crosland, Jessie R. *The Old French Epic.* Oxford, 1951.

Daiches, David. *Poetry and the Modern World.* Chicago, 1940.

Dangerfield, George. *The Strange Death of Liberal England.* New York, 1935.

Darton, J. Harvey. *From Surtees to Sassoon: Some English Contrasts.* London, 1931.

Day Lewis, C. A *Hope for Poetry.* Oxford, 1934.

Dixon, W. Macneile. *English Epic and Heroic Poetry.* London, 1912.

Eliot, T. S. *Collected Poems.* New York, 1936.

Evans, B. Ifor. *English Literature Between the Wars.* London, 1948.

Falls, Cyril. *The Great War.* New York, 1959.

———. *War Books: A Critical Guide.* London, 1930.

Ford, Ford Madox. *Parade's End.* New York, 1950.

Frankau, Gilbert. *The City of Fear and Other Poems.* London, 1917.

———. *The Guns.* London, 1916.

Garnett, David. *The Flowers of the Forest*. London, 1956.

Gibbs, Sir Philip. *Now It Can Be Told*. New York, 1920.

Goldring, Douglas. *Reputations*. New York, 1920.

Graves, Robert. *Collected Poems*. London, 1948.

————. *Fairies and Fusiliers*. London, 1917.

————. *Good-bye to All That*. London, 1929.

————. *Over the Brazier*. London, 1916.

Graves, Robert, and Alan Hodge. *The Long Week End: A Social History of Great Britain, 1918-1939*. New York, 1941.

Gregory, Horace. "The Isolation of Isaac Rosenberg," *Poetry*, LXVIII, 1 (April 1946), 30-39.

Hardie, Alec M. *Edmund Blunden*. (The British Council and the National Book League: Writers and Their Work, No. 93.) London, 1958.

Harvey, F. W. *A Gloucestershire Lad*. London, 1916.

Hassall, Christopher. *Edward Marsh: A Biography*. London, 1959.

Hodgson, William Noel. *Verse and Prose in Peace and War*. London, 1916.

Jerrold, Douglas. *The Lie about the War*. London, 1930.

Jones, David. *In Parenthesis*. London, 1937.

Keeling, Frederick. *Keeling Letters and Recollections*, ed. E. Townshend. London, 1918.

Kennedy, Charles W. *The Earliest English Poetry*. New York, 1943.

Ker, W. P. *Epic and Romance*. London, 1896.

Kipling, Rudyard. *Something of Myself*. London, 1937.

Lawrence, T. E. *Seven Pillars of Wisdom*. Garden City, N.Y., 1935.

Lawrence, William W. *Beowulf and Epic Tradition*. Cambridge, Mass., 1928.

Leavis, F. R. *New Bearings in English Poetry*. London, 1932, new ed., 1950.

Ledwidge, Francis. *Complete Poems*. New York, 1919.

Liddell Hart, B. H. *The War in Outline, 1914-1918.* New York, 1936.

Loiseau, J. "A Reading of Wilfred Owen's Poems," *English Studies*, xxi (1939), 97-108.

Mabinogion, The, trans. Lady Charlotte Guest. London, 1906.

Manning, Frederic. *Her Privates We.* London, 1930.

Marsh, Sir Edward. *A Number of People.* London, 1939.

——. *Rupert Brooke: A Memoir.* New York, 1918.

Masefield, John. *Gallipoli.* London, 1916.

Meynell, Viola. *Julian Grenfell.* London, 1917.

Monro, Harold. *Some Contemporary Poets.* London, 1920.

Montague, C. E. *Disenchantment.* London, 1922.

Moore, T. Sturge, ed. *Some Soldier Poets.* New York, 1920.

Mottram, R. H. *The Spanish Farm Trilogy.* New York, 1927.

Murray, Gilbert. *The Classical Tradition in Poetry.* Cambridge, Mass., 1930.

Murry, John Middleton. *The Evolution of an Intellectual.* London, 1920.

Nevinson, C. R. W. *Paint and Prejudice.* London, 1937.

Nichols, Robert, ed. *Anthology of War Poetry, 1914-1918.* London, 1943.

——. *Ardours and Endurances.* London, 1917.

——. *Invocation: War Poems and Others.* London, 1915.

Osborn, E. B., ed. *The Muse in Arms.* London, 1917.

Owen, Wilfred. *Poems,* ed. Siegfried Sassoon. London, 1921.

——. *Poems,* ed. Edmund Blunden. New York, 1931.

Parry, Thomas. *A History of Welsh Literature,* trans. H. Idris Bell. Oxford, 1955.

Pinto, Vivian de Sola. *Crisis in English Poetry.* London, 1951.

Pritchett, V. S. *The Living Novel.* New York, 1947.

Read, Sir Herbert. *Collected Poems.* Norfolk, Conn., 1951.

——. "Definitions towards a Modern Theory of Poetry," *Art and Letters,* i, 3 (January 1918).

——. *English Prose Style.* Rev. ed., New York, 1952.

————. *In Retreat*. London, 1925.

————. *The Innocent Eye*. New York, 1947.

————. "A Malory of the Trenches," *London Mercury*, XXXVI (July 1937), 304-305.

————. *Naked Warriors*. London, 1919.

————. *Paul Nash*. Harmondsworth, Eng., 1944.

————. *The Philosophy of Modern Art*. London, 1952.

————. "The Present State of Poetry," *Kenyon Review*, I, 4 (Autumn 1939), 359-369.

Rosenberg, Isaac. *Collected Works*, ed. Gordon Bottomley and Denys Harding. London, 1937.

————. *Poems*, ed. Gordon Bottomley. London, 1922.

Routh, H. V. *English Literature and Ideas in the Twentieth Century*. New York, 1950.

————. *God, Man, and Epic Poetry*. 2 vols. Cambridge, Eng., 1927.

Sassoon, Siegfried. *Collected Poems*. London, 1947.

————. *Counter-Attack and Other Poems*. London, 1918.

————. *The Memoirs of George Sherston*. Garden City, N.Y., 1937.

————. *The Old Century and Seven More Years*. London, 1938.

————. *The Old Huntsman and Other Poems*. London, 1917.

————. *Picture Show*. London, 1919.

————. *Siegfried's Journey*. New York, 1946.

————. *The Weald of Youth*. New York, 1942.

Savage, D. S. "Two Prophetic Poems," *Western Review*, XIII, 2 (Winter 1949), 67-78.

Schinz, Albert. *French Literature of the Great War*. New York, 1920.

Scott-James, R. A. *Fifty Years of English Literature: 1900-1950*. London, 1951.

Sitwell, Osbert. *Noble Essences*. Boston, 1950.

Sorley, Charles H. *Letters*. Cambridge, Eng., 1919.

Sorley, Charles H. *Marlborough and Other Poems.* Cambridge, Eng., 1916; fourth ed., enlarged and rearranged, 1919.

Spender, Stephen. *The Destructive Element.* London, 1935.

Thomas, Edward. *Collected Poems.* London, 1936.

Tindall, William York. *Forces in Modern British Literature.* New York, 1947.

Treece, Henry, ed. *Herbert Read: An Introduction to His Work by Various Hands.* London, 1944.

Tschumi, Raymond. *Thought in Twentieth-Century English Poetry.* London, 1951.

Waller, Willard, ed. *War in the Twentieth Century.* New York, 1940.

Waugh, Arthur. *Tradition and Change: Studies in Contemporary Literature.* New York, 1919.

Welland, D. S. R. "Half-Rhyme in Wilfred Owen: Its Derivation and Use," *RES,* 1 (n.s.), 3 (July 1950), 226-241.

———. *Wilfred Owen: A Critical Study.* London, 1960.

———. "Wilfred Owen's Manuscripts," *TLS,* June 15, 1956, p. 368; June 22, 1956, p. 384.

West, Arthur Graeme. *The Diary of a Dead Officer.* London, 1919.

Williams, Gwyn. *An Introduction to Welsh Poetry.* Philadelphia, 1952.

Wright, Quincy. *A Study of War.* 2 vols. Chicago, 1942.

Yeats, William Butler. *Letters on Poetry to Dorothy Wellesley.* New York, 1940.

———, ed. *The Oxford Book of Modern Verse.* New York, 1936.